Mathematica for the Sciences

Mathematica for the Sciences

Richard E. Crandall

Addison-Wesley Publishing Company, Inc.
The Advanced Book Program
Redwood City, California • Menlo Park, California
Reading, Massachusetts • New York • Don Mills, Ontario
Wokingham, United Kingdom • Amsterdam • Bonn
Sydney • Singapore • Tokyo • Madrid • San Juan

NeXT, NeXTStep, and Interface Builder are registered trademarks of NeXT, Inc.
POSTSCRIPT and DISPLAY POSTSCRIPT are registered trademarks of Adobe Systems Inc.
Mathematica is a registered trademark of Wolfram Research, Inc.
Mathematica is not associated with Mathematica, Inc., Mathematica Policy Research, Inc.
  or MathTech, Inc.

Publisher: *Allan M. Wylde*
Production Manager: *Jan Benes*
Marketing Manager: *Laura Likely*
Cover Design: *Iva Frank*

Library of Congress Cataloging-in-Publication Data

Crandall, Richard E., 1947–
    Mathematica for the sciences / Richard Crandall.
    p.   cm.
    Includes index.
    ISBN 0-201-51001-4
    1. Science–Mathematics–Data processing. 2. Mathematica (Computer program) I. Title.
    Q172.C73   1991   501'.51–dc19   91-319

This book was prepared by the author, using the NeXT computer.

Copyright ©1991 by Addison-Wesley Publishing Co., The Advanced Book Program,
350 Bridge Parkway, Redwood City, CA 94065.

ISBN 0-201-51001-4

ABCDEFGHIJ-MA-94321

Foreword

"Mathematica for the Sciences" is a new kind of science book. Until very recently, the basic form of science books had not changed much for a long time. In fact, in many respects the last major change happened nearly three hundred years ago, when mathematical formulae began to replace words and diagrams as the primary way to describe scientific theories.

In just the last few years, however, things have started to change again. What is happening is that through the widespread availability of computers and high-level programming languages, it is becoming possible to use computer programs as a way to express science. That is what *"Mathematica for the Sciences"* does. In *"Mathematica for the Sciences,"* programs in the *Mathematica* language carry the main message, with words, diagrams and formulae providing support.

There are many advantages to expressing science using *Mathematica* programs. Traditional mathematical formulae can give relations and results, but typically cannot capture the processes of calculation which lead to them. Thus, for example, a traditional formula might give the solution to a particular kind of equation, but cannot describe the process by which such a solution is found. In a *Mathematica* program, however, you can describe the complete computational process that is required.

Traditional science books are passive. It is up to the reader to take the ideas in the book and implement them. But *"Mathematica for the Sciences"* includes active implementations in the form of *Mathematica* programs. To reproduce computations in the book, all you need do is execute the *Mathematica* programs on a computer. And you can apply these programs directly to problems you are trying to solve.

By making it easy to do the calculations it describes, *"Mathematica for the Sciences"* allows you immediately to become a researcher. You can do experiments with the programs in the book, changing them slightly and re-running them. Very probably, you will end up doing calculations that have never been done before. So every result you get will be a discovery.

Using *Mathematica* helps *"Mathematica for the Sciences"* not only in describing the implementation of scientific models, but also in many cases in describing the models themselves. Particularly in emerging areas of science such as complex systems research, traditional mathematical formulae are increasingly inadequate tools. Instead, models are often best represented directly as algorithms. Thus, for example, the genetics model on page 186 is easily expressed as an algorithm in *Mathematica,* even though it could not easily be expressed in terms of traditional algebraic or other formulae.

It comes as no surprise that Richard Crandall would create a state-of-the-art science book like this. For twenty years, Crandall has taken the latest in computer technology and applied it to teach science and to create new science. Sometimes he has also had to create new computer technology. Often Crandall has done this by immersing himself in the computer industry, then injecting science there.

Crandall is in many respects the epitome of a modern computational scientist. And in this book he shares some of the power available to modern computational scientists.

There are, I am told, still scientists who do not use computers at all. I hope this book will show them some of the things they could do with computers. And more than that, I hope the book will give aspiring scientists a glimpse of the tools they can use in doing science now and in the future.

Stephen Wolfram
Champaign, Illinois
July 19, 1990

Preface

It has been said that the evolution of humankind took a substantial, discontinuous swerve about the time when our forepaws left the ground. Once in the air, our hands were free for "other things". Toolmaking. Communication. The emergence of new levels of environmental control. A population geneticist might say that what we do with our hands does not chemically affect our genes. But what we do manually certainly must change the import of natural selection. How we alter the physical or intellectual environment, what we do with our tools, may alter the meaning of the elusive concept of "success" for future generations.

This admittedly conjectural rambling occured to me in a natural way as I prepared this *Preface*. I developed the ideas of this book over the period 1987-1990, as an Educational Fellow at NeXT, Inc., where I sought fortuitous ways to obviate, through computer-based tools, unnecessary intellectual effort. Just as NeXT is a relatively new force in the computing arena, so too *Mathematica* is a relatively new, many-person-years software package. The combination of *Mathematica* and NeXT technology has altered irrevocably but happily my own scientific perspective. Because of this symbiotic marriage of power tools and the new efficiencies they bring I am often enough left "free for other things".

Here are examples of how one's hands may "leave the ground". You think you have a theorem but cannot yet prove it. Then *Mathematica* says the theorem fails for some outlying case. You are able to move on, knowing there is no use in spending time on a proof for this false theorem. Much time is saved. Or say that you require systematic means to send daily problems of some specific ilk–such as fluid mechanics or particle physics problems–to a solver. You can contemplate and design an easy NeXT application that messages *Mathematica* in a convenient way, sending any number of problems via the resulting friendly interface. Another example: you need to distribute, amongst many fast machines, some parallel algorithm. It can happen that *Mathematica* symbolic simplifications, obtained prior to code implementation of the main project, improve the overall parallel performance by astounding factors. This approach helped this author once, when *Mathematica* indicated correctly that a certain abstruse polynomial in a variable t possessed non-zero coefficients only for powers t^0, t^8, t^{16}, t^{24}, ...; thereby reducing by a factor of eight the effort expected from a brace of fast parallel machines. In this regard *Mathematica* can be a catalyst *par excellence*.

In a word, what I wish to direct toward the reader is the hope that the book will create for you more free time than its reading usurps. May I dare wish that the book comes close to violating in this way the Second Law of Thermodynamics?

During the preparation of this book I was aided by colleagues at Wolfram Research: S. Wolfram, J. Keiper, and D. Grayson. I received clutch advice on programming style from B. Sawhill, T. Gray, P. Abbott, and C. Wolfram.

At NeXT Computer, Inc., S. Jobs has been a perpetual source of encouragement and insight as regards the importance of efficient human-machine interface. It is he who more than anyone propagates the idea that tools should free you rather than bind you. I was aided by NeXT's Director of Software G. Tribble in the presentation of some scientific problems herein. The practical aspects of the book–from graphical output problems to cures for versionitis–were made possible through the aid of NeXT colleagues J. Capela, L. Hourvitz, J. Newlin, M. Paquette, J. Coursey, J. Adams, B. Yamamoto, and J. Anderson. Certain philosophical observations herein arose in conversations with R. Weissman. For operating systems insights I have depended upon the expertise of NeXT colleagues A. Tevanian, T. Matteson, M. Meyer, J. Seamons, J. Smith, P. Hegarty, R. Poor and J. Doenias. I am indebted to J. Welch for inspiration pertinent to the supreme cultural importance of academic software.

For research problems discussed herein I wish to thank J. Buhler, J. Dudman, R. Kaplan, S. Arch, G. Gwilliam, P. Russell, C. Wagner, G. Whitney, M. McClellan, D. Griffiths, H. Aref, R. Leary, B. Bense and S. Christenson for their profound contributions to the exploratory aspects of the book.

Gratitude must also be directed toward my Addison-Wesley publisher gentlemen, J. Benes and A. Wylde, for their undying patience, not to mention their intrepid manner of handling radical book ideas with notably polite aplomb.

Finally, I wish to thank N. Stucki for her book design insight, aid in manuscript preparation, and unwavering moral encouragement during the protracted creative phases of this work.

Richard E. Crandall
San Carlos, California
June 1990

Table of contents

Chapter 3: Graphics for the sciences

Chapter 4: Mathematical examples

Chapter 1:
Epistemology

1.1 The purpose of this book

What a rich, suggestive, mysterious word: *epistemology*, the philosophy of knowledge. Just what is it that we should study, and the goal is to know what? Do we attempt to quantify the workings of the head of the beast, or do we analyze the intricate guiding dynamics of the tail? A classic piece of scientific folklore comes to mind. When the first great radio dishes came to life in the 1950's–these were massive parabolic radio antennae aimed at the stars–some engineers would speak of the computer bank back in the personnel shed as a mere component of the driving circuitry of the dish. But the more computing-inclined workers would envision the giant radio dish itself as a peripheral, that is, just another input device presented to a computer port.

Here we have *Mathematica*, a powerful analysis medium that is applicable, in ways heretofore unrealized in the technological sector, to all branches of science. It certainly is tempting to immerse oneself in a study of the *Mathematica* universe: its language, powers, and properties; finding from time to time interesting scientific dilemmas that provide erudite challenges to the *Mathematica* programmer. But on the other hand, one may adopt the point of view that scientific problems stand foremost, that *Mathematica* is a welcome addition to the cultural tools of history. So, do we enumerate, categorize, and collate scientific exercises in order to sound the profundity of this new *Mathematica* software, or do we use *Mathematica* as a new fulcrum upon which to leverage scientific inquiry?

The author claims no fundamental philosophical bias in the matter, and would claim further that the settlement of such epistemological issues is not a task to which mortals should fairly be assigned. Nevertheless the author, an aspiring scientist himself, has written this book in a one-sided fashion, to provide information for other scientists who may, from time to time, make good use of the new tools.

So the book leans more toward the career purpose of scientists than toward the fulfillment of programmers' needs. The forthcoming chapters adopt a vantage point from which one looks *from* the scientific periphery, looking *in* to the programming concepts. To put it another way: programming techniques are introduced in an as-needed fashion. The author therefore apologizes in advance for the implicit vectorial nature of the book. The reader should not expect that *Mathematica* methods be covered in a comprehensive manner.

In a word, this book is not a programmer's book *per se*.

This book is about science.

The reader may perceive that the actual program code herein varies in style from problem to problem. There are two reasons for this style variance. One is that the author endeavored to show how scientific disciplines can be investigated via more than one essential coding style. A second reason is that the author's own preference is to suit the coding style to the discipline at hand, not the other way around. So, for example, a numerical problem in neurobiology, pp. 197-203, is handled in a FORTRAN-esque manner; while a quantum theory problem, as on pp. 181-185 is heavy in symbolics and formal manipulations. It therefore behooves the aspiring *Mathematica* programmer always to have at arm's length the standard guide *Mathematica: A System for Doing Mathematics by Computer* [Wolfram 1988]. For more rarified programming techniques and language specifications one may consult *Programming in Mathematica* [Maeder 1990]. These excellent references represent the authority perspective and as such are indispensable to the serious *Mathematica* aspirant. In addition there have already appeared *Mathematica* books for teachers and researchers in specific disciplines. A good example of this kind of professional treatment is [Skiena 1990].

The author has worked out the ensuing examples exclusively on the NeXT Computer, running *Mathematica* in NeXT Software Release 1.0. Programming considerations for custom applications, examples of which are discussed next in Chapter 2, are to be found in the official technical document: *NeXT Programming Reference 1.0*. The philosophical and practical bases for attempting to do science with a NeXT Computer are described in a lay article [Crandall 1990], while methodologies are discussed in a forthcoming text [Crandall and Colgrove 1990].

1.2 *Mathematica* for education and research

There are still some amongst us who remember when hand-held calculator engines were virtually non-existent. One still can hear the hue of teachers who claim that arithmetical skills decayed coincidentally with the advent of low-cost calculating apparatus. This complaint is by no means unreasonable. To the author's mind there is no historical evidence whatsoever to induce one to believe that a technological advance necessarily brings about intellectual improvement on the part of that technology's practitioners.

But software environments such as the *Mathematica* environment show promise that the–shall we say, "calculator crisis"–can be turned around. And turned around with force! What a hand-held calculator cannot normally do, but a package such as *Mathematica* can do, is to exhibit the beauty of deep algebraic interrelations, to realize the power of arbitrary file-based data analysis, and to exercise the ability to interconnect with other programs and systems.

The author sees *Mathematica* as an "emergent" type of calculator, one whose utility is sufficiently profound that a student is now able to work beyond what may be called the mechanistic mode, to see the intrinsic beauty of mathematical manipulations that arise from within a machine.

In the ensuing chapters of this book we attempt to exploit in a positive way the irony implicit in the preceding paragraph. Machine manipulations will be used to convey understanding, sometimes to establish new methods of analysis. In this way the same technology that may have stifled intellectual expansion can be used in reverse: to provide incentive.

The author has used some of the techniques to follow in normal research efforts. Specifically, experiments with the NeXT Computer have benefitted from *Mathematica* analysis with respect to problems involving high precision at high speed. For example, if one can establish via *Mathematica* an internally consistent finite-element formalism for a quantum-chemical calculation, then one may port this algorithm to a network of fast machines. The same transfer from interpretive code to tightly compiled code proves useful for large-integer arithmetic. In the author's experience it has happened more than once that a

complicated identity was, as a practical matter, discoverable *only* through
Mathematica prototyping; said identity then to be applied in a parallel manner
on a machine network.

Figure 1.2.1 shows a collection of projects, a sampling of the scientific
problems one may expect to investigate with efficiency, and hopefully with
fervor, via *Mathematica*.

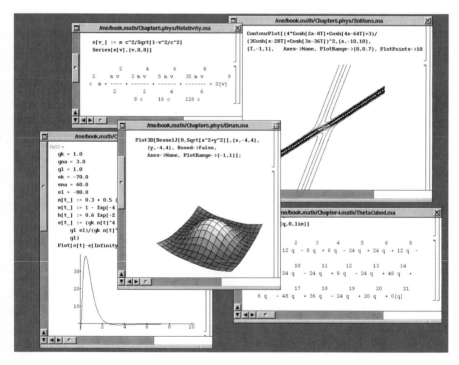

Figure 1.2.1: Suite of *Mathematica* projects appearing in NeXT
windows. Center: Bessel function membrane eigenstate.
Clockwise from upper left: relativity algebra, soliton collision,
Jacobi theta function identity, Hodgkin-Huxley nerve
action potential.

Figure 1.2.1 is intended to represent approximately the ratiometric coverage of
this book. We do some symbolics, some graphics, some numerical analysis. In
addition, special features of the NeXT Computer were used herein to analyze
"real world" data such as sounds and images via *Mathematica*.

1.3 Book presentation

In this book the general trend of discussion within a chapter section is:

1) Theoretical motivation and preliminary analysis
2) *Mathematica* input pertaining to some aspect of the problem
3) *Mathematica* output from (2).

Mathematica output in this book is displayed according to the NeXT Computer software Release 1.0 front end scheme, in which final expression assignments (but not function assignments) will be output. In addition, intermediate Print[ ] or Plot[ ] statements will also produce output.

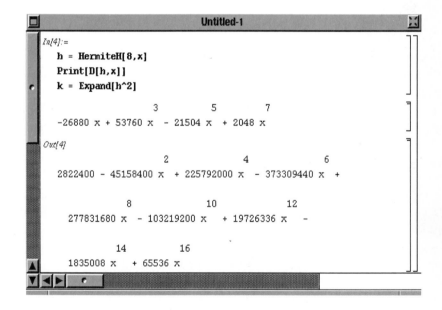

Figure 1.3.1: In the NeXT *Mathematica* front end, a final assignment such as k = Expand[h^2] will produce output, as will an intermediate Print[ ] statement.

Figure 1.3.1 shows a NeXT window in which the Print[] statement of a derivative of a Hermite polynomial produces the required output; but also the final assignment produces an output. This output scheme is mirrored in the book sections. Generally, our *Mathematica* programs will appear in the form:

                                                                    (C.S.XXm)
```
Mathematica input source text
```

occasional discussion prior to output...

▬▬▬▬▬▬▬▬▬▬▬▬▬▬▬▬▬▬▬▬▬▬   **(Gray bar means start of output)**

```
Mathematica output (text and/or graphics)
```

The gray delimiter bar is used herein to indicate the start of output. For chapter number C and section number S, conventional text mathematics is labelled (C.S.XX), while explicit *Mathematica* sources are labelled with a trailing "m", as in the above enumeration (C.S.XXm).

The reader who tries out program examples should beware of pre-initialization of variables. For example, if one has just run program A, and then starts program B immediately thereafter, variables for B may have already been initialized, or typed, or sized previously by A. At any rate program B might suffer from the effects of A. One may use such as the Clear[] function to initialize variables, but the safe–if monotonous–way to be fair to one's next program is to re-initialize the *Mathematica* kernel itself.

At the close of each of the Chapters 3-9 there appear suggestions for further exploration. These suggestions vary from simple calculations to full-blown research projects. It is the author's hope that these explorations will provide some incentive to the aspiring *Mathematica* programmer; or to put it more appropriately given the book's purpose, to the aspiring scientist.

Chapter 2:
NeXT interfaces and projects

2.1 Standard NeXTstep interface

The NeXT *Mathematica* front end application provides a standard NeXTstep window interface. Scientific programs and packages one creates and saves with this application may later be opened via the same application, resulting in a typical window configuration as exemplified in Figure 2.1.1.

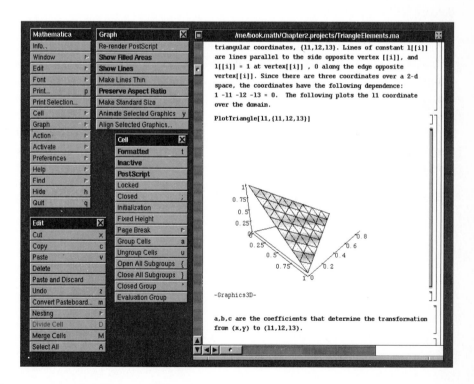

Figure 2.1.1: Typical project as it appears via the NeXT front end.

The figure shows a window segment from a finite-element package that supports triangular grid mesh calculations [Bense 1990]. The author of this package made adroit use of cell organization to combine tutorial motif with actual calculations–a combination that is well-supported by *Mathematica*. The NeXT menus are thorough, detachable and moveable. One may evaluate existing cells, create new cells, start or interrupt the *Mathematica* kernel, and so on. There is provision for animation of selected graphics cells. When one invokes such options the animation proceeds in the selected window, conveniently within a fixed frame in real time.

As one creates, edits and runs a NeXT *Mathematica* program, one has at every stage the support of the full power of the PostScript imaging model. High-resolution screen fonts may be changed, screen and printer graphics will be mutually consistent, and all the features of resizeability and arbitrary graphics density will be available.

When a scientific problem demands that data be read from a file, NeXT *Mathematica* will properly load such data via standard UNIX pathnames, these pathnames being entirely consistent with the browser paths in the standard NeXTstep Workspace.

A strong aspect of the NeXT front end is that *Mathematica* will run concurrently with other applications. One may cut and paste PostScript graphics to or from a *Mathematica* window. One may further use a standard Mail application to mail colleagues program text, graphics, or complete packages at will.

2.2 **Example applications that talk *Mathematica***

One of the simplest methods by which a NeXT application may communicate with *Mathematica* is to display explicit source text into one of the application's windows. The text may be copied and then pasted into *Mathematica* front end windows. Later we shall show examples of automated messaging of *Mathematica*, but for now a good example of the single-shot manual pasting approach is an application called CircuitBuilder. Figure 2.2.1 exhibits the typical configuration of the CircuitBuilder windows.

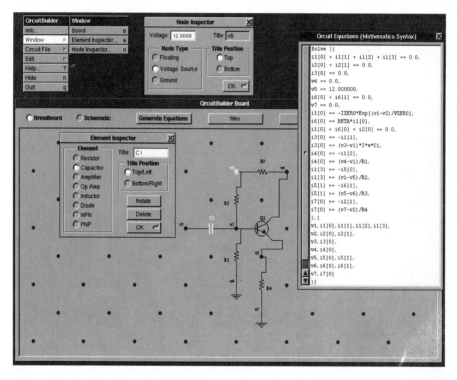

Figure 2.2.1: The CircuitBuilder application generates *Mathematica* source. A circuit–in this case a transistor amplifier–was built, with its mathematical description ready for copying and pasting into the *Mathematica* front end.

CircuitBuilder was created by [Lydgate and Crandall 1989] as an experiment in object-oriented programming. Electronic circuit elements are determined or edited via an Element Inspector window, while wiring or unwiring uses a Node Inspector window. The application will, on demand, generate the correct *Mathematica* format describing the complete circuit equations. This generation is done by tracking through the object structure of a circuit, noting Kirchhoff's and Ohm's Laws as appropriate. For the transistor circuit of Figure 2.2.1 the equations are non-linear and only numerical analysis may be expected to produce useful results. A linear active filter circuit, on the other hand, is solved completely in Section 8.1.

A second example of an application that generates *Mathematica* format is ExpressionBuilder [Doenias and Crandall 1989]. This (experimental, unreleased) application is another example of object-oriented development that shows how the NeXT Computer has the facility to bridge the gap between PostScript equation-setting and symbolic processing. A typical window configuration is shown in Figure 2.2.2.

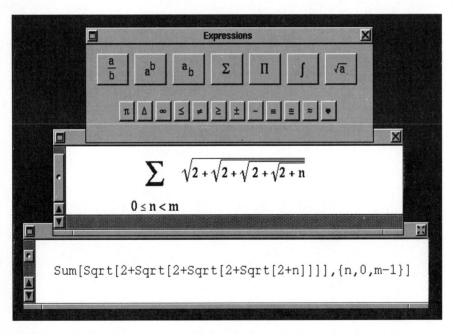

Figure 2.2.2: The ExpressionBuilder application allows the construction of PostScript expression definitions. The application can usually parse the object structure of the expression into valid *Mathematica* input format.

ExpressionBuilder maintains an object structure defining the equation at hand. The program has instructive features such as expression subclasses and a recursive display method. A fraction, for example, when asked to display itself will first ask its numerator and denominator to display themselves; said parts of the fraction asking their subexpressions (if any) to display themselves and so on. It is not hard to see that, given the object structure of a complete expression, *Mathematica* syntax may be automatically generated as shown for the nested radicals of Figure 2.2.2. Again, the user may copy and paste the *Mathematica* format into the front end window(s) in order to further analyze the expression.

To the author's mind the ExpressionBuilder is a kind of harbinger of future developments in mathematical typesetting. It should be pointed out that J. Doenias succeeded in a code implementation of the following feature: that after an expression's PostScript is pasted into a text processor window, such as may be done with WriteNow on the NeXT Computer, one may at a future date copy this expression back out of WriteNow and into ExpressionBuilder for re-editing. This is accomplished using a simple but devilish scheme for condensing an expression's object structure into a PostScript comment [Anderson and Yamamoto 1988]. Much work remains to be done in this field of typesetting/symbolic evaluation/re-editing/re-evaluation, but now we know that sufficient tools exist.

2.3 Automated messaging

The previous application examples involve manual copying/pasting of *Mathematica* source text.   But the manual restriction can be lifted as appropriate. The Application Kit segment of the NeXTstep software provides for a Speaker/Listener paradigm in which two separate applications may communicate automatically.   A good example is the application RealTimeAlgebra, also subtitled "Mathematics for the Impatient" [Gray 1989], exhibited in Figure 2.3.1.

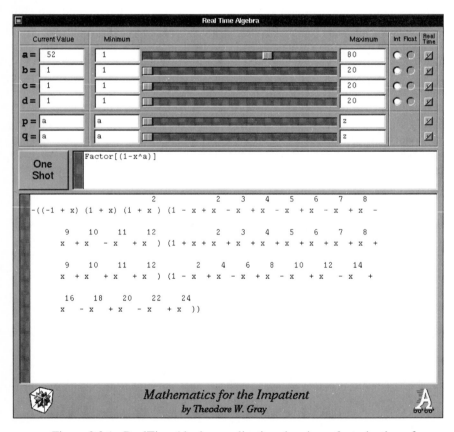

Figure 2.3.1: RealTimeAlgebra application showing a factorization of $(1-x^a)$ where the parameter a is slider-adjusted.

RealTimeAlgebra itself launches the *Mathematica* front end and through the Speaker/Listener connection sends to *Mathematica* parameterized expressions; i.e. expressions with parameters determined via standard Slider controls and/or TextFields, receives the answers, and finally displays the result in the lower portion of the main window. In Figure 2.3.1 the polynomial $(1-x^{52})$ is factored. The reader should imagine that, as sliders are moved about, the result from *Mathematica* updates in a real-time fashion.

Our second and final example of automation is an application called Gourmet. This project was an attempt on the author's part to create a calculator that would insulate the user from many of the intricacies of *Mathematica* syntax.

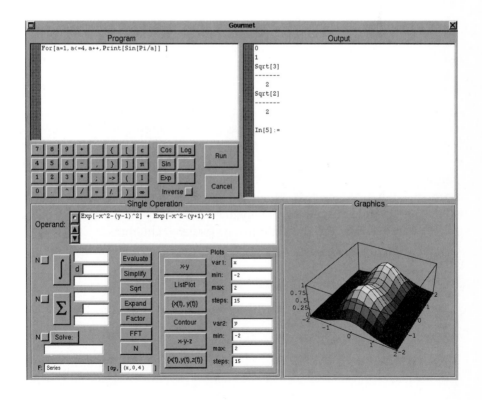

Figure 2.3.2: The Gourmet calculator application, in which *Mathematica* programs can be edited (upper left) and run. Expressions (left center) may be evaluated (upper right) or plotted (lower right).

Gourmet allows the user to compute such functionals as integrals and summations, solve equations, and graph functions in one or more variables all in one window.

The Gourmet application instantiates a special object called a Droid. This Droid can be thought of as a process–in this case the *Mathematica* kernel–that is launched by the application. Strings are sent back and forth asynchronously between the application and the Droid, with graphics handled via temporary PostScript files. The effect is similar to that of RealTimeAlgebra, except that Gourmet uses only the raw *Mathematica* kernel.

The competent systems or application programmer should consider the relatively new development *MathLink* [Cejtin, et. al. 1990] for all such communication scenarios. The *MathLink* protocol is intended as a standard, through which one may support direct exchange of expressions between programs. What *MathLink* will provide, which the examples of this chapter do not, is the ability to call external programs from within *Mathematica*.

At any rate the applications of this chapter are intended to show what is now possible in the way of modern interfaces and interprocess communication. Having toured the modern NeXT interface concepts, we devote the remainder of the book to scientific inquiry. We leave it to the reader to decide independently how much personal effort to expend on interface issues and how much to expend on science. If there is any luck to be had in the future experience of mathematical technology, then eventually such decisions should, through advances in software platforms, be rendered automatic.

Chapter 3:
Graphics for the sciences

3.1 The interplay of 2D and 3D graphics

Let us introduce the typical interplay of 2D and 3D graphics by commencing with a clear, elementary example. The basic 2D plotting mechanism of *Mathematica* is exemplified in a simple plot of the Gamma function $\Gamma(x)$. This function is essentially the analytic version of the factorial in the sense that $\Gamma(x) = (x-1)!$ when x is a positive integer.

$$(3.1.1m)$$

```
Plot[Gamma[x],{x,0.1,5}]
```

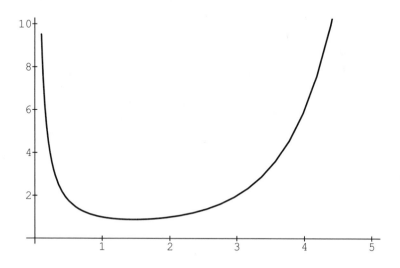

Figure 3.1.1: Simple plot of the Gamma function $\Gamma(x)$.

Note that an example value verified from the graph is $\Gamma(4) = 3! = 6$. The plot also shows the interesting theoretical local minimum at $x \sim 1.5$. Independent of the present graphics exercise is the interesting task of finding this minimum more precisely.

Further study of the Gamma function might involve its analytic continuation into the complex plane. For complex z, $\Gamma(z)$ is defined everywhere except for a pole at $z = 0 + 0i$. This pole corresponds to the divergence at the left of Figure 3.1.1. There are many interesting ways to study the analytic Gamma function's properties. One may analyze $1/\Gamma(z)$ which has a zero at the origin and an infinite number of poles on the negative real axis; or explore the asymptotic behavior of $\Gamma(z)$ for $|z|$ large (Stirling's formula comes into play here); or work out efficient numerical expansions for $\Gamma(z)$.

We choose in this treatment to analyze the behavior of the Gamma function as the imaginary part of the argument varies, with the real part fixed. Let us look at a plot of the absolute value of the function over a certain region of complex points. The Plot3D function will be invoked, and we take care to ask for a plot of the absolute value of Gamma, since we must plot something real-valued:

$$(3.1.2m)$$

```
Plot3D[Abs[Gamma[x + I y]],
        {x,0.1,3},{y,-3,3},PlotPoints->35,
        PlotRange->{0,4.0}]
```

This operation will suggest, via a tall spike, the simple pole at $z = x + iy = 0$. One should remember that if such tall structures (or strongly negative-going structures) appear to have a flattened, stublike appearance at the limits of the graph box, such flat ends can be omitted using the ClipFill->None or similar option.

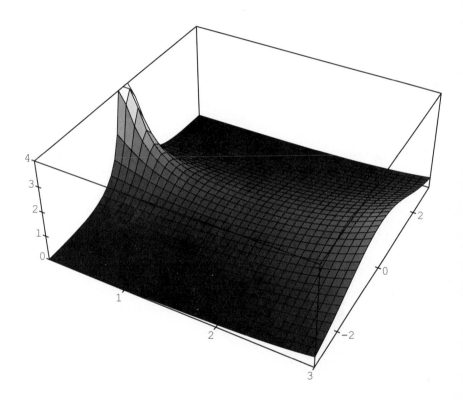

Figure 3.1.2: Plot of the absolute value of $\Gamma(x + iy)$, $0.1 < x < 3$ and $|y| < 3$.

This 3D plot shows, down its central spine $y = 0$, the same behavior as exhibited by the 2D plot for $x < 3$. An interesting feature of the continued Gamma function is now apparent: the function decays in either the $+y$ or $-y$ direction away from the real axis. This decay in $|y|$, which is essentially exponential for appropriate fixed x, is an important analytical property of the Gamma function. It can be shown in theory that the decay on the line $x = 1$ is dominated by $e^{-\pi|y|}$ in the sense that [Abramowitz and Stegun, eds. 1970]:

$$\mid \Gamma(1 + \frac{i\,y}{\pi})\mid^2 = \frac{y}{\sinh y} \tag{3.1.3}$$

It is an interesting graphics task to verify this relation using a 2D plot:

(3.1.4m)

```
epsilon = 10^(-14)
Plot[Abs[Gamma[1 + I y]]^2-(Pi y/Sinh[Pi y]),{y,0.1,3},
     PlotRange->{-epsilon,epsilon}]
```

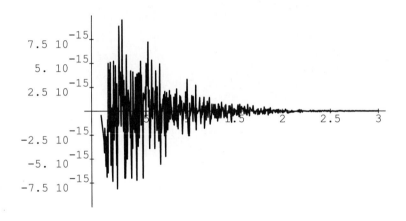

Figure 3.1.3: Verification of a theoretical result to 14 decimals.

Note the excellent behavior of the *Mathematica* numerics for this verification. The error in the theoretical formula is on the order of 10^{-14}; what is more this error is chaotic and fairly symmetrically distributed about zero–two signs of a good numerical processor.

3.2 The importance of resolution

The previous brief study of the Gamma function uses a common *Mathematica* task circuit: try 2D, graduate to 3D, maybe reverting to 2D again to study detail. We next take up various options that extend vanilla 2D and 3D, the idea being to flavor one's graphics study to taste; i.e. to adapt to specific problems and settings.

A primary graphics dilemma is that of deciding on proper spatial resolution. The cost of high resolution is due to the very nature of computer technology: resolution is another aspect of information density. On the one hand, low resolution takes less computation. On the other, one may be confronted with a situation in which some function to be plotted has a fine grain that resists, because of a shortage in either time or expense, a graphics attack. These issues are especially important in modern settings for which chaotic phenomena–often possessed of infinite information density in some sense–are to be faithfully represented in graphical form.

We take up an example, not of chaos, but of a smooth function that is nevertheless not trivial to plot. Consider the radial function surface sinc(r/a) = a sin(r/a)/r, where r is a radial coordinate in the plane and a is some real constant. A moment's reflection indicates that the resolution required to properly represent this surface over the plane, for virtually any measure of "properly", increases as a increases. For example, a plotting mechanism should have its resolution doubled in each dimension if a is doubled. This means that if a is replaced by $2a$, a good plotting routine should then take about four times longer to execute. To study how this works it is therefore sufficient to fix $a = 1$ and investigate some different options for PlotPoints–>:

$$(3.2.1m)$$

```
Sinc[x_] := Sin[x]/x /; x!=0
Sinc[x_] := 1 /; x==0
Plot3D[Sinc[1.5*Sqrt[x^2+y^2]],{x,-25,25},{y,-25,25},
      PlotRange->{-0.5, 1}]
```

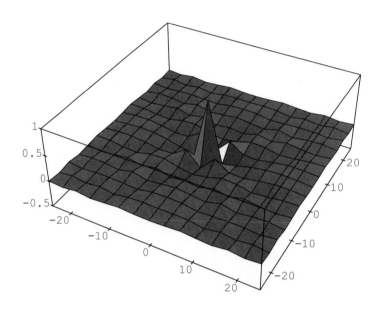

Figure 3.2.1: Bad plot of the radial sinc function. Aliasing and
crude surface effects appear: there is insufficient graphics
resolution. One would prefer the characteristic spatial
oscillation wavelength of the function to be significantly
larger than a grid cell (shaded surface polygon).

The plot Figure 3.2.1 has poor enough resolution that one cannot adequately
glean the true nature of the function. We suffer from *aliasing*, in this case
meaning certain relative extrema in the function are sampled too infrequently,
so the plot belies the detailed undularity of said function. The sinc function in
this case has faster changes per unit distance than our default plotting resolution
supports. Let us try then a higher resolution, using the PlotPoints–> option:

(3.2.2m)

```
Plot3D[Sinc[1.5*Sqrt[x^2+y^2]],
      {x,-25,25},{y,-25,25},
      PlotRange->{-0.5, 1}, PlotPoints->70]
```

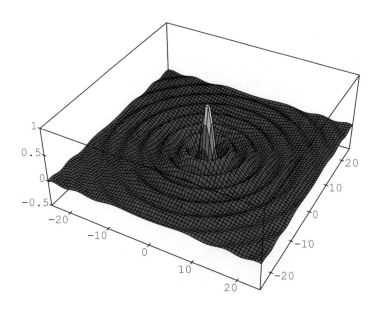

Figure 3.2.2: Better plot of the radial sinc function. The resolution is
tight enough to capture the natural oscillations.

The plot in Figure 3.2.2 is reminiscent of such phenomena as optical
diffraction. In physical instances there might exist a fundamental wavelength;
for the resolution of which one's camera film must have sufficient grain. The
situation with *Mathematica* plots is analogous: the number of plot junctures in
any one dimension must possess at least twice the spatial frequency of the most
rapidly changing phenomena.

3.3 Insight via the contour option

Another valuable graphics option is contour mode. Consider the following plot of a section of a helicoid surface. Such a surface can be defined by:

$$\tan z \ = \ \frac{y}{x} \tag{3.3.1}$$

with a continuity condition applied to z in order to establish the proper branches of the arctan function. A section of this surface can be plotted like so:

(3.3.2m)

```
Plot3D[ArcTan[y/x],{x,-1.5,1.5},{y,-1.5,1.5}]
```

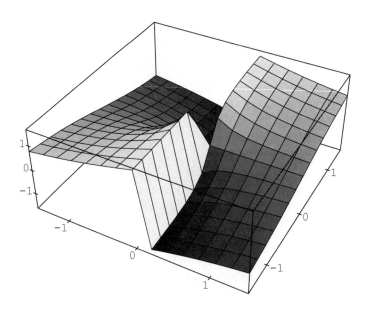

Figure 3.3.1: A section of a helicoid surface.

One way to gain more more insight into the nature of this surface is to perform a contour plot:

(3.3.3m)

```
ContourPlot[ArcTan[y/x],{x,-1.5,1.5},
            {y,-1.5,1.5}, PlotPoints->40]
```

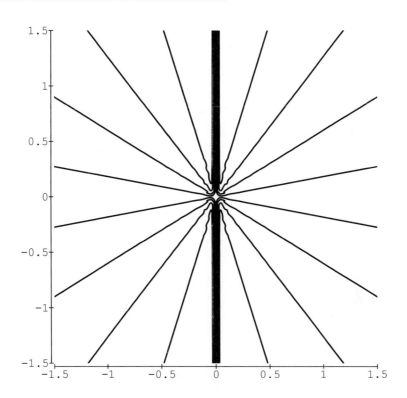

Figure 3.3.2: Contour plot of a helicoid section reveals the ruled
         property of the surface. The darker lines correspond to the
         branch discontinuities of the surface.

Sure enough, through every point of a helicoid there is a straight ray that lies snugly on the surface. In Figure 3.3.2 the darker lines arise from the discontinuity of surface height.

3.4 3D animation of rigid structures

The Graphics3D function is useful for the viewing of rigid structures whose three-space orientations may be chosen to taste. The ViewPoint–> option then looms in importance because, at least until holographic-level display densities become commonplace, we are committed to two dimensional visual projections. The reader who wishes to gain intuition for the ViewPoint–> option might consider writing a simple *Mathematica* program that displays three mutually orthogonal axis vectors with respective labels *x*, *y*, *z*, under different choices for the viewpoint.

Herein we show an example of how one can inspect a rigid shape by generating an automated sequence of incremental views. Consider the following plot of a series of animation frames for a certain assembly of polygonal faces:

$$(3.4.1\text{m})$$

```
t = Table[(a=2 Pi j/5;{Cos[a],Sin[a],0}),{j,0,5}]
apex = {0,0,1.5}
pentapyramid =
      Table[Polygon[{t[[n]],t[[Mod[n,5]+1]],apex}],
            {n,1,5}
      ]
x = Graphics3D[pentapyramid]
Do[Show[x, Boxed->False,
            ViewPoint->{10,-30 Sin[2 Pi j/10.0],
                        -30 Cos[2 Pi j/10.0]}
      ],
      {j,0,9}
]
```

This program creates a sequence of ten rigid pyramidal shells. On systems such as the NeXT Computer, one may animate the figures via menu options after having drawn incremental orientations. Some typical orientations are exhibited in Figures 3.4.1 and 3.4.2.

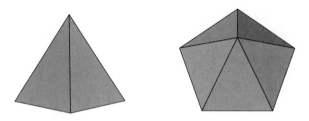

Figure 3.4.1: Two particular views of a rigid structure during
animation. Not enough visual information is yet
provided to ascertain the structure's topology.

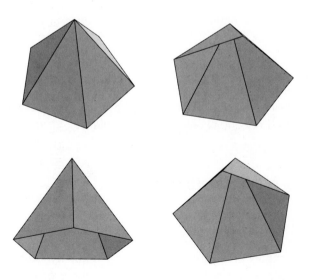

Figure 3.4.2: The nature of the object is now more apparent.

The new views in Figure 3.4.2 show the object for what it is supposed to be: a right pyramid of pentagonal base with that base removed. This pyramidal shell was executed by first creating the pentagonal base's vertices in the initial Table[]. This is just one way to proceed for such a figure. A more advanced programming approach, which also generalizes to more complex shapes, is exemplified in the following sequence for an heptapyramid [Abbott 1990]:

$$(3.4.2m)$$

```
shape[n_] :=
Block[{j,pts,size,apex = {{0,0,1}}},
     pts = Table[{Cos[2 Pi j/n],Sin[2 Pi j/n],0},
                {j,0,n}
            ] // N;
     sides = Partition[pts,2,1];
     Polygon /@ (Join[apex,#]& /@ sides) // Graphics3D
]
Show[shape[7],Boxed->False,ViewPoint->#]& /@
     Table[{10,-30 Sin[2 Pi j/10.0],
           -30 Cos[2 Pi j/10.0]},
          {j,0,3}
     ]
]
```

When (3.4.2m) is run, we obtain an animation sequence of a pyramid with an heptagonal base.

Just as we have seen resolution and contour options play a role in the interpretation of functional or geometrical structure, so too the orientation options can be important, especially when the object in question has many qualitatively distinct projections onto the picture plane.

3.5 When *y* is not a function of *x*

Two dimensional parametric plots are called for when the *y*-coordinate is not a unique function of the *x*-coordinate. A simple 2D example of a parametric plot is the following exponential spiral, which is commonly referenced as the envelope of a nautilus sea shell, or the trajectory curve of a sunflower seed array:

(3.5.1m)

```
r[t_] := Exp[-0.1 t]
ParametricPlot[{r[t]*Cos[t], r[t]*Sin[t]},
               {t,0,30}, AspectRatio->Automatic
]
```

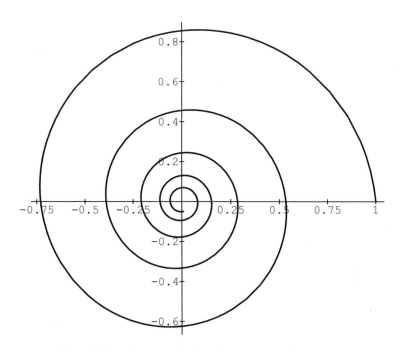

Figure 3.5.1: Parametric plot of an exponential spiral.

This curve, which is nowhere a legitimate function $y = y(x)$, is nevertheless easy to plot if the radius r is determined as in (3.5.1m) as a function of the polar angle t.

Another example of the need for parametric plots arises when we wish to draw some family of 2D trajectories, with each trajectory indexed by some meaningful parameter. Consider the example of Newtonian ellipses, of the polar form:

$$r \;=\; \frac{1}{1 - e \cos t} \tag{3.5.2}$$

These curves are possible gravitation-driven orbits, described in terms of polar angle t and radius r, for eccentricty parameter $|e| < 1$. The heavy attracting body resides at the origin (actually a focus of the relevant conic) in such problems. A typical study of the orbits might call for a simultaneous orbital plot such as the following:

$$\tag{3.5.3m}$$

```
r[t_, e_] := 1/(1 - e Cos[t])
list = {r[t,#] Cos[t], r[t,#] Sin[t]}& /@
       {0.7,0.5,0.2,0.1}
ParametricPlot[Release[list],{t,0,2 Pi},
            AspectRatio->Automatic]
```

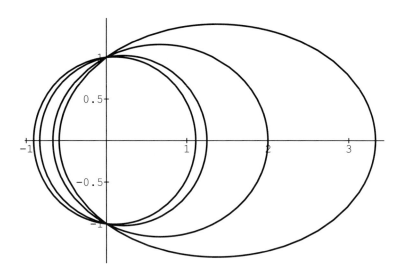

Figure 3.5.2: Family of parametric ellipses of varying eccentricities.

3.6 3D parametric plots

The 3D extension of parametric plotting is a powerful option that exhibits *Mathematica* graphics at its finest. The parametric notion is that a collection of Cartesian coordinates comprise either a space curve or a spatial surface. For a space curve, a vector *r* on the curve is assumed to be given as:

$$r = \{x(t),\, y(t),\, z(t)\} \tag{3.6.1}$$

where *t* is a real parameter. For surfaces, we require two real parameters and the general vector r is of the form

$$r = \{x(t,u),\, y(t,u),\, z(t,u)\} \tag{3.6.2}$$

Using ParametricPlot[] and the standard package ParametricPlot3D.m, we can investigate instructive examples of these two cases. Consider the space curve parameterized like so:

$$\rho(t) = a + b\,\cos(3t/2) \tag{3.6.3}$$
$$x(t) = \rho(t)\,\cos(t)$$
$$y(t) = \rho(t)\,\sin(t)$$
$$z(t) = c\,\sin(3t/2)$$

where *t* runs over the interval $(0, 4\pi)$. This curve is a trefoil knot which was chosen because of its resistance to plotting schemes: only when we have properly plotted this curve, with certain embellishments, will we see an acceptable topological picture. The radius $\rho(t)$ can be used to plot a 2D projection of the curve:

$$\tag{3.6.4m}$$

```
a = 1.0
b = 0.4
r[t_] := a + b Cos[3 t/2]
ParametricPlot[{r[t] Cos[t], r[t] Sin[t]},
      {t,0,4 Pi + 0.1}, AspectRatio->Automatic]
```

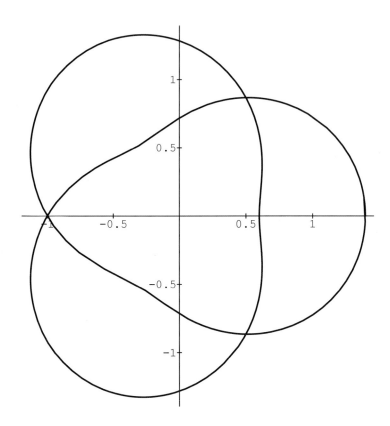

Figure 3.6.1: 2D projection of a parametric knot. More advanced graphics
options are required if one wishes to see the true topological character.

Now when we invoke the Parametric3D package we can infer more from this
curve because the *z*-coordinate will come into play:

$$(3.6.5m)$$

```
Needs["Graphics `ParametricPlot3D` "]
(* << ParametricPlot3D.m *)
a = 1.0
b = 0.4
c = 0.5
r[t_] := a + b Cos[3 t/2]
z[t_] := c Sin[3 t/2]
SpaceCurve[{r[t]*Cos[t], r[t]*Sin[t], z[t]},
```

```
{t,0,4 Pi + 0.1,0.2},
  ViewPoint->{20,30,-70} ]
```

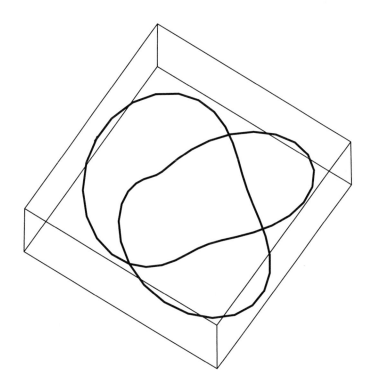

Figure 3.6.2: The z-coordinate for the trefoil knot comes into play via
the SpaceCurve function.

The plot of Figure 3.6.2 still does not adequately reveal the topological nature
of the space curve. Depth perception is problematic: the "over-under" features
of the knot are yet difficult to see.

At this juncture it is a good idea to enter what might be called "sausage mode",
in which a space curve is fattened, to appear as a tubular surface whose local
axis coincides with the space curve in question. Assume as before that a
general vector $r(t)$ describes the space curve of Figure 3.6.2. A vector q that is
always tangent to the space curve is the following:

$$q(t) \ = \ \frac{dr}{dt} \qquad\qquad\qquad (3.6.6)$$

To create a sausage surface axial to the curve we start with a vector that is always perpendicular to the tangent. One such vector is:

$$v(t) = \{ \, q(t)_y, -q(t)_x, 0 \, \} \qquad\qquad\qquad (3.6.7)$$

Perpendicularity follows from the fact that the dot-product of q and v is identically zero. Next we establish a third vector that is perpendicular to both q and v. This is easy: a vector that works is the cross-product $w = q$ X v. All of this means that for a real parameter u ranging from 0 to 2π, the vector

$$p(t,u) \ = \ \frac{v}{|v|} \, \cos u \ + \ \frac{w}{|w|} \sin u \qquad\qquad\qquad (3.6.8)$$

describes a unit circle centered at the origin but oriented in such a way that its plane is perpendicular to the space curve tangent $q(t)$. It is easy to check that the dot product of q and p vanishes. Therefore the circle $\{r(t) + p(t, u): 0 \le u < 2\pi\}$, as t evolves, describes a "sausage" surface that is locally coaxial with the space curve.

To visualize these ideas, let the radius of each sausage circle be denoted by a constant d. Then a surface rendition of our trefoil knot can be programmed thus:

$$(3.6.9\text{m})$$

```
Needs["Graphics `ParametricPlot3D` "]
(* << ParametricPlot3D.m *)

a = 1.0
b = 0.4
c = 0.5
d = 0.3
```

```
r[t_]  := a + b Cos[1.5 t]
z[t_]  := c Sin[1.5 t]
x[t_]  := r[t] Cos[t]
y[t_]  := r[t] Sin[t]
qqx[t_] :=
 -((1. + 0.3*Cos[1.5*t])*Sin[t]) - 0.45*Cos[t]*Sin[1.5*t]
qqy[t_] :=
     Cos[t]*(1. + 0.3*Cos[1.5*t]) - 0.45*Sin[t]*Sin[1.5*t]
qqz[t_]  := 0.75*Cos[1.5*t]
norm[t_] := Sqrt[qqx[t]^2 + qqy[t]^2 + qqz[t]^2]
qx[t_] := qqx[t]/norm[t]
qy[t_] := qqy[t]/norm[t]
qz[t_] := qqz[t]/norm[t]
normv[t_] := Sqrt[qx[t]^2 + qy[t]^2]
vx[t_]  := qy[t]/normv[t]
vy[t_]  := -qx[t]/normv[t]
wx[t_]  := -qz[t] vy[t]
wy[t_]  := qz[t] vx[t]
wz[t_]  := qx[t] vy[t] - vx[t] qy[t]
xx[t_, u_] := x[t] + d (vx[t] Cos[u] + wx[t] Sin[u])
yy[t_, u_] := y[t] + d (vy[t] Cos[u] + wy[t] Sin[u])
zz[t_, u_] := z[t] + d (wz[t] Sin[u])
ParametricPlot3D[
        {xx[m,n], yy[m,n], zz[m,n] },
        {m, 0, 4 Pi + 0.31, 0.3}, {n, 0, 2 Pi, Pi/4},
        ViewPoint->{20,30,-70}
]
```

We have performed the vector calculus explicitly, but the reader should contemplate working out such examples using the full *Mathematica* vector-matrix apparatus. An elegant cross-product is given, for example, in a later program (3.6.12m).

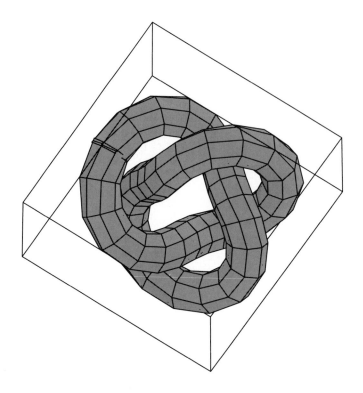

Figure 3.6.3: The ParametricPlot3D function is used with a "sausage" model of
the trefoil knot. We finally obtain an adequate picture of the topology.

These examples show the importance of deciding whether to plot space curves
or space surfaces.

Our final example of 3D parametric plotting is a celebrated one-sided surface,
the Moebius band. A possible parameterization is

$$r(t, v) = a + b\, v \cos(t/2) \qquad\qquad (3.6.10)$$
$$x(t, v) = r(t, v) \cos(t)$$
$$y(t, v) = r(t, v) \sin(t)$$
$$z(t, v) = b\, v \sin(t/2)$$

Where a and b are constants, t runs through $[0, 2\pi)$ and v runs through $[-1, 1)$.

It is the half-angle argument *t*/2 that causes the band thus defined to meet itself with only a half-twist after *t* runs through its full range. A *Mathematica* sequence to plot this wonderful surface might run like so:

(3.6.11.m)

```
Needs["Graphics `ParametricPlot3D` "]
(* << ParametricPlot3D.m *)

a = 1.0; b = 0.5
r[t_,v_] := a + b*v*Cos[t/2]
x[t_,v_] := r[t,v] Cos[t]
y[t_,v_] := r[t,v] Sin[t]
z[t_,v_] := b*v*Sin[t/2]
ParametricPlot3D[{x[t,v], y[t,v], z[t,v]},
      {t,0., 2 Pi,2 Pi/30}, {v, -1.,1.,2/4.0}]
```

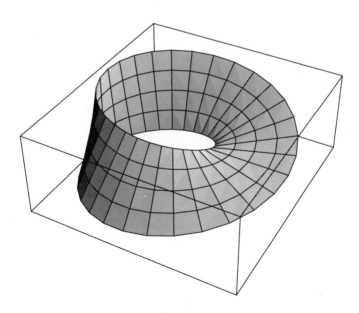

Figure 3.6.4: A Moebius band as a parametric surface.

The topological character of the Moebius surface can be further studied using the notion of normal surface vector. For surfaces parameterized by pairs (t, v), a surface normal can be defined as the cross-product n_t X n_v, where n_t and n_v are surface tangent vectors given by:

$$n_t = \{ \frac{\partial x}{\partial t}, \frac{\partial y}{\partial t}, \frac{\partial z}{\partial t} \}$$ (3.6.12)

$$n_v = \{ \frac{\partial x}{\partial v}, \frac{\partial y}{\partial v}, \frac{\partial z}{\partial v} \}$$

Now a fundamental property of the Moebius surface is that it does not possess a continuous normal surface vector. That is, if we slide a vector, initially normal to the Moebius surface, and staying normal to the surface; around the circuit as t runs through $[0,2\pi)$, the final vector is in the opposite direction to the initial vector. A *Mathematica* sequence that shows this violation of continuity can be performed like so:

(3.6.12m)

```
a = 1.0
b = 0.5
r[t_,v_]  := a + b*v*Cos[t/2]
x[t_,v_]  := r[t,v] Cos[t]
y[t_,v_]  := r[t,v] Sin[t]
z[t_,v_]  := b*v*Sin[t/2]
cross[c_List, d_List]  := Det[{IdentityMatrix[3],c,d}]
tant[t_,v_]  := D[{x[t,v], y[t,v], z[t,v]},t]
tanv[t_,v_]  := D[{x[t,v], y[t,v], z[t,v]},v]
nz[t_,v_]  := cross[tant[t,v], tanv[t,v]][[3]]
nz[t,v]
```

```
0.5*Cos[t/2]*Sin[t]*(-0.25*v*Cos[t]*Sin[t/2] -
    (1. + 0.5*v*Cos[t/2])*Sin[t]) -
  0.5*Cos[t/2]*Cos[t]*((1. + 0.5*v*Cos[t/2])*Cos[t] -
    0.25*v*Sin[t/2]*Sin[t])
```

So far this has printed out the *z*-component of the normal vector as a function of *t* and *v*. One may proceed in several ways beyond this point in order to visualize the discontinuity of the normal. A density plot such as

(3.6.13.m)

```
DensityPlot[%,{t,0,12 Pi},{v,-1,1}]
```

will result in a picture such as Figure 3.6.5.

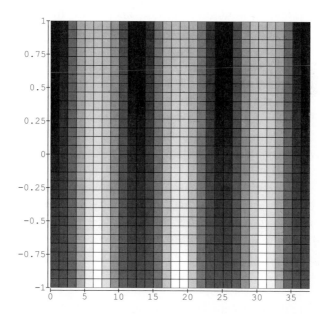

Figure 3.6.5: The z-component of a normal vector to the Moebius
surface of Figure 3.6.4 does not return to its original value
after one full circuit. As the parameter t runs from 0 to 12π
(horizontal axis), the density plot here spans six complete
circuits around the surface, whilst the magnitude of the
z-component undergoes only *three* cycles.

An attempt to construct a normal surface vector to Figure 3.6.4 thus results in a
vector that requires two complete circuits around the Moebius band to arrive at
its original value, as shown in Figure 3.6.5. This exercise shows how symbolic
manipulation together with plotting options can be used to verify fundamental
topological concepts.

3.7 Further explorations

E3.1) Find an extremely accurate x value for the minimum of the gamma function $\Gamma(x)$ near $x \sim 1.5$. Try this directly using Gamma[ ], and also using a standard integral representation of gamma (forcing Γ' to vanish formally).

E3.2) Perform a 3D plot of several windings of the helicoid surface (3.3.1).

E3.3) It is known that an arbitrarily elastic "inner tube", that is a torus with a small side airhole, can be deformed continuously into another torus for which the original airhole becomes the new torus' central circular hole, while the original central hole becomes the new inner tube airhole. Show such an overall deformation in an animated sequence.

E3.4) Plot a 3D rendition of a Klein bottle. This might be, for example, a sausage surface in our trefoil knot motif; but rendered such that the sausage starts out, moving coaxially upward along the z-axis, then turning off and around, intersecting itself at some midway place, finally meeting its original cross-section *inside* the original sausage segment. One way to effect such a rendition is to work out first a space curve shaped like an upper case "P", then to posit appropriate sausage radius along the trajectory.

E3.5) Plot the electric field lines of a dipole: one charge of $+q$ is situated at $+a$ on the x-axis, while a charge of $-q$ sits at $x = -a$.

E3.6) Plot the field lines of the Earth's magnetic field, under the assumption that a cylindrically symmetric circulating current persists inside the planet.

E3.7) Plot the diffraction intensity of light passing a hard, straight edge. This edge diffraction can be expressed in terms of Fresnel integrals.

E3.8) Plot the far-field diffraction pattern due to light of given wavelength impinging on a circular aperture. This should involve J_1, the Bessel function of order one.

Chapter 4:
Mathematical examples

4.1 Identities and expansions

A good way to tune up one's *Mathematica* skills is to verify established identities and expansions, perhaps even to discover new ones. In such explorations one also may witness the internal consistencies of *Mathematica*. Three categories of activity along these lines are: verification, test, discovery. One may verify pre-established identities, as we do shortly, or test a postulated identity, or discover a new identity.

Let us start with an example of verification: we recreate part of the celebrated formal generating function identity for the Legendre polynomials P_n. These orthogonal polynomials arise in many studies; to mention a few: electromagnetic theory, atomic physics, astrophysics and scattering theory. The generating identity reads:

$$(1 - 2zt + t^2)^{-1/2} = \sum_{n=0}^{\infty} P_n(z) \ t^n \qquad (4.1.1)$$

Binomial expansion of the left-hand side (with respect to the variable t) may be accomplished thus:

$$(4.1.2m)$$

```
legendreGen = Series[(1 - 2z t + t^2)^(-1/2),{t,0,4}]
```

```
                                                        2
                                        5 z (-1 + 3 z )        3
                          2   2   (-2 z + ---------------) t
                (-1 + 3 z ) t                    2
1 + z t + --------------- + --------------------------- +
                2                          3


                                                2
                                  5 z (-1 + 3 z )
                  2       7 z (-2 z + ---------------)
    -3 (-1 + 3 z )                    2                4
  (------------- + ---------------------------) t
        2                          3
  --------------------------------------------------- +
                          4


        5
  O[t]
```

It is evident that the coefficients of the *t* power series are themselves polynomials in the *z* parameter. We look at a particular coefficient by picking out the t^3 term:

(4.1.3m)

```
Coefficient[Normal[legendreGen],t,3]
```

```
          3
-3 z    5 z
---- + ----
  2      2
```

Sure enough, this is the order-3 Legendre polynomial, as can be verified by invoking the LegendreP[ ] function directly:

(4.1.4m)

```
LegendreP[3,z]
```

```
            3
 -3 z + 5 z
 -----------
      2
```

Another way to obtain a Legendre polynomial is through the Rodrigues identity:

$$P_n(z) = \frac{1}{2^n \, n!} \frac{d^n}{dz^n} (1 - z^2)^n \qquad (4.1.5)$$

Still another is to use the appropriate recursion relation to generate a polynomial from known polynomials of lesser order. The Rodrigues formula can be implemented as follows:

(4.1.6m)

```
leg[n_, z_] := D[(z^2-1)^n,{z,n}]/(2^n n!)
Print[Simplify[leg[3,z]]]
```

```
          2
 z (-3 + 5 z )
 -------------
       2
```

Again this is a correct expression for the Legendre polynomial $P_3(z)$. These example techniques can readily be applied to a good number of special orthogonal functions of chemistry and physics. With more work one may even guess sophisticated orthogonality relations, such as exact inner products, using such techniques.

For our second example let us go beyond mere verification and establish a rigorous identity, that is, to prove an exact result symbolically. Our next application of *Mathematica* techniques will rigorously resolve a particular Poisson sum identity. The general Poisson identity involves two sums, each taken over all integers $Z = \{-\infty, ...,0,..., +\infty\}$:

$$\sum_{n \, \varepsilon \, Z} f(n) \; = \; \sum_{m \, \varepsilon \, Z} \int_{-\infty}^{\infty} f(x) \, e^{2\pi i x m} \, dx \qquad (4.1.7)$$

valid for a wide class of complex functions *f*. The interesting feature of the Poisson summation is that the two integer-indexed sums over *n* and *m* often appear quite different in structure. One hopes for example that either the left- or right-hand side can be evaluated in closed form, in this way providing a practical identity. Our goal here will be to evaluate in closed form the sum:

$$S = \sum_{m \, \varepsilon \, Z} \frac{1}{1 + m^2} \qquad (4.1.8)$$

We invoke the Poisson identity for the function $f(x) = e^{-|2\pi x|}$. From (4.1.7) we have:

$$\sum_{n \, \varepsilon \, Z} e^{-|2\pi n|} \; = \; \frac{1}{\pi} \sum_{m \, \varepsilon \, Z} \int_{0}^{\infty} e^{-y} \cos my \, dy \qquad (4.1.9)$$

The *m*-summand of the right-hand side can be obtained as follows:

$$(4.1.10\text{m})$$

```
term = Integrate[Exp[- y] Cos[m y],{y,0,Infinity}]
```

```
   1
 ------
    2
1 + m
```

The desired sum S in (4.1.8) is thus equal to π times the left-hand side of (4.1.7), or:

$$S = \pi \, (... + e^{-4\pi} + e^{-2\pi} + 1 + e^{-2\pi} + e^{-4\pi} + ...) \qquad (4.1.11)$$

It is evident from the symmetry of this infinite series that:

$$e^{2\pi} \, S = \pi \, (... + e^{-2\pi} + 1 + e^{2\pi} + 1 + e^{-2\pi} + ...) \qquad (4.1.12)$$
$$= S + \pi \, (1 + e^{2\pi})$$

We may therefore find the final value of S via:

$$\text{(4.1.13m)}$$

```
Solve[E^(2Pi) s == s + Pi(1+E^(2Pi)), s]
```

```
                2 Pi
        -Pi - E        Pi
{{s ->  -(--------------)}}
                2 Pi
        -1 + E
```

Of course one may easily solve the linear problem of (4.1.13m) in one's head, but it is instructive to see just how much of a proof can be expected to rely on *Mathematica*. At any rate we have finally established the attractive identity:

$$\sum_{m \, \varepsilon \, Z} \frac{1}{1+m^2} = \pi \, \frac{e^{2\pi} + 1}{e^{2\pi} - 1} \qquad (4.1.14)$$

Such identities, especially when generalized to higher dimensional sums, play an important role in the theory of crystal structure [Crandall and Buhler 1987].

The beautiful theta function identities of Jacobi, worked out by him in the early 19th century, stand to this day as a fertile arena for connecting various fields of inquiry, such as algebra, elliptic function theory, number theory, and even relativistic string theories. Next we investigate some examples of how the Jacobi identities, which at first might appear only as algebraic oddities, actually can yield meaningful number theoretic information. One of the Jacobi functions is defined as:

$$\Theta_3(q) = \sum_{n \, \varepsilon \, Z} q^{n^2} \qquad (4.1.15)$$

The following identity is just one of many examples worked out originally by Jacobi [Glasser and Zucker 1980]:

$$\Theta_3(q)^2 = 1 + 4 \sum_{n=1}^{\infty} \frac{q^n}{1+q^{2n}} \qquad (4.1.16)$$

Let us verify this identity to some finite number of terms:

$$(4.1.17m)$$

```
theta3[q_] := Sum[q^(n^2),{n,-5,5}]
left = Expand[theta3[q]^2]
```

$$1 + 4\,q + 4\,q^2 + 4\,q^4 + 8\,q^5 + 4\,q^8 + 4\,q^9 + 8\,q^{10} +$$

$$8 \, q^{13} \; + \; 4 \, q^{16} \; + \; 8 \, q^{17} \; + \; 4 \, q^{18} \; + \; 8 \, q^{20} \; + \; 12 \, q^{25} \; + \; 8 \, q^{26} \; +$$

$$8 \, q^{29} \; + \; 4 \, q^{32} \; + \; 8 \, q^{34} \; + \; 8 \, q^{41} \; + \; 4 \, q^{50}$$

This result is the left-hand side of (4.1.16), correct at least through $O(q^{25})$. Now for the right-hand side:

(4.1.18m)

```
sum2[q_] := 1 + 4 Sum[q^n/(1+q^(2n)),{n,1,25}]
right = Series[sum2[q],{q,0,25}]
```

$$1 \; + \; 4 \, q \; + \; 4 \, q^{2} \; + \; 4 \, q^{4} \; + \; 4 \, q^{5} \; + \; 8 \, q^{8} \; + \; 4 \, q^{9} \; + \; 4 \, q^{10} \; +$$

$$8 \, q^{13} \; + \; 4 \, q^{16} \; + \; 8 \, q^{17} \; + \; 4 \, q^{18} \; + \; 8 \, q^{20} \; + \; 12 \, q^{25} \; + \; O[q]^{26}$$

It is easiest in such verification exercises to simply print out the difference of the two presumably equal forms:

(4.1.19m)

```
right-left
```

$$O[q]^{26}$$

which verifies the identity (4.1.16) through $O(q^{25})$. Another way to verify this kind of identity is to successively differentiate both left- and right-hand sides, trying to equate for each order of derivative the two sides evaluated at q = 0.

The number-theoretic connection comes in for Θ_3 when we ponder the right-hand side of (4.1.16) and realize that, due to the geometric series expansion for $(1+q^{2n})^{-1}$, a general power q^m comes in on the right-hand side with coefficient:

$$r_2(m) = 4 \sum_{\text{odd } d \mid m} (-1)^{(d-1)/2}$$

(4.1.20)

But on the left-hand side of (4.1.16) the coefficient of q^m is the number of ways of expressing m as the sum of two squares, that is, $m = a^2 + b^2$. Thus we obtain (4.1.20) as an exact formula giving the number of such two square representations. Let us quickly verify the relation for $r_2(m)$ for say $m = 25$:

(4.1.21m)

```
right2[m_] := 4 Sum[If[Mod[m,d]==0,(-1)^((d-1)/2),0],
                {d,1,m,2}
              ]
left2[m_] := Sum[If[a^2+b^2==m,1,0],
                 {a,-m,m},{b,-m,m}
              ]
Print[right2[25]," ", left2[25]]
```

```
12 12
```

Indeed, the representations of 25 as sums of two squares are:

(4.1.22)

$25 = 0^2 + (\pm 5)^2$

$\quad = (\pm 5)^2 + 0^2$

$\quad = (\pm 3)^2 + (\pm 4)^2$

$\quad = (\pm 4)^2 + (\pm 3)^2$

for a total of 12 representations when we count ($\pm$) multiplicities, as expected. As a practical matter one observes that the function right2[] is a much more efficient means by which to compute $r_2(n)$.

The Jacobi identities' further connections to elliptic integrals yield many attractive results in mathematics and science [Zucker 1984]. What is more, such connections, and even other identities such as Andrews' recent and remarkable identities involving cubes of theta functions, are still being uncovered [Andrews 1986].

It may have occurred to the reader that the idea of "verifying" an exact identity via a finite subset of cases in *Mathematica* is a dangerous procedure. That is so, because there are numerous examples, some not even far-fetched, where an identity breaks down for some case lying beyond the convenient range of calculation. The author, for example, uses verification only when there is compelling reason to believe the truth of the identity. For example, one may have thought to have proved a theorem and then *Mathematica* can be used to check cases. In this way one may find errors, such as overall constant factors or hidden singularities, in a presumed formula. Let us indicate next a classic example in which what may seem to be a fact falls down if the cases are pushed far enough.

Define the cyclotomic polynomial of order k to be the product of $(z - r)$ where r runs through the primitive k-th roots of unity:

$$\Phi_k(z) \;=\; \prod_{0 < j \leq k, \; (j,k) = 1} \left(z - e^{2\pi i j/k}\right) \tag{4.1.23}$$

The notation $(j,k) = 1$ means that j and k be relatively prime. It is possible to generate with *Mathematica* the cyclotomic polynomials directly from (4.1.23). But there is a built-in function Cyclotomic[ ] that gives the polynomials, and we use this to show an example of the pitfalls of case-by-case verification:

$$\tag{4.1.24m}$$

```
Do[Print["C",j," = ",Cyclotomic[j,z]],{j,10}]
```

```
C1 = -1 + z
C2 = 1 + z
              2
C3 = 1 + z + z
          2
C4 = 1 + z
```

```
          2    3    4
C5 = 1 + z + z  + z  + z
              2
C6 = 1 - z + z
              2    3    4    5    6
C7 = 1 + z + z  + z  + z  + z  + z
          4
C8 = 1 + z
              3    6
C9 = 1 + z  + z
               2    3    4
C10 = 1 - z + z  - z  + z
```

Having printed out Φ_1 through Φ_{10}, it is tempting to guess that every coefficient of powers of z in a cyclotomic polynomial is -1, 0, or $+1$. This is *false*, as evidenced by the classic example of Φ_{105}:

$$(4.1.25m)$$

```
Print["C",105," = ",Cyclotomic[105,z]]
```

```
              2     5     6        7     8     9      12      13
C105 = 1 + z + z  - z  - z  - 2 z  - z  - z  + z   + z   +

      14      15      16      17      20      22      24      26      28
      z   + z   + z   + z   - z   - z   - z   - z   - z   +

      31      32      33      34      35      36      39      40        41
      z   + z   + z   + z   + z   + z   - z   - z   - 2 z   -

      42      43      46      47      48
      z   - z   + z   + z   + z
```

Sure enough, the coefficient of z^{41} in $\Phi_{105}(z)$ is -2. This result destroys any naive conjecture based on the output of (4.1.24m) that the cyclotomic coefficients be restricted to the values -1, 0, $+1$.

In summary, we have seen that one may verify a suspected identity by cases (but with due caution), and sometimes derive formal identities rigorously.

4.2 Real and complex analysis

The primary *Mathematica* tools for analysis are the options for limits, derivatives, and integrals. We begin with an exact evaluation of the sum

$$\zeta(4) = \sum_{n=1}^{\infty} \frac{1}{n^4} \tag{4.2.1}$$

This evaluation of the Zeta function can be found immediately in *Mathematica*, because $\zeta(2n)$ is well-known (and built in) for integers n; but here we wish to derive the exact expression in a convincing fashion. For real constants a and b define a periodic function f of period 2, by demanding:

$$f(x) = ax^2 + bx^4 \quad ; \ -1 \leq x < 1 \tag{4.2.2}$$

The condition of periodicity acts to duplicate this polynomial curve over the entire x-axis. Now f will have a Fourier expansion:

$$f(x) = \sum_{n=-\infty}^{\infty} f_n e^{i\pi nx} \tag{4.2.3}$$

where the coefficients $\{f_n\}$ can be obtained via the inversion formula:

$$f_m = \frac{1}{2} \int_{-1}^{+1} f(x) \cos \pi mx \, dx \tag{4.2.4}$$

this last integral following from the reality of a,b and the even symmetry of $f(x)$. The point of the choice (4.2.2) is that we shall be able to demonstrate:

$$(4.2.5)$$

$$f_m = 2\,(-1)^m\,((a+2b)\,/\,(\pi^2 m^2)\, -\, 12b/(\pi^4 m^4))\quad;\quad m \neq 0$$

$$= a/3 + b/5\quad;\quad m = 0$$

because of which we can cast the Fourier sum (4.2.3) in a form containing inverse fourth powers of the index *n*. Turning then to a proof of (4.2.5) we proceed:

$$(4.2.6m)$$

```
p1 = Integrate[(a x^2 + b x^4) Cos[Pi n x]/2, {x,-1,1}]
```

```
-12 b Cos[-(Pi n)]      a Cos[-(Pi n)]      2 b Cos[-(Pi n)]
------------------  +  --------------  +  ----------------  -
      4  4                  2  2                 2  2
    Pi   n                Pi   n              Pi   n


  12 b Cos[Pi n]      a Cos[Pi n]      2 b Cos[Pi n]
  --------------  +  -----------  +  -------------  -
       4  4              2  2             2  2
     Pi   n            Pi   n          Pi   n


  12 b Sin[-(Pi n)]       a Sin[-(Pi n)]      6 b Sin[-(Pi n)]
  ----------------  +  --------------  +  ----------------  -
       5  5                  3  3                 3  3
     Pi   n                Pi   n              Pi   n


  a Sin[-(Pi n)]      b Sin[-(Pi n)]      12 b Sin[Pi n]
  --------------  -  --------------  +  --------------  -
     2 Pi  n            2 Pi  n              5  5
                                          Pi   n


  a Sin[Pi n]      6 b Sin[Pi n]      a Sin[Pi n]      b Sin[Pi n]
  -----------  -  -------------  +  -----------  +  -----------
     3  3              3  3             2 Pi  n          2 Pi  n
   Pi   n            Pi   n
```

This unwieldy expression needs some reduction formulae:

(4.2.7m)

```
rules1 = {Cos[Pi n_] -> (-1)^n,
            Sin[Pi n_] -> 0
          }
p = Simplify[p1 /. rules1]
```

```
          2 n                  2   2           2    2
(1 + (-1)    ) (-12 b + Pi   a n   + 2 Pi   b n  )
------------------------------------------------
                        n    4   4
                   (-1)   Pi   n
```

Still more reduction is needed:

(4.2.8m)

```
rules2 = {(-1)^(2 n_) -> 1}
p = Simplify[p /. rules2]
```

```
              2   2         2    2
2 (-12 b + Pi   a n   + 2 Pi   b n  )
-----------------------------------
                n    4   4
           (-1)   Pi   n
```

We are almost finished with this stage, needing only the case $n = 0$ which we can handle as follows:

(4.2.9m)

```
q = Limit[p1,n->0]
Simplify[q]
```

```
a     b
- + -
3     5
```

Now (4.2.5) is proven for all integer indices m. If we assign $a = 1/2$, $b = -1/4$ we may now write (4.2.3) as:

$$\frac{x^2}{2} - \frac{x^4}{4} = \frac{7}{60} + \frac{12}{\pi^4} \sum_{n=1}^{\infty} (-1)^n \frac{\cos \pi n x}{n^4} \tag{4.2.10}$$

This equation is valid for all x in the interval $[-1,1]$ and we need only choose a convenient value of x to get our required result. For $x = 1$ we finally obtain an evaluation of $\zeta(4)$:

$$\zeta(4) = \sum_{n=1}^{\infty} \frac{1}{n^4} = \frac{\pi^4}{90} \tag{4.2.11}$$

The last example having made use of limits and integrals, we turn now to the use of derivatives. We shall consider the calculation of mean curvature for two-dimensional surfaces imbedded in 3-space. Let us restrict attention to so-called Monge surfaces in Cartesian (x,y,z) coordinates, where the height of the surface above the x-y plane is some sufficiently smooth function $z(x,y)$. The mean curvature C of the surface can be defined in many equivalent ways, one of which is to posit the pair of relations:

$$C = -\frac{1}{2} \left(\frac{\partial}{\partial x} \frac{\frac{\partial z}{\partial x}}{d} + \frac{\partial}{\partial y} \frac{\frac{\partial z}{\partial y}}{d} \right) \tag{4.2.12}$$

$$d = \sqrt{1 + \left(\frac{\partial z}{\partial x}\right)^2 + \left(\frac{\partial z}{\partial y}\right)^2}$$

To calculate the mean curvature of a spherical surface we can proceed as follows, starting with the expression $z = \sqrt{(r^2 - x^2 - y^2)}$ for a hemispherical cap of radius r:

(4.2.13m)

```
f[x_,y_] := Sqrt[r^2 - x^2 - y^2]
fx = D[f[x,y],x]; fy = D[f[x,y],y]
den = Sqrt[1 + fx^2 + fy^2]
meanCurvature = -1/2 (D[fx/den,x] + D[fy/den,y])
Simplify[meanCurvature]
```

```
1
-
r
```

This result $1/r$, which is a constant value obtained for all points of the surface, is the natural, intuitive result for a sphere. But there is a fascinating class of surfaces whose mean curvature is everywhere zero. These are minimal surfaces, so called because they solve the variational problem of least surface area connecting a given boundary curve. The properly posed minimum-area problem in fact results in an Euler-Lagrange relation amounting to the vanishing of the derivative form on the right of (4.2.12). A simple plane is such a surface, but there are beautiful surfaces far from planar that have the zero mean curvature property. A physical manifestation of this problem is the attainment by a soap film of a minimal surface subject to a wire boundary constraint. A minimal surface has already been witnessed as the helicoid example of Section 3.3, for which the wire boundary is a helix in union with a coaxial straight wire along the z-axis. Another fine minimal surface is given by:

$$z = \log \frac{\cos x}{\cos y}$$

(4.2.14)

For this Monge surface mean curvature may be calculated, then the surface plotted, like so:

(4.2.15m)

```
f[x_,y_] := Log[Cos[x]/Cos[y]]
fx = D[f[x,y],x]; fy = D[f[x,y],y]
```

```
den = Sqrt[1 + fx^2 + fy^2]
meanCurvature = -1/2 (D[fx/den,x] + D[fy/den,y])
Print[Simplify[meanCurvature]]
subpi = Pi/2 - 0.1
Plot3D[f[x,y],{x,-subpi,subpi},{y,-subpi,subpi},
      PlotPoints->60, ViewPoint->{10,10,5}, Mesh->False]
```

0

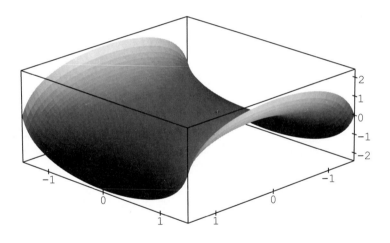

Figure 4.2.1: The minimal surface z = log(cos x/cos y) has the
requisite zero mean curvature at all surface points.

Note that the surface of Figure 4.2.1 indeed has zero mean curvature, as proved
by the printout of "0" just before the plot.

For complex analysis a natural application of *Mathematica* is the evaluation of
contour integrals. An integral such as:

$$I(a) \;=\; \int_{-\infty}^{\infty} \frac{\cos at}{1+t^2}\, dt \tag{4.2.16}$$

where a is assumed real, may be evaluated exactly using the method of residues. In this approach, one generally finds the poles and associated residues of the integrand, deforms the domain of integration to (possibly) encompass some poles, then uses the result that a (counterclockwise) line integral is equal to $2\pi i$ times the sum of the encompassed residues. If the integrand is some function $f(z)$, we start by writing:

$$f(z) \;=\; \frac{n(z)}{d(z)} \tag{4.2.17}$$

such that the zeros of $d(z)$ correspond to the poles of $f(z)$. When this form for f is adopted, a (first-order) residue for a (first-order) zero z_0 of d can be obtained via:

$$\mathrm{Res}(z_0) \;=\; \lim_{z\rightarrow z_0} n(z)\,(z-z_0)/d(z) \tag{4.2.18}$$

With *Mathematica* we can generate a list of poles, a list of associated residues, and even a Boolean function describing whether a pole lies within the encompassed region. For the integral (4.2.16) we can, by the even symmetry of the cos function, use an integrand:

$$f(z) \;=\; \frac{e^{\,i\,|a|\,z}}{1+z^2} \tag{4.2.19}$$

and contemplate a contour running from $-\infty$ to ∞ along the real axis, then circling back counterclockwise through an arbitrarily large semicircular arc back to $-\infty$. Only those poles having positive imaginary part will contribute their residues to the final integral (4.2.16):

$$(4.2.20m)$$

```
n[z_] := Exp[I a z]
d[z_] := 1 + z^2
f[z_] := n[z]/d[z]
encompassed[z_] := (Im[N[z]]>0)
poleList = Solve[d[z] == 0,z]
zero = Table[z /. poleList[[j]], {j,Length[poleList]}]
residueList = Table[Limit[(z-zero[[j]]) f[z],
                    poleList[[j]]],
                    {j,Length[poleList]}
              ]
result = 2 Pi I Sum[If[encompassed[z /. poleList[[j]]],
                    residueList[[j,1]], 0
                  ],
                  {j,Length[residueList]}
              ]
```

```
 Pi
 --
  a
 E
```

Therefore the exact value for the integral (4.2.16) is:

$$I(a) = \pi\, e^{-|a|} \qquad\qquad (4.2.21)$$

A wide class of contour integrals may be evaluated with this *Mathematica* scheme. One should take care, however, to properly interpret fractional powers that may appear in those problems for which the denominator pole function $d(z)$ is a suffuciently complicated polynomial in z.

4.3 Factorization and primality testing algorithms

Mathematica has a built-in FactorInteger[ ] routine that provides the prime factorization of the integer argument. For example, the number 54444439 can be factored thus:

$$(4.3.1m)$$

```
FactorInteger[54444439]
```

```
{{7, 2}, {239, 1}, {4649, 1}}
```

indicating that:

$$54444439 = 7^2 * 239 * 4649 \qquad (4.3.2)$$

Independent of the FactorInteger[ ] routine we shall implement in this section several factorization algorithms so that the reader may see how such algorithms can be programmed.

A convenient factorization method is the Pollard "rho" scheme [Riesel 1985]. Let n be the number to be factored. For some initial integer x_0 define further x_j via the recurrence:

$$x_{j+1} = x_j^2 + a \pmod{n} \qquad (4.3.3)$$

where the constant integer a is neither 0 nor -2. It is believed to be so that the sequence $\{ x_j \}$ is effectively pseudorandom (mod p) for a prime factor p of n. But if this is true, then eventually some x_k (mod p) should equal a previous member of the sequence (mod p). When that happens, the iteration (4.3.3) is, by its deterministic nature, "stuck" in a periodic loop (mod p). There is a novel way to detect such a loop, which is to use the so-called Floyd cycle-finding algorithm. It turns out that when periodic loops are present there will eventually be some instance of the equality $x_{2m} = x_m$. Pollard's application of Floyd's algorithm is to continually check the greatest common divisor of n and $(x_{2m} - x_m)$. If indeed $x_{2m} = x_m$ (mod p), then the common divisor will likely be p itself. An easy way to track both x_{2m} and x_m is to initialize with an x_0 and a second integer $w = x_0$, then iterate (4.3.3) twice for w every time the x sequence is iterated once:

$$(4.3.4m)$$

```
n = 11111111111111111
x = 3
w = 3
g = 1
While[g==1,
            x = Mod[x^2+1,n];
            w = Mod[w^2+1,n];
            w = Mod[w^2+1,n];
            g = GCD[n, w-x];
]
Print[g, " ", n/g]
```

```
2071723 5363222357
```

This example shows the factorization:

$$11111111111111111 = 2071723 * 5363222357 \qquad (4.3.5)$$

The widespread conjecture, in absence of rigorous results about the pseudorandom properties of the Pollard sequence, is that the number of iterations of the While[ ] loop of (4.3.4m) should be roughly $p^{1/2}$. Even though several other factorization algorithms have much better theoretical efficiencies, the "rho" method has enjoyed some isolated spectacular successes, such as the factorization of the eighth Fermat Number, $F_8 = 2^{2^8} + 1$ by [Brent and Pollard 1981] who investigated higher-order recursion polynomials such as $x_j^{1024} + a$ in (4.3.3). Generally, a polynomial $x_j^m + a$ is an efficient choice if the mystery prime factor is known to be congruent to 1 (mod m).

Another factorization algorithm, in modern form also due to Pollard, is one whose chance of success depends wildly on the nature of the unknown factor p of n. This "$p-1$ method" can provide stunning results if a factor p of n has the property that $(p-1)$ is divisible only by relatively small primes. Since we do not of course know p in advance, the success of the method is a matter of luck. An implementation of the $(p-1)$ method starts with some integer x, for example we might choose $x = 3$, from which we compute the expression:

$$y = x^q \pmod{n} \tag{4.3.6}$$

where q is some product of small primes to powers; that is $q = 2^a 3^b 5^c...$ where all primes 2,3,5,... not exceeding some limit B are involved . We continually take $GCD[n, y - 1]$ and hope for a factor p of n. The idea is that if the number $(p-1)$ divides q, which will happen if q has enough primes to powers that all the prime powers in $(p-1)$ appear in q; then $x^q = 1 \pmod{p}$ by Fermat's Theorem that $a^{p-1} = 1 \pmod{p}$ for any $a \neq 0 \pmod{p}$. But if $x^q - 1 = 0 \pmod{p}$ then $GCD[n, x^q-1]$ is likely to produce the factor p. Let us try with this method to find a factor of the 103rd Mersenne number M_{103}:

$$n = 2^{103} - 1 = 10141204801825835211973625643007 \tag{4.3.7}$$

For small primes $p = 2,3,5,...$not exceeding B we take the power of p entering into q as the least integer greater than or equal to $\log_p \sqrt{n}$. This is enough to capture virtually any factor p of n for which no prime divisor of $(p-1)$ exceeds B. For the number $n = 2^{103} - 1$ we choose $B = 1000$:

$$\tag{4.3.8m}$$

```
n = 10141204801825835211973625643007   (* 2^103-1 *)
x = 3
b = 600
c = Sqrt[n]
p = 2
j = 1
While[p<b,
            d = Ceiling[N[Log[c]/Log[p]]];
            x = PowerMod[x, p^d, n];
            ++j;
```

```
        p = Prime[j];
]
g = GCD[x-1,n]
If[g > 1, Print["n = ",g," * ",n/g]]
```

n = 2550183799 * 3976656429941438590393

Indeed we have found the pretty factorization of the 103rd Mersenne number. It can further be proved that the two factors of this n are themselves prime, so the factorization is complete. It should be pointed out that there is also a $(p+1)$ method in which the prime factors of $(p+1)$ are important to the algorithm [Riesel 1985].

A fairly recent, powerful algorithm which is a kind of generalization of the idea behind the $(p-1)$ method is the elliptic curve factorization method [Lenstra 1986][Koblitz 1987]. Whereas any success of the $(p-1)$ method can be thought of as depending on the structure of the unique field of residue classes (mod p), the elliptic curve method's success depends on a host of abelian groups constructed as follows. For a number n to be factored we define an elliptic curve as the locus of coordinate pairs (t_1, t_2) related according to:

$$t_2{}^2 = t_1{}^3 + at_1 + b \qquad (4.3.9)$$

where a,b are constants such that $4a^3 + 27b^2$ is prime to n, ensuring that roots of the cubic are generally distinct (mod n). In fact, in this formalism all arithmetic is to proceed (mod n). An abelian group may be envisioned as having elements (t_1, t_2), actually these are points on the curve (4.3.9), together with a "point at infinity" identity element O. The group operation + is defined by the following rules. First, $O + (t_1, t_2) = (t_1, t_2)$. Second, a doubled point $v = (t_1, t_2) + (t_1, t_2) = 2(t_1, t_2)$ is defined by the relations:

$$
\begin{aligned}
m &= (3t_1{}^2 + a)/(2t_2) \\
v_1 &= m^2 - 2t_1 \\
v_2 &= -t_2 + m(t_1 - v_1)
\end{aligned}
\qquad (4.3.10)
$$

Third, when two points to be added are unequal a sum $v = (t_1, t_2) + (u_1, u_2)$ is defined by the relations:

$$m = (u_2 - t_2)/(u_1 - t_1)$$
$$v_1 = m^2 - u_1 - t_1 \qquad\qquad (4.3.11)$$
$$v_2 = -t_2 + m(t_1 - v_1)$$

It is to be remembered that all operations are performed (mod n), for example in (4.3.10) the slope m is computed as $(3t_1^2 + a)(2t_2)^{-1}$ (mod n). An inverse such as $(2t_2)^{-1}$ may not exist, but this turns out to be a key to the whole algorithm as we see shortly. The idea of elliptic curve factorization is that the abelian group defined by the above relations (mod n) often has a fair number of elements of relatively small order (mod p) if p divides n. Another way to say this is that for some initial point (t_1, t_2) on the curve, a relatively small integer k may well exist such that $k(t_1, t_2) = O$ (mod p). When some k multiple of an initial point has this last property, some inversion in (4.3.10) or (4.3.11) is eventually *illegal*, because x^{-1} (mod n) does not exist if some p divides both x and n.

To implement the elliptic curve algorithm we therefore choose constants a,b and an initial point (t_1, t_2). Then we compute multiples $k(t_1, t_2)$ using the doubling and adding relations above. Whenever an inversion operation involving a denominator d is illegal, we likely have a non-trivial GCD[d, n] and thus a factor of n. From the deeper theory of the elliptic curves [Koblitz 1987] it turns out that good choices of multiplier k are essentially the choices of q in (4.3.6); i.e. k should be the product of small primes to powers. To implement the method one other observation is needed: we can compute a multiple $k(t_1, t_2)$ using a binary-ladder technique, similar to what one uses to raise a number to a power (mod n). For example,

$$11(t_1, t_2) = 2(2(2(t_1, t_2))) + (2(t_1, t_2) + (t_1, t_2)) \qquad (4.3.12)$$

That is, multiples $k(t_1, t_2)$ can be obtained in a straightforward way using the binary representation of k together with doubling and adding operations. The following example finds a factor of the sixth Fermat number $F_6 = 2^{2^6} + 1 = 18446744073709551617$ using a parameter relation $b = -a$, so that the initial point $(1,1)$ lies on the curve (4.3.9):

(4.3.13m)

```
ellipticAdd[t_List, u_List, n_] :=
        Block[{v, slope, iList},
            v = {0,0};
        iList = ExtendedGCD[u[[1]]-t[[1]],n];
        If[iList[[1]] != 1,
                foundOne = True;
                Print[iList[[1]]];
                Return[{0,0}];
        ];
        slope = Mod[(u[[2]]-t[[2]])
                            * iList[[2]][[1]],n];
        v[[1]] = Mod[slope^2 - u[[1]] - t[[1]], n];
        v[[2]] = Mod[-t[[2]] + slope*(t[[1]]
                            - v[[1]]), n];
        Return[v];
        ]
ellipticDouble[t_List, a_, n_] :=
        Block[{v, slope, iList},
            v = {0,0};
        iList = ExtendedGCD[2 t[[2]],n];
        If[iList[[1]] != 1,
                foundOne = True;
                Print[iList[[1]]];
                Return[{0,0}];
        ];
        slope = Mod[(3*t[[1]]^2 + a)
                        * iList[[2]][[1]],n];
        v[[1]] = Mod[slope^2 - 2 t[[1]], n];
        v[[2]] = Mod[-t[[2]] + slope*(t[[1]]
                        - v[[1]]), n];
        Return[v];
        ]
ellipticMul[m_, z_List, a_, n_] :=
        Block[{k, t, u},
            k = m;
            u = z;
            While[Mod[k,2]==0,
                    u = ellipticDouble[u, a, n];
                    k /= 2;
            ];
            k = Floor[k/2];
            t = u;
            While[k>0,
```

```
                              t = ellipticDouble[t, a, n];
                              If[Mod[k,2]==1,
                                    u = ellipticAdd[t, u, n]
                              ];
                              k = Floor[k/2];
                        ];
                  Return[u];
]
n = 2^(2^6) + 1
a = 23
blim = 100
c = Sqrt[n]  (* A ceiling on possible factors.*)
t = {1,1}
p = 2
j = 1
foundOne = False
While[p<blim,
            d = Floor[N[Log[c]/Log[p]]];
            Print[p," ",d];
            t = ellipticMul[p^d, t, a, n];
            If[foundOne, Break[]];
            ++j;
            p = Prime[j];
]
```

```
2 32
3 20
5 13
7 11
11 9
13 8
17 7
19 7
23 7
29 6
31 6
37 6
274177
```

The reported factor is correct; indeed F_6 = 274177 * 67280421310721. The output shows that the initial point $t = (1,1)$ satisfies kt = O (mod 274177) for some k all of whose prime factors are ≤ 37. In the program (4.3.13m) the

ExtendedGCD[] calls, which simultaneously find GCD's and (when GCD is unity) the relevant inverse (mod n), are used to avoid illegal inversions. Another way to handle the illegal inversions that signal success in the elliptic curve algorithm is to use PowerMod[., −1, .] and invoke the Check[ ] function to detect error messages. The reader interested in pursuing elliptic curve algorithms should note that the calculations can be effected without explicit inversions, as reported by [Montgomery 1987] who also explains speedup techniques for the Pollard methods. In practice, it is important to carefully choose *blim* and the ceiling c in (4.3.13m), perhaps fixing these values and whenever the final While[] loop runs out without a factor found, choosing another a parameter (i.e. another elliptic curve). Heuristic analyses show that, if you have an idea of the rough magnitude of an unknown factor p, then an efficient choice of fixed parameters is $blim \sim c \sim p^{\sqrt{(\log \log p)/(2 \log p)}}$.

The elliptic curve method is one of the best available, especially for n in the 50-100 decimal digit region. Other methods of roughly comparable asymptotic performance include the quadratic sieve of [Pomerance et. al. 1988], the continued fraction method of [Morrison and Brillhart 1975] and several others. Very recently there has appeared a supposedly stronger (in the asymptotic sense) algorithm called the Number Field Sieve that appears quite efficient for numbers n having special form [Lenstra, et. al. 1990]. This algorithm very recently enjoyed spectacular success in the completion of the factorization of F_9, the ninth Fermat Number [Manasse and Lenstra 1990].

Primality testing in *Mathematica* can be performed directly using the routine PrimeQ[ ]. But it is instructive to create one's own primality proof using more fundamental routines such as PowerMod[ ]. A standard theorem [Riesel 1985] is that p is prime if and only if there exists a number a such that

$$a^{p-1} = 1 \pmod{p} \qquad\qquad (4.3.14)$$

$$a^{(p-1)/q} \neq 1 \pmod{p}$$

where q runs through all primes dividing $(p-1)$. If the first modular equality in (4.3.14) holds then we say p is a pseudoprime with base a, but this property is not enough for primality: the second condition (or some equivalent set of side conditions) must also hold. Just one example of the insufficiency of pseudoprimality is $2^{2046} = 1$ (mod 2047) but $2047 = 23*89$. We can invoke the complete set of conditions in (4.3.14) to prove the primality of some interesting integer, say, $p = (10^{23} - 1)/9 = 11111111111111111111111$:

$$(4.3.15m)$$

```
p = 11111111111111111111111
factors = FactorInteger[p-1]
Print[factors]
a = 11
isPseudo = (PowerMod[a,p-1,p] == 1)
isPrime = True
If[isPseudo,
      For[j=1,j<=Length[factors],j++,
            If[PowerMod[a,(p-1)/factors[[j]][[1]],p] == 1,
                 isPrime = False; Break[] ];
      ];
]
If[!isPseudo, Print["p is composite."],
      If[isPrime, Print["Proof complete, p is prime."],
            Print["unresolved."]
      ]
]
```

```
{{2, 1}, {5, 1}, {11, 2}, {23, 1}, {4093, 1}, {8779, 1},
   {21649, 1}, {513239, 1}}
Proof complete, p is prime.
```

Note that this "prover" program had to run through 8 separate prime divisors q of $(p-1)$ to finish the proof. The choice of base $a = 11$ is exhibited with hindsight since in this case $a = 3, 5, 7$ all fail to resolve this particular p value.

Sometimes the special nature of a number p allows more direct primality proofs. The Mersenne numbers $M_q = 2^q - 1$ provide a fine example of direct methods, thanks to the Lucas-Lehmer threorem [Hardy and Wright 1979], which states that M_q is prime if and only if the sequence defined:

$$x_1 = 4$$

$$(4.3.16)$$

$$x_{n+1} = x_n^2 - 2$$

has $x_{q-1} = 0 \pmod{M_q}$. Let us try this test on $M_{1279} = 2^{1279} - 1$:

(4.3.17m)

```
q = 1279
p = 2^q-1
x = 4
Do[x = Mod[x^2-2,p], {j,q-2}]
Print[p]
If[x != 0, Print["is composite."], Print["is prime."]]
```

10407932194664399081925240327364085538615262247266670480531\

91123504036080596733602980122394417323241848424216139542\

81007791383566248323464908139906605677320762924129509389\

22034577318334966158355047295942054768981121169367714754\

84788669625013844382602917323488853111608285384165850282\

55604666224831890918801847068222203140521026698435488732\

958028878050869736186900714720710555703168729087

is prime.

This exercise (which takes a few minutes on a NeXT Computer running Release 1.0 *Mathematica*) shows that, at least for certain special integers, *Mathematica* can be used in rigorous primality proofs for integers having hundreds of digits.

New and increasingly powerful primality testing algorithms continue to be discovered. Many of these are based on the theory of residues and on the formalism of Jacobi sums [Cohen and Lenstra 1984].

4.4 Fast algorithms

In this section we explore a few "fast algorithms." The claim is not that *Mathematica* will necessarily perform blindingly fast on such problems. The point is that fast algorithms can be studied and refined via *Mathematica*. The author has found that an effective approach is to solidify an algorithm in *Mathematica*, then to move said algorithm to a suitable machine whose software and/or hardware have been optimized for the problem class in question.

One interesting problem is that of fast multiplication of very large integers. We can do this via convolution. Whereas the conventional "grammar school" method of long multiplication of two numbers that have m digits each takes a time of order m^2, the convolution method requires in practice a compute time $O(m \log^k m)$ for some small integer $k \sim 2$. Assume two large integers x, y are represented by their digits $\{x_j\}$ and $\{y_j\}$ in some base W:

$$x = \sum_{j=0}^{m-1} x_j W^j \qquad\qquad (4.4.1)$$

$$y = \sum_{j=0}^{m-1} y_j W^j$$

Choose the least h such that $n = 2^h$ is greater than or equal to $2m$. We extend the x,y digit sequences by "zero-padding" them so that the sums (4.4.1) can be taken from $j = 0$ through $n-1$ inclusive. It is not hard to see that the desired product $z = xy$ has digits $\{z_k\}$, where

$$z_k = \sum_{j=0}^{n-1} x_j \, y_{k-j} \qquad\qquad (4.4.2)$$

Let Fx, Fy denote the Fourier transforms of the respective zero-padded x, y sequences (these transforms are defined explicitly in Section 8.2). A standard result is that the convolution sequence $\{z_k\}$ arises as the inverse transform of the sequence $\{Fx[q]\ Fy[q]\}$ for $q = 0,1,...,n-1$. One must take care to correctly incorporate the prefactors such as $1/\sqrt{n}$ that may appear in various equivalent *Mathematica* definitions of the transforms. After one finds the digits of z, one may perform a simple add-with-carry operation to produce a final base-W representation of z. Let us apply these ideas to an example of integer multiplication. Let the integers to be multiplied be specified:

$$x = 555221453977032891233 \qquad\qquad (4.4.3)$$

$$y = 442186118023559174$$

For this example we shall work in base $W = 1000$. A program that calculates xy via convolution can be written thus:

$$(4.4.4m)$$

```
w = 1000
x = {233, 891, 32, 977, 453, 221, 555}
y = {174, 559, 23, 118, 186, 442}
lenx = Length[x]
leny = Length[y]
len = Max[{lenx, leny}]
n = 2^(1 + Ceiling[N[Log[len]/Log[2]]])
Do[AppendTo[x,0],{j,n-lenx}]    (* Or Join[] may be used. *)
Do[AppendTo[y,0],{j,n-leny}]
x = Fourier[x]
y = Fourier[y]
x *= y
x = InverseFourier[x]
x = Round[N[Re[x*Sqrt[n]]]]
z = Sum[x[[s]] w^(s-1), {s,n}]
```

245511219377500394175414413382281321542

The result is a the correct product. This technique is more efficient than "grammar school" multiplication for sufficiently large n, with the critical n being (very) roughly 2000 decimal digits, depending naturally on the type of hardware and software used. When one studies this convolution technique further, one confronts interesting issues involving floating-point precision. The author has found that the convolution technique as explored in *Mathematica* can be applied with some care to multiplication of one million bit numbers on 48-bit floating point machines, or 4 million bit numbers when 64-bit precision is available.

We next investigate a fast polynomial inversion algorithm based on the age-old idea of computing reciprocals via Newton's method. For an appropriate guess x the iteration:

$$x := 2x - yx^2 \tag{4.4.5}$$

will force x to converge on the reciprocal $1/y$. If one pays proper attention to the current precision at every step of the iteration, this Newton formula will work in polynomial domains. Let us apply this idea to evaluate some Bernoulli numbers $B_n \pmod{p}$ which are useful in the analyses of Section 9.2. The key identity is (also written as (9.2.9)):

$$\frac{t}{e^t - 1} = \sum_{n=0}^{\infty} \frac{B_n}{n!} t^n \tag{4.4.6}$$

If this identity is written out to $O(t^{p-2})$ the left-hand side can be written as the reciprocal of a particular polynomial y:

$$\frac{1}{y(t)} = \frac{1}{\dfrac{1}{1!} + \dfrac{t}{2!} + \dfrac{t^2}{3!} + \ldots + \dfrac{t^{p-2}}{(p-1)!}} \tag{4.4.7}$$

$$= \sum_{n=0}^{p-2} \frac{B_n}{n!}\, t^n + O(t^{p-1})$$

The following program shows how to adjust precision in Newton's method in order to compute the numbers B_n (mod p) for $p = 37$:

$$\tag{4.4.8m}$$

```
p = 37
y = Sum[Mod[PowerMod[Factorial[j+1],-1,p],p] t^j,
       {j,0,p-2}
    ]
prec = 1
x = 1
While[prec < p-1,
      prec *= 2;
      If[prec > p-1, prec = p-1];
      z = x;
      z = Mod[z^2,p];
      w = Normal[Series[y,{t,0,prec-1}]];
      z = Mod[w*z, p];
      x = Mod[2x - z, p];
      x = Normal[Series[x,{t,0,prec-1}]];
]
Print[x]
```

```
                  2         4         6         8          10
1 + 18 t + 34 t  + 13 t  + 27 t  + 28 t  + 12 t     +

        12        14        16      18        20         22
 13 t    + 2 t  + 25 t   + t  + 9 t   + 19 t     +

        24        26        28        30         34
 29 t    + 33 t  + 31 t  + 3 t   + 33 t
```

This "fast" reciprocal is equivalent (up to a factor -1) to the direct result of (9.2.11m). The fast methods relating to the identity (9.2.17) for proof of cases of Fermat's "Last Theorem" use the present Newton's method for reciprocation and the convolution methods of this section for polynomial multiplication within the Newton's loop.

One attractive design approach for large-integer number theoretic packages is to use Fourier multiplication in the inner loops of a Newton's method integer divide, the latter described in [Knuth 1969]. In this way a divide is asymptotically only a fixed multiple (usually about twenty in practice) times slower than an FFT-based multiply. The author has found that the divide time can further be brought down to roughly 3/2 a multiply time, provided that some fixed number n is always the divisor, as happens in most factoring problems. One may achieve this asymptotic equivalence of divide and multiply speeds by computing just once, via Newton's method say, the Fourier transform of the digits of the reciprocal of n, continuing to use this (stored) reciprocal to perform div and mod operations with FFT-based multiplies alone.

Fast polynomial reciprocation can also be used to expand generating functions. The first example of this chapter (4.1.1) can be handled in this way, where one uses a Newton's method for the $-1/2$ power. Furthermore, there are higher-order Newton's methods [Knuth 1969] requiring even less overall multiplication.

As a last example of fast algorithm development we consider the Chinese Remainder Theorem (CRT). This theorem is thought to have been known to the Chinese at least by the first century AD [Hardy and Wright 1979]. The implied method was supposedly used to count soldiers by lining them up successively in ranks of relatively prime lengths, in this way deducing the total troop population. The CRT, then, must certainly represent one of the very first examples of advanced war technology. Given relatively prime numbers $\{p_1, p_2, ..., p_k\}$ we are given that some mystery number n has respective residues u_i (mod p_i). The question is, given the $\{p_i\}$ and the $\{u_i\}$ alone, what is the least non-negative n having such residues? The CRT answers this question with the formula:

$$n = \sum_{i=1}^{k} c_i d_i u_i \ (\text{mod } \pi) \qquad\qquad (4.4.9)$$

where π is the product of all the p_i, $c_i = \pi/p_i$, and d_i is the inverse of c_i (mod p_i). We interpret the (mod π) operation in (4.4.9) as applying after the sum, and producing a residue n out of the set 0, 1, 2, ..., π–1. This specification is necessary because clearly if some integer m has the respective residues $\{u_i\}$ then $m + \pi$ also has these residues. The prescription (4.4.9) is an exact solution to the remainder problem.

If the number k of relatively prime numbers p_i is small, one may compute the mystery n from (4.4.9) directly. But if k is large there is a divide-and-conquer style fast algorithm for obtaining n. This "preconditioned" Chinese Remainder algorithm can be treated following the description in [Aho, et. al. 1974]. Let us find the least non-negative n such that:

$$(4.4.10)$$

$n = 1 \ (\text{mod } 3)$

$n = 6 \ (\text{mod } 7)$

$n = 5 \ (\text{mod } 11)$

$n = 67 \ (\text{mod } 101)$

$n = 87 \ (\text{mod } 103)$

$n = 230 \ (\text{mod } 257)$

$n = 321 \ (\text{mod } 701)$

$n = 5999 \ (\text{mod } 7001)$

The algorithm is, like its FFT counterpart, highly efficient when k is a power of 2, as in the present case where $k = 8$. We do not go into the details of the derivation here; instead we write out a working program for the fast remainder calculation:

$$(4.4.11m)$$

```
p = {3, 7, 11, 101, 103, 257, 701, 7001}
u = {1, 6, 5, 67, 87, 230, 321, 5999}
k = Length[p]
t = Round[N[Log[k]/Log[2]]]
d = Table[PowerMod[Product[p[[m]],{m,k}]/p[[n]],
                    -1,p[[n]]
             ],
             {n,k}
      ]
q = Table[0,{i,k},{j,t+1}]
s = Table[0,{i,k},{j,t+1}]
Do[For[i=1,i<=k,i+=2^(j-1),
            q[[i,j]] = Product[p[[m]],{m,i,i+2^(j-1)-1}]];
   ],
   {j,t+1}
]
Do[s[[b,1]] = d[[b]]*u[[b]], {b,k}]
Do[For[i=1,i<=k,i+=2^(j-1),
            s[[i,j]] = s[[i,j-1]]*q[[i+2^(j-2),j-1]] +
                       s[[i+2^(j-2),j-1]]*q[[i,j-1]];
   ],
   {j,2,t+1}
]
answer = Mod[s[[1,t+1]],q[[1,t+1
```

1746582896641918

It is not hard to verify that $n = 1746582896641918$ indeed satisfies all eight congruences (4.4.10), and furthermore that n is less than the overall product $\pi = 3030971113232601$.

The fast Chinese remainder algorithm is useful in situations where fast number theoretic transforms (essentially discrete arithmetic versions of the FFT) are used. If one can compute an integer convolution, say, modulo various p_i, then with sufficiently many p_i the desired final integer can be reconstructed along these lines.

4.5 Further explorations

E4.1) Verify by cases some additional orthogonal polynomial generating functions. Hermite, Laguerre, and Gegenbauer polynomials are possible choices. Establish orthogonality integral identities by formally integrating squares of the respective generating functions.

E4.2) Find a proof, using *Mathematica* whenever possible, that every non-negative integer is a sum of four non-negative squares.

E4.3) Use the new theta function identities of [Andrews 1986] to prove Gauss' classic epithet: "num = $\Delta + \Delta + \Delta$", meaning that every non-negative integer is the sum of three non-negative triangular numbers. The triangular numbers are those of the form $n(n+1)/2$ where n is a non-negative integer. The idea is to use an identity involving the cube of a certain theta function.

E4.4) Generate cyclotomic polynomials directly from the definition (4.1.21).

E4.5) Show that the helicoid surface (3.3.1) is also a minimal surface, that is, possesses identically zero mean curvature. Show that a catenoid, which is a catenary of revolution, is also a minimal surface. This is the surface connecting, for example, two closely-spaced, coaxial wire rings. The "barreled" surface achieved by a soap film will break when the rings are separated sufficiently far. Model the dynamics of this breakage, where one presumes the breaking results in two planar soap-film discs.

E4.6) Work out a package that computes Gaussian (instead of mean) curvature.

E4.7) Work out a *Mathematica* package to deal with general contour integration. Such a package should at least be able to find numerical values of integrals of $1/p(x)$, over $(-\infty, \infty)$, where p is a polynomial having no real zeros.

E4.8) As a practical matter, how large a Mersenne number $M_q = 2^q - 1$ can be assessed as to its primality via *Mathematica* on your system? How large a Fermat number defined $F_n = 2^{2^n} + 1$ can you prove composite (by showing for example that $3^{(F_n - 1)/2} \neq -1 \pmod{F_n}$)?

Chapter 5:
Physics

5.1 Classical mechanics

The Hamiltonian formalism of classical physics is a fertile domain for *Mathematica* analysis. Denote by $\{q_i\}$ the coordinates and by $\{p_i\}$ the momenta for a given classical system. The index i runs through 1,....,N with N denoting the dimension of the space. The equations of motion are [Goldstein 1965] :

$$\frac{dq_i}{dt} = \frac{\partial H}{\partial p_i} \qquad (5.1.1)$$

$$\frac{dp_i}{dt} = -\frac{\partial H}{\partial q_i}$$

where the Hamiltonian $H = H(p_i, q_i)$ will be assumed to be defined without explicit time dependence. The system (5.1.1) is comprised of $2N$ equations involving a total of $2N$ functions: the $q_i(t)$ and $p_i(t)$. A standard example system is the simple harmonic oscillator in one dimension, with Hamiltonian

$$H(p, q) = \frac{p^2}{2m} + \frac{m}{2}\omega^2 q^2 \qquad (5.1.2)$$

where m is the particle mass and the spring constant $m\omega^2$ implicitly determines the natural angular frequency ω. For potentials other than the oscillator potential we can substitute $V(q)$ for the q-dependent term. For example, the pendulum shown in Figure 5.1.1 can be described via the Hamiltonian:

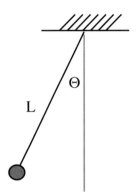

Figure 5.1.1: The physical setting for pendulum analysis. When
we go beyond the simple harmonic approximation the
analysis is non-trivial and instructive.

$$H(l, \Theta) \;=\; \frac{l^2}{2mL^2} \;-\; mgL(1 - \cos \Theta) \tag{5.1.3}$$

Here the Earth's gravitational acceleration g and pendulum length L are
constants for the problem, while l is interpreted as angular momentum. It is
common to invoke the pedagogical approximation $\cos \Theta \sim 1 - \Theta^2/2$; in so
doing we obtain just another oscillator Hamiltonian of the type (5.1.2). The
"true pendulum" obtained when one *avoids* such quadratic approximations can
be envisioned as an harmonic oscillator with perturbation.

Let us proceed with *Mathematica* manipulations by starting with a symbolic
experiment for the simple harmonic case. Hamilton's equations of motion
(5.1.1) read, for the system (5.1.2):

$$\frac{dq}{dt} = \frac{p}{m}$$

(5.1.4)

$$\frac{dp}{dt} = -m\omega^2 q$$

Assume now that $p(t)$ and $q(t)$ are power series in t with coefficients $\{a_i\}$ and $\{b_i\}$ respectively. For initial conditions we can take $q(0) = 1, p(0) = 0$ which correspond to the mass m residing initially at rest at coordinate value 1. The following session computes the Hamiltonian relation amongst all the coefficients through degree 15:

(5.1.5m)

```
deg = 15
qexpansion = Sum[a[i] t^i, {i,1,deg}] + 1
pexpansion = Sum[b[i] t^i, {i,1,deg}]
q = Series[qexpansion,{t,0,deg}]
p = Series[pexpansion,{t,0,deg}]
f = LogicalExpand[D[q,t]  ==  p/m &&
                  D[p,t]  ==  -m w^2 q]
```

Note that Hamilton's equations appear in the LogicalExpand statement. When the sequence (5.1.5m) is evaluated, we obtain the logical expansion:

```
a[1]  ==  0 && 2*a[2]  - b[1]/m  ==  0 &&
   3*a[3]  - b[2]/m  ==  0 && 4*a[4]  - b[3]/m  ==  0 &&
   5*a[5]  - b[4]/m  ==  0 && 6*a[6]  - b[5]/m  ==  0 &&
   7*a[7]  - b[6]/m  ==  0 && 8*a[8]  - b[7]/m  ==  0 &&
   9*a[9]  - b[8]/m  ==  0 && 10*a[10]  - b[9]/m  ==  0 &&
   11*a[11]  - b[10]/m  ==  0 && 12*a[12]  - b[11]/m  ==  0 &&
   13*a[13]  - b[12]/m  ==  0 && 14*a[14]  - b[13]/m  ==  0 &&
   15*a[15]  - b[14]/m  ==  0 && m*w^2 + b[1]  ==  0 &&
   m*w^2*a[1]  + 2*b[2]  ==  0 && m*w^2*a[2]  + 3*b[3]  ==  0 &&
   m*w^2*a[3]  + 4*b[4]  ==  0 && m*w^2*a[4]  + 5*b[5]  ==  0 &&
   m*w^2*a[5]  + 6*b[6]  ==  0 && m*w^2*a[6]  + 7*b[7]  ==  0 &&
   m*w^2*a[7]  + 8*b[8]  ==  0 && m*w^2*a[8]  + 9*b[9]  ==  0 &&
```

```
m*w^2*a[9]  + 10*b[10]  == 0 &&
m*w^2*a[10] + 11*b[11]  == 0 &&
m*w^2*a[11] + 12*b[12]  == 0 &&
m*w^2*a[12] + 13*b[13]  == 0 &&
m*w^2*a[13] + 14*b[14]  == 0 &&
m*w^2*a[14] + 15*b[15]  == 0
```

These are the necessary conditions on the coefficients. We may further solve these relations, remembering to specify exactly what is to be recovered (for example we do not wish to solve for the constants such as *m*):

$$(5.1.6m)$$

```
aList = Table[a[h],{h,15}]
bList = Table[b[h],{h,15}]
solute = Solve[f,Join[aList,bList]]
```

```
{{a[1] -> 0, a[2] -> -w^2/2, a[3] -> 0, a[4] -> w^4/24,
  a[5] -> 0, a[6] -> -w^6/720, a[7] -> 0,
  a[8] -> w^8/40320, a[9] -> 0, a[10] -> -w^10/3628800,
  a[11] -> 0, a[12] -> w^12/479001600, a[13] -> 0,
  a[14] -> -w^14/87178291200, a[15] -> 0,
  b[1] -> -(m*w^2), b[2] -> 0, b[3] -> (m*w^4)/6,
  b[4] -> 0, b[5] -> -(m*w^6)/120, b[6] -> 0,
  b[7] -> (m*w^8)/5040, b[8] -> 0,
  b[9] -> -(m*w^10)/362880, b[10] -> 0,
  b[11] -> (m*w^12)/39916800, b[12] -> 0,
  b[13] -> -(m*w^14)/6227020800, b[14] -> 0,
  b[15] -> (m*w^16)/1307674368000}}
```

These results are still considerably opaque, but it is not easy to solve Hamiltonian problems formally. Everything becomes clear, though, when we ask for explicit series for the coordinate and momentum. First, the coordinate expansion:

$$(5.1.7.m)$$

```
qqq = q/. solute[[1]]
```

$$1 - \frac{w^2 t^2}{2} + \frac{w^4 t^4}{24} - \frac{w^6 t^6}{720} + \frac{w^8 t^8}{40320} - \frac{w^{10} t^{10}}{3628800} + \frac{w^{12} t^{12}}{479001600} -$$

```
      14  14
      w   t                  16
   ----------- + O[t]
   87178291200
```

Next, the momentum expansion:

```
psolution = p/. solute[[1]]
```

```
               4  3       6  5       8  7       10  9
        2     m  w  t    m  w  t    m  w  t    m  w   t
- (m  w   t) + ------- - ------- + ------- - -------- +
               6          120       5040       362880

    12  11       14  13           16  15
   m  w   t     m  w   t         m  w   t                16
   --------- - ---------- + ------------- + O[t]
   39916800    6227020800   1307674368000
```

What we actually have produced here are the leading Taylor series terms of the exact theoretical solutions

$$q(t) = \cos \omega t \tag{5.1.8}$$
$$p(t) = -m\omega \sin \omega t$$

To visualize the approximation through degree 15 in the time variable, we can plot a specific case:

$$\tag{5.1.9m}$$

```
m = 1.5; w = 1.0
ParametricPlot[{Normal[qqq],Normal[ppp]},{t,0,2 Pi},
    AspectRatio->Automatic]
```

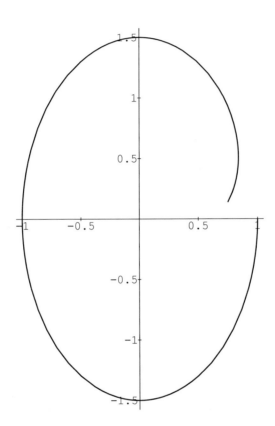

Figure 5.1.2: Symbolically derived (q,p) plot of an oscillator Hamiltonian
system to a finite degree in time t. Sufficiently higher degree
would show the correct, closed phase-space ellipse.

where for the purpose of plotting we have taken care to set explicit (unity)
values for the constants and to remove the O[ ] terms via the Normal[ ]
function.

Of course there are more efficacious ways to produce a closed ellipse for the
oscillator's phase-space plot. But Figure 5.1.2, despite its approximation error,
has the feature that nothing was assumed *a priori* about sinusoidal motion, or
periodicity. The exercise is intended to show what is possible in the way of
symbolic dynamics. These methods can be generalized to analyze dynamical
systems within the framework of other formalisms, such as Lagrangian, non-

linear Hamilton-Jacobi, and Poisson-bracket formalisms. In each of these settings *Mathematica* symbolics can be applied in the guise of operator calculus, to produce trajectories that can be arbitrarily precise given high enough orders of approximation.

Let us turn to numerical analysis, this time concentrating on the true pendulum as described by (5.1.3). We begin with direct Eulerian integration of the motion. Since

$$\frac{d\Theta}{dt} = \frac{l}{mL^2} \qquad\qquad (5.1.10)$$

$$\frac{dl}{dt} = -mgL \sin \Theta$$

we infer

$$\frac{d^2\Theta}{dt^2} = -\frac{g}{L} \sin \Theta \qquad\qquad (5.1.11)$$

which is the celebrated second-order pendulum differential equation. It is true that this equation is more easily obtained from a Lagrangian formalism, but after the present example of Eulerian integration it will be convenient to revert to coupled Hamilton's equations, with a view to more unified and powerful numerical solving. Imagine now that in Figure 5.1.1 we release the mass from an initial angle $\Theta = \pi/2$. The algorithm is as simple as can be; we loop on assignments of the angle–call it *theta*–and its time derivatives *dtheta, ddtheta* (heretofore setting $g = L$ for convenience; e.g. a 9.8 meter long pendulum rod gives this equality for M.K.S. physical units):

$$ddtheta = -\sin \Theta \qquad\qquad (5.1.12)$$
$$dtheta += ddtheta * dt$$
$$theta += dtheta * dt$$

A *Mathematica* sequence that follows the motion in this way and reports an estimate for the period is the following:

$$(5.1.13.\text{m})$$

```
theta = N[Pi/2.0]
dtheta = 0
dt = 0.02
t = 0.0
While[theta>0,
      ddtheta = -Sin[theta];
      dtheta += ddtheta dt;
      theta += dtheta dt;
      t += dt;
]
period = 4 t
```

```
7.44
```

This session thus reports that for the simplified units' system $g = L$, the period should be 7.44 seconds. How good is this estimate? For one thing the simple harmonic approximation is the exact period $2\pi\sqrt{(L/g)}$, about 6.28 seconds. Either the Eulerian integration of the motion is off, or the simple harmonic oscillator model is off. It turns out to be the latter: for wide release angles, the discrepancy between true motion and simple harmonic motion is quite noticeable.

A theoretical analysis of the exact period may proceed as follows. From standard theory [Goldstein 1965] we know that the Hamiltonian (5.1.3) must be a constant of the motion. Since angular momentum is $l = mL^2 \, d\Theta/dt$ which is zero at the initial angle Θ_0 at time $t = 0$, we conclude that

$$l^2/(2mL^2) \;=\; mgL \, (1 - \cos \Theta(t)) - mgL \, (1 - \cos \Theta_0) \qquad (5.1.14)$$

By direct integration we obtain the exact period P, which is four times the time to traverse from the initial angle Θ_0 down to zero angle:

$$P = \sqrt{\frac{8L}{g}} \int_0^{\Theta_0} \frac{d\Theta}{(\cos\Theta - \cos\Theta_0)^{1/2}} \tag{5.1.15}$$

The integral is, up to a constant multiplier, a complete elliptic integral of the first kind [Abramowitz and Stegun, ed.s 1970]. The exact period can thus be written:

$$P = 4\sqrt{\frac{L}{g}}\, \mathrm{K}(\sin\frac{\Theta_0}{2}) \tag{5.1.16}$$

From this point there are several interesting ways to test the theory. Let us first perform a direct numerical integration of (5.1.15) in the case $\Theta_0 = \pi/2$:

$$\tag{5.1.17m}$$

```
p = Sqrt[8] NIntegrate[1/Sqrt[Cos[theta]],
                 {theta,0,Pi/2}]
N[p,10]
```

```
7.416298673
```

This result vindicates the direct Eulerian approach of (5.1.13m) where the approximate result was a period of 7.44 seconds.

One could of course evaluate EllipticK[] or EllipticF[] functions numerically in *Mathematica* in order to obtain values for the period. But it is instructive to work out means for calculating such integrals ourselves. A great discovery of Gauss was that certain elliptic integrals can be computed via the arithmetic-geometric mean, or AGM method [Borwein and Borwein 1987]. The AGM is defined for two numbers, call them a and b. Then replace the pair $\{a, b\}$ by the two means $\{(a+b)/2, \sqrt{ab}\}$. Iterating this way, always computing the two means for the most recent pair, the two components of the pair generally approach a common limit. This limit is the AGM which we denote $M(a,b)$. The wonderful connection with elliptic integrals is the relation:

$$2\,K(k)\,M(1,\sqrt{1-k^2}) \;=\; \pi \tag{5.1.18}$$

In particular this means that the exact pendulum period P, for initial release angle $\pi/2$, is given by

$$P \;=\; \frac{2\pi}{M(1, \cos\frac{\pi}{4})} \tag{5.1.19}$$

A numerical value for this period can be obtained with *Mathematica* by way of a direct call to an AGM function like so:

$$\tag{5.1.20m}$$

```
N[2 Pi/ArithmeticGeometricMean[1,Cos[Pi/4]],10]
```

```
7.416298709
```

which agrees, as expected, with the result of the direct numerical integration (5.1.17m).

There is still one more valuable analysis we may apply to the true pendulum. We have seen that Eulerian integration of the equation of motion, direct numerical integration of the period integral, and a result from the theory of elliptic integrals all give about the same value 7.4163 seconds for the period. But it is well to have at hand a general, powerful tool for dynamical integration. A prime candidate is the deservedly popular fourth-order Runge-Kutta differential solver method [Press, et. al. 1987][Stump 1986]. We next give a simplified version of the Runge-Kutta package found in [Maeder 1990]:

(5.1.21m)

```
BeginPackage["RK`"]

RK::usage = "RK[{e1,e2,..}, {y1,y2,..}, {a1,a2..},{t1,dt}]
            numerically integrates dyi/dt = ei,
            with initial values yi(0) = ai."

Begin["`Private`"]

RKStep[f_, y_, y0_, dt_] :=
    Block[{k1, k2, k3, k4},
    k1 = dt N[f /. Thread[y->y0]] ;
    k2 = dt N[f /. Thread[y->y0+k1/2]] ;
    k3 = dt N[f /. Thread[y->y0+k2/2]] ;
    k4 = dt N[f /. Thread[y->y0+k3]] ;
    y0 + (k1 + 2 k2 + 2 k3 + k4)/6
    ]

RK[f_List, y_List, y0_List, {t1_,dt_}] :=
    NestList[RKStep[f, y, #,
            N[dt]]&, N[y0], Round[N[t1/dt]]
    ] /; Length[f] == Length[y] == Length[y0]

End[]
EndPackage[]
```

It turns out to be delightfully easy to use the Runge-Kutta technique for arbitrary first-order differential systems. The package (5.1.21m) solves numerically the system:

$$\frac{dy_i}{dt} = e_i \tag{5.1.22}$$

subject to the initial conditions $y_i(0) = a_i$. This format is ideal for Hamiltonian systems whose motion is described by (5.1.1). Just allow the functions y_i to denote N coordinate functions and N momentum functions, for a total of $2N$ functions of time. The elegance of *Mathematica* now comes to bear on dynamical problems, for all we need do to iterate a Hamiltonian system is to invoke:

$$(5.1.23.m)$$

```
RK[ {D[ham[p,q], p], -D[ham[p,q], q]},
       {q, p}, {q0, p0}, {tmax,dt}]
```

where "ham" is a suitably defined Hamiltonian ham[p,q]. This RK function returns a phase-space list of the form:

$$(5.1.24)$$

$$\{\{q(0), p(0)\}, \{q(dt), p(dt)\}, \{q(2dt), p(2dt)\}, ...\{q((n-1)dt), p((n-1)dt)\}\}$$

where n is the round of (*tmax/dt*), obtainable *a posteriori* via the Length[ ] function applied to the list. Let us apply these ideas to a numerical analysis of the true pendulum for which, as before, the Hamiltonian is (5.1.3) with the simplifying relations $m = g = L = 1$:

$$(5.1.25m)$$

```
h[v_, x_] := v^2/2 - Cos[x]
dt = 0.02
phaseplot = RungeKutta[ {D[h[v,x],v], -D[h[v,x],x]},
             {x,v},{Pi/2, 0}, {8,dt}
             ]
ListPlot[phaseplot, PlotJoined->True,
         AspectRatio->Automatic
]
```

This sequence creates a phase plot that upon inspection is not really an ellipse (as it would be for the naive simple harmonic approximation):

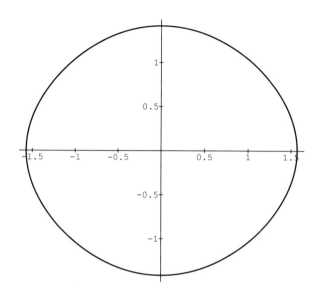

Figure 5.1.3: Runge-Kutta methods yield the true pendulum's
phase-space plot, which is not quite an ellipse due to
natural anharmonicity.

We may finally estimate the period of the true pendulum within the Runge-Kutta context. Note that the elements of phasedata can be accessed according to the rule

$$phasedata[[j]] = \{theta((j-1)dt), l((j-1)dt)\} \qquad (5.1.26)$$

The following sequence picks out two points just before and just after a zero-crossing of the variable *theta*, then uses linear interpolation to estimate the time of zero-crossing to report an estimate for the period:

(5.1.27m)

```
Do[If[phaseplot[[k]][[1]]<0, Break[]],
    {k,Length[phaseplot]}
]
before = phasedata[[j-2]][[1]]
after = -phasedata[[j-1]][[1]]
period = 4*dt*((j-3)after + (j-2)*before)/
    (after + before)
N[period,10]
```

```
7.416298261
```

The resulting period value fares quite well when compared to our previous calculations. In summary,

Period P from Euler method, $dt = 0.01$: 7.44   (5.1.28)

Period P from numerical integral: 7.416298673

Period P from AGM method: 7.416298709

Period P from Runge-Kutta, $dt = 0.02$: 7.416298261

Period P from Runge-Kutta, $dt = 0.01$: 7.416298739

The AGM result is actually correct to the implied precision, so we see the remarkable result that Runge-Kutta methods, for $dt \sim 10^{-2}$, can give overall integration errors better than one part in 10^{-8} for such problems.

5.2 Quantum mechanics

A quantum phenomenon that lends itself readily to *Mathematica* analysis is the tunnel effect. This effect involves the penetration of potential regions that are classically inaccessible. In a word, a quantum particle of energy E may pass a barrier of potential $V > E$ with non-zero probability. We begin with the time-dependent Schroedinger equation:

$$i \frac{\partial \Psi}{\partial t} = - \frac{\partial^2 \Psi}{\partial x^2} + V(x)\, \Psi$$

(5.2.1)

for which we have adopted units such that mass $m = 1/2$ and the Planck constant $h = 2\pi$.

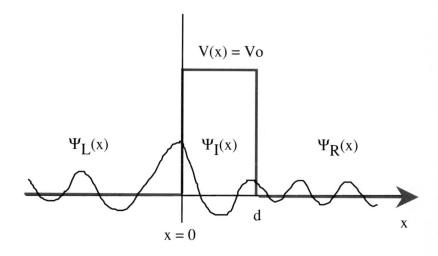

Figure 5.2.1: Geometrical setting for the tunnel effect. The potential
function has a steady value V_0 for $0 \le x \le d$, and zero
otherwise. The wave function is comprised of left, interior
and right parts: Ψ_L, Ψ_I, and Ψ_R respectively.

A solution $\Psi(x,t) = e^{-iEt+ikx}$ to (5.2.1) on any x interval over which V is steady must satisfy:

$$E = k^2 + V \qquad\qquad (5.2.2)$$

We conclude that the wave function Ψ is given by, up to overall normalization factor, the relations:

$$\Psi_L(x) = e^{ikx} + r\,e^{-ikx} \qquad\qquad (5.2.3)$$
$$\Psi_I(x) = a\,e^{Kx} + b\,e^{-Kx}$$
$$\Psi_R(x) = t\,e^{ikx} + u\,e^{-ikx}$$

with $k = \sqrt{E}$ and $K = \sqrt{(V_0 - E)}$. We now take the coefficient $u = 0$, in order to analyze the situation in which all waves to the right of $x = d$ are outgoing (positive momentum k). Accordingly, we need to solve for the four unknowns $\{r, a, b, t\}$ where r will turn out to be the reflection amplitude (for the backward wave in the left region), and t will be the transmission amplitude (for the forward-going wave in the right region). The four unknowns are determined via four standard boundary conditions:

$$\Psi_L(0) = \Psi_I(0) \qquad\qquad (5.2.4)$$
$$\Psi_L'(0) = \Psi_I'(0)$$
$$\Psi_I(d) = \Psi_R(d)$$
$$\Psi_I'(d) = \Psi_R'(d)$$

These four conditions amount to continuity criteria for the wave function and its derivatives at the discontinuites of the potential pictured in Figure 5.2.1. These boundary criteria can be cast in a useful logical form via a *Mathematica* sequence:

$$(5.2.5m)$$

```
psiL[x_] := Exp[I k x] + r Exp[-I k x]
psiI[x_] := a Exp[K x] + b Exp[-K x]
psiR[x_] := t Exp[I k x]
set = LogicalExpand[(psiL[x] /. x->0)  ==  (psiI[x] /. x->0)
      &&
      (psiI[x] /. x->d)  ==  (psiR[x] /. x->d) &&
      (D[psiL[x],x] /. x->0)  ==  (D[psiI[x],x] /.
          x->0) &&
      (psiI[x],x] /. x->d)  ==  (D[psiR[x],x] /. x->d)]
```

```
                        1. K           b           1. I k
1 + r == a + b && E         a +  -----  == E            t &&
                        1. K
                      E


  I k + -I k r == K a - K b &&

    1. K          K b            1. I k
  E       K a -  -----  == I E            k t
                  1. K
                E
```

The *Mathematica* output thus obtained is enough to determine the exact reflection and transmission amplitudes $\{r, t\}$. It is perhaps most illustrative at this point to move straight on to some exemplary numerical values:

(5.2.6m)

```
d = 1.0
params = {K -> 2, k -> 4.0}
sol = Solve[set /. params,{r,t,a,b}]
```

```
{{r -> 0.5721620444279645 - 0.7913494817689292*I,
   t -> -0.2096081120783268 + 0.04960878925169297*I,
   a -> -0.00526845955494696 + 0.03216321468757098*I,
   b -> 1.577430503982912 - 0.8235126964565*I}}
```

It may readily be verified that probability is conserved, in the sense that reflected matter plus transmitted matter equals original matter:

$$|r|^2 + |t|^2 = 1 \qquad\qquad (5.2.7)$$

as follows:

(5.2.8m)

```
(Abs[r]^2 + Abs[t]^2) /. sol
```

```
{1.}
```

The phenomenon of tunneling may be visualized by way of a *Mathematica* plot of the wave function's real part:

(5.2.9m)

```
psi[x_] := psiL[x] /; x<0
psi[x_] := psiI[x] /; (x>=0)&&(x<d)
psi[x_] := psiR[x] /; x>=d
Plot[Re[psi[x] /. sol[[1]] /. params],{x,-8,8}]
```

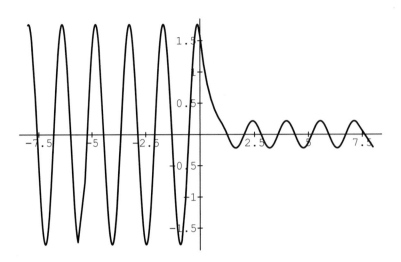

Figure 5.2.2: Graphical verification of the tunnel effect. The wave
function shown solves the Schroedinger equation for
incident energy E less than the barrier height V_o. The
incident particle wave (from left) thus "tunnels" through
the barrier and appears on the right with non-zero
probability.

A good starting example for quantum eigenvalue studies is the quantum
harmonic oscillator. In the current system of units the time-independent
Schroedinger equation for the harmonic potential x^2 reads:

$$-\frac{\partial^2 \Psi}{\partial x^2} + x^2 \Psi = E \Psi \qquad (5.2.10)$$

Symbolic solutions in this context may be effected by invoking a fortuitous
substitution:

$$\Psi(x) = g(x)\, e^{-x^2/2} \qquad (5.2.11)$$

At this juncture it is common to use the power series method to establish
recurrence relations for the coefficents of g. Let us look for even-parity

eigenstates, so that g can be expanded in even powers of x:

$$g(x) \;=\; \sum_{i=0}^{\infty} a_i x^{2i}$$

(5.2.12)

We proceed by finding the coefficents a_i to some order, with a_0 set equal to unity to fix a particular normalization. The opening *Mathematica* lines will represent identities (5.2.10-5.2.12) in reverse sequence:

(5.2.13m)

```
g = 1 + Sum[a[i] x^(2i), {i,1,5}]
psi = Series[g Exp[-x^2/2],{x,0,10}]
LogicalExpand[-D[psi,{x,2}] + x^2 psi == e psi]
```

```
         1
-e - 2 (-(-) + a[1])  == 0 &&
         2

       1                1    a[1]
 1 - e (-(-) + a[1]) - 12 (- - ---- + a[2]) == 0 &&
        2                8     2

   1                1    a[1]
 -(-) + a[1]  - e (- - ---- + a[2]) -
   2                8     2

       1      a[1]    a[2]
 30 (-(--) + ---- - ---- + a[3]) == 0 &&
       48      8      2

 1    a[1]               1      a[1]    a[2]
 - - ---- + a[2] - e (-(--) + ---- - ---- + a[3]) -
 8     2                48      8      2

      1     a[1]    a[2]    a[3]
 56 (--- - ---- + ---- - ---- + a[4]) == 0 &&
     384    48      8      2
```

$$-\left(\frac{1}{48}\right) + \frac{a[1]}{8} - \frac{a[2]}{2} + a[3] \; -$$

$$e\left(\frac{1}{384} - \frac{a[1]}{48} + \frac{a[2]}{8} - \frac{a[3]}{2} + a[4]\right) \; -$$

$$90\left(-\left(\frac{1}{3840}\right) + \frac{a[1]}{384} - \frac{a[2]}{48} + \frac{a[3]}{8} - \frac{a[4]}{2} + a[5]\right) \; == \; 0$$

The conditions are just enough to solve for a_1 through a_5:

(5.2.14m)

```
solute = Solve[%,{a[1], a[2], a[3], a[4], a[5]}]
```

$$\{\{a[1] \to \frac{1 - e}{2}, \; a[2] \to$$

$$\frac{(267544166400 - 44590694400\ e)\ (1 - e)}{1070176665600} + \frac{-1 + e}{24},$$

$$a[3] \to \frac{1 - e}{240} + \frac{(22295347200 - 1486356480\ e)\ (-1 + e)}{1070176665600} +$$

$$\frac{(1 - e)\ (84722319360 - 22295347200\ e + 1486356480\ e^2)}{1070176665600}\backslash$$

$$, \; a[4] \to$$

$$\frac{(2229534720 - 79626240\ e)\ (1 - e)}{1070176665600} + \frac{-1 + e}{2688} +$$

```
                                                    2
     (-1 + e) (6370099200 - 743178240 e + 26542080 e )
     ------------------------------------------------- +
                      1070176665600


                                                     2
     ((1 - e) (20065812480 - 6688604160 e + 743178240 e  -

                3
       26542080 e )) / 1070176665600,

            1 - e   (199065600 - 4423680 e) (-1 + e)
     a[5] -> ----- + ------------------------------- +
            34560             1070176665600


                                                2
     (1 - e) (606928896 - 39813120 e + 884736 e )
     -------------------------------------------- +
                    1070176665600


                                                    2
     ((-1 + e) (1327104000 - 211156992 e + 13271040 e  -

                3
       294912 e )) / 1070176665600 +


                                                      2
     ((1 - e) (3821174784 - 1486356480 e + 214695936 e  -

                3            4
       13271040 e  + 294912 e )) / 1070176665600}}
```

This correct but unwieldy set of solutions can be brought down to a much more illustrative form:

$$(5.2.15m)$$

```
Simplify[solute]
```

```
            -(-1 + e)              (-5 + e) (-1 + e)
{{a[1] -> ----------, a[2] -> ------------------,
              2                       24
```

```
                -((-9 + e)  (-5 + e)  (-1 + e))
    a[3]  ->    ------------------------------,
                             720


                (-13 + e)  (-9 + e)  (-5 + e)  (-1 + e)
    a[4]  ->    ---------------------------------------,
                                 40320


    a[5]  ->

        -((-17 + e)  (-13 + e)  (-9 + e)  (-5 + e)  (-1 + e))
        ----------------------------------------------------}}
                              3628800
```

This result exhibits the celebrated quantization of eigenvalues. Indeed, if the energy E is any one of a certain set of values:

$$E = 1, 5, 9, 13, 17, ... \qquad (5.2.16)$$

then the coefficients a_i vanish from a certain index i onward. We did not prove this rigorously, but the result (5.2.15m) supports the fact. When the power series for g is thus a finite polynomial in x^2, it follows immediately that the wave function (5.2.11) is normalizable. Conversely, one can show through theoretical effort that if E is not one of the values in (5.2.16), then as x increases the g function (which is now an infinite series) grows so large that the exponential damping in (5.2.11) is insufficient and Ψ is not normalizable. This is all to say that the eigenvalues for even parity states of the harmonic oscillator are given precisely by (5.2.16). A similar *Mathematica* analysis may be carried through for the odd-parity eigenstates, in which case we find the relevant energy eigenvalues to be $E = 3, 7, 11, 15, ...$; meshing neatly with the even-parity eigenvalues (5.2.16). The exact normalized eigenstates for the Schroedinger equation (5.2.10) can be represented as [Schiff 1968]:

$$\Psi_n(x) = c_n H_n(x)\, e^{-x^2/2} \qquad (5.2.17)$$

where $c_n = (2^n n! \sqrt{\pi})^{-1/2}$ and H_n is the Hermite polynomial of order n. The energy eigenvalue E_n associated with the quantum number n is, as we have already seen for the first few n,

$$E_n = 2n + 1 \tag{5.2.18}$$

It is instructive to inspect a specific wave function using the *Mathematica* results just obtained:

(5.2.19m)

```
g /. solute[[1]] /. e->17
```

```
                    6         8
      2      4   32 x      16 x
1 - 8 x  + 8 x  - ----- + -----
                   15       105
```

This should be, up to an overall constant multiplier, the Hermite polynomial $H_8(x)$, because the energy is $17 = 2*8+1$. Sure enough, we call HermiteH[ ] directly as a check, remembering to adjust the overall constant by dividing through by $H_8(0)$:

(5.2.20m)

```
HermiteH[8,x]/HermiteH[8,0]
```

```
              2            4          6          8
1680 - 13440 x  + 13440 x  - 3584 x  + 256 x
------------------------------------------------
                    1680
```

This is just the output of (5.2.19m) in disguise. We can split the fraction into pieces via:

(5.2.21m)

```
Apart[%]
```

```
                    6         8
      2      4   32 x      16 x
1 - 8 x  + 8 x  - ----- + -----
                   15       105
```

It is also instructive to plot the wave function $\Psi_8(x)$:

(5.2.22m)

```
Plot[Normal[g Exp[-x^2/2] /. solute[[1]]
                       /. e->17], {x,-7,7}]
```

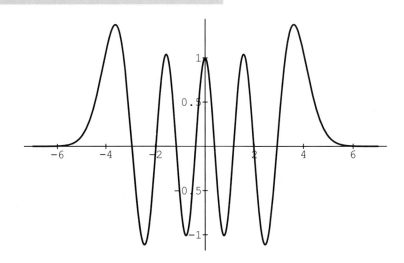

Figure 5.2.3: Symbolic manipulation can sometimes find exact
solutions, such as this eigenstate $\Psi_8(x)$ for the quantum
harmonic oscillator.

Many interesting techniques are available for *Mathematical* calculations
involving Hermite polynomials; or in fact most any orthogonal polynomial
system.   One may use the generating function for the orthogonal series, or
establish stored tables of definite integrals, or use recurrence relations between
orthogonal functions, and so on. Along such lines we next explore an example
from perturbation theory. In the standard theory for non-degenerate systems,
one begins with a perturbed Hamiltonian:

$$H' = H + \Delta H \tag{5.2.23}$$

where ΔH denotes the perturbation. Let $|n>$ denote the general eigenstate of
the unperturbed H, and let E_n denote the associated unperturbed energy. Then
the new energy is given by a perturbation series [Schiff 1968][Gottfried 1989]:

$$E_n' = E_n + M_{nn} + \sum_{m \neq n} \frac{|M_{mn}|^2}{E_n - E_m} + \dots \qquad (5.2.24)$$

where the matrix elements M_{mn} are given by:

$$M_{mn} = <m \mid \Delta H \mid n> \qquad (5.2.25)$$

We have exhibited the perturbation series only to second-order in the matrix element. But often in quantum studies just the first order correction M_{nn} is sufficient to yield useful results.

We shall demonstrate by way of example that *Mathematica* can be used to find the formal perturbation terms if an harmonic potential is perturbed by *any* polynomial in x. Consider a perturbed harmonic oscillator, whose original Hamiltonian is, as in (5.2.10):

$$H = -\frac{\partial^2}{\partial x^2} + V(x) \qquad (5.2.26)$$

with $V(x) = x^2$. Let this potential be perturbed by a quartic term:

$$V'(x) = x^2 + \lambda x^4 \qquad (5.2.27)$$

where the perturbation parameter λ is suitably minute. The theory tells us that

$$E_n' = E_n + M_{nn} + \frac{1}{2} \sum_{m \neq n} \frac{|M_{mn}|^2}{n - m} + \dots \qquad (5.2.28)$$

where the matrix element may be computed from the oscillator wave functions (5.2.17):

$$M_{mn} = \int_{-\infty}^{\infty} \Psi_m(x)\, \lambda\, x^4\, \Psi_n(x)\; dx \qquad (5.2.29)$$

One way to evaluate the indicated integral is to find x^4 as a linear combination of Hermite polynomials. Since H_0, H_2, and H_4 will be involved, we assume a linear combination of these three, and demand that the coefficients of x^0 and x^2 vanish; while the coefficient of x^4 be unity:

(5.2.30m)

```
f[x_]  := a HermiteH[0,x] + b HermiteH[2,x] +
                    c HermiteH[4,x]
Solve[f[0]  ==  0  &&
        f''[0]  ==  0  &&
        f''''[0]  ==  Factorial[4],  {a,b,c}
]
```

```
{{a -> 3/4,  b -> 3/4,  c -> 1/16}}
```

which establishes that

$$x^4 = 3H_0(x)/4 + 3H_2(x)/4 + H_4(x)/16 \qquad (5.2.31)$$

This expansion may then be used together with the integral [Gradshteyn and Ryzhik 1965]:

$$I_{mnk} = \int_{-\infty}^{\infty} H_m(x)\, H_n(x)\, H_k(x)\; e^{-x^2}\, dx \qquad (5.2.32)$$

$$= \frac{2^s \, m! \, n! \, k! \sqrt{\pi}}{(s-k)! \, (s-n)! \, (s-m)!}$$

valid when $s = (m+n+k)/2$ is an integer (otherwise the integral is zero). Note that factorials of negative integers are taken to be Infinity. The idea is to evaluate this interesting integral for H_k running through the list of Hermite polynomials appearing in the expansion (5.2.31). The exact result for the matrix element (5.2.29) under the perturbation $\Delta H = \lambda \, x^4$ is:

$$(5.2.33)$$

$$M_{mn} = \lambda \sqrt{m!} \sqrt{n!} \, (p! q!)^{-1} \, (\, 3\delta_{mn}/4 + 3p\delta_{q<2}/(q+1) +$$
$$6p(p-1)(\delta_{q<3} - \delta_{qo}/2)/((q+1)(q+2)))$$

where $m + n$ must be even, $2p = m + n$, $2q = |\, m - n\,|$, and δ denotes Kronecker delta. When $m + n$ is odd M_{mn} vanishes. Various corrections in (5.2.28) may now be evaluated readily:

$$(5.2.34m)$$

```
mat[m_,n_] := Block[
            {p, q, d0, d1, d2},
            If[Mod[m+n,2]>0, Return[0]];
            p = (m+n)/2;
            q = Abs[(m-n)/2];
            d0 = If[q==0,1,0];
            d1 = If[q >2,1,0];
            If[q==0,d2=1/2,If[q<3,d2=1,d2=0]];
            Return[lam *Sqrt[m! n!] *
                  (1/(p! q!) *
                  (3/4 d0 + 3p/(q+1) d1 +
                  6p(p-1) d2/((q+1)*(q+2)))
            ];
]
Print[mat[n,n]]
Print[mat[0,2]]
Print[mat[0,4]]
Print[mat[0,6]]
```

```
        3                   3 (-1 + n) n
lam (- + 3 n + ------------)
        4                   2
3 Sqrt[2] lam
-------------
        2
Sqrt[6] lam
-----------
        2
0
```

The first output of M_{nn} gives us the first-order energy correction in the form:

$$E_n{}' = E_n + M_{nn} + O(\lambda^2) \tag{5.2.35}$$
$$= E_n + 3\lambda(2n^2 + 2n + 1)/4 + O(\lambda^2)$$

This shows the first-order ground-state correction is $3\lambda/4$, and also that the first-order correction grows with the quantum number of the perturbed state. Later we shall check such results numerically. The three outputs of matrix elements of the form M_{0m} are enough to establish the second-order term for the perturbation of ground state energy. From (5.2.28) we know to set $n = 0$ and compute the sum:

$$\tag{5.2.36m}$$

```
Sum[mat[0,m]^2/(-2m), {m,2,4,2}]
```

```
        2
-21 lam
-------
    16
```

This result gives a neat expression for the ground state energy (recall $E_0 = 1$) as:

$$E_0{}' = 1 + 3\lambda/4 - 21\lambda^2/16 + O(\lambda^3) \tag{5.2.37}$$

This ends our symbolic tour of perturbation theory for the λx^4 perturbation. Before passing on to numerical approaches, we note that formal matrix elements of the form (5.2.33) can always be obtained using these procedures, as long as the perturbation is a polynomial in x.

Numerical solutions of the Schroedinger equation (5.2.1) can be obtained via many methods [Koonin and Meredith 1990]. A popular class of methods is comprised of shooting methods, in which trial E values are posited, and the wave function is integrated until it either blows up (or down), or violates the requisite number of zero-crossings, and so on. Information about the nature of the violation is used to update the E value, and the process continues with E converging hopefully to a good approximation of the exact energy. One shooting method that is easy to use when the potential is monotonic, as with $V(x) = x^2 + \lambda x^4$ for positive λ, is a certain trajectory method found in [Crandall and Reno 1982]. In this approach one reduces the eigenvalue problem to that of solving the first-order differential equation satisfied by a trajectory $g(z)$:

$$\frac{dg}{dz} = 1 - \frac{V(zE^{-1/2})}{E} \cos^2 g \qquad (5.2.38)$$

subject to boundary conditions $g(0) = 0$ (even-parity states), $g(0) = -\pi/2$ (odd-parity states). The key to finding eigenvalues is the observation that if $E = E_n$, then the exact function $g(z)$ approaches the value $(2[n/2]+1)\pi/2$ asymptotically, as $z \to \infty$, where [ ] denotes the integer floor. The actual formal substitution that yields (5.2.38) from the Schroedinger equation (5.2.1) is:

$$g(z) = \tan^{-1}\left(\frac{-\Psi'(zE^{-1/2})}{E^{1/2}\,\Psi(zE^{-1/2})}\right) \qquad (5.2.39)$$

from which it can be seen how the number of zeros of the wave function is related to the asymptotic value of the "trajectory function" g. Let us reproduce the first excited energy ($n = 1$) of the quantum oscillator using the trajectory equation (5.2.38) together with the Runge-Kutta solver (5.1.21m):

$$(5.2.40\text{m})$$

```
<<RK.m
v[x_] := x^2   (* Put monotonic potential function here. *)
n = 1   (* The quantum number. *)
```

```
If[Mod[n,2]==0, gam0=0, gam0 = -Pi/2.0]
asympt = N[(2 Floor[n/2.0]+1) Pi/2]
elow =   0
ehigh = 8
dz = 0.05
zlim = 7.0
While[ehigh-elow > 10^(-14),
    e = (elow+ehigh)/2.0;
    Print[N[e,20]];
      s = Sqrt[e];
    traj = RungeKutta[ {1,1-v[z/s]/s^2 Cos[gam]^2},
            {z, gam}, {0, gam0}, {zlim, dz}];
    final = traj[[Length[traj]]][[2]];
      If[final > asympt, ehigh = e, elow = e];
]
```

```
4.
2.
3.
3.5
3.25
3.125
3.0625
3.03125
3.015625
3.0078125
3.00390625
3.001953125
3.0009765625
3.00048828125
3.000244140625
3.0001220703125
3.00006103515625
3.000030517578125
3.000015258789063
3.000022888183594
3.000019073486328

. . .
```

The result 3.00002... is in good agreement with the exact eigenvalue $E_1 = 3$. We can use this technique to verify various results from our previous perturbation analysis. For the potential $V(x) = x^2 + \lambda\, x^4$, $\lambda = 1/100$ we proceed to calculate the perturbed ground state energy:

(5.2.41m)

```
v[x_] := x^2 + 0.01 x^4
n = 0
If[Mod[n,2]==0, gam0=0, gam0 = -Pi/2.0]
asympt = N[(2 Floor[n/2.0]+1) Pi/2]
elow =  1
ehigh = 1.01
dz = 0.02
zlim = 5.0
While[ehigh-elow > 10^(-14),
    e = (elow+ehigh)/2.0;
    Print[N[e,20]];
     s = Sqrt[e];
    traj = RungeKutta[ {1,1-v[z/s]/s^2 Cos[gam]^2},
                {z, gam}, {0, gam0}, {zlim, dz}];
    final = traj[[Length[traj]]][[2]];
     If[final > asympt, ehigh = e, elow = e];
]
```

```
1.005
1.0075
1.00625
1.006875
1.0071875
1.00734375
1.007421875
1.0073828125
1.00736328125
1.007373046875
1.0073779296875
1.00737548828125
1.007374267578125
1.007373657226562
1.007373962402344
1.007373809814453
1.007373733520508
1.007373695373535
1.007373676300049
1.007373666763306
1.007373671531677
. . .
```

Recall that the first-order correction for E_0 is $3\lambda/4 = 0.0075$, and that the second-order correction is $-21\lambda^2/16 = -0.0001312...$; the full correction through second order is embodied in (5.2.37):

$$E_0' \sim 1 + 0.0075 - 0.0001312 = 1.0073688... \qquad (5.2.42)$$

This is in good agreement with the result of (5.2.41m), the error being five parts per million of the unperturbed energy. The trajectory method in *Mathematica* can give results to at least twelve correct significant digits in some cases. For the pure-quartic oscillator with $V(x) = x^4$, the result of running (5.2.40m) with $n = 0$, $dz = 0.001$, $zlim = 4.5$ is:

$$E_0 \sim 1.0603620904841 \qquad (5.2.43)$$

which is presumably correct in its first thirteen significant digits.

There exist a multitude of further directions one may take for quantum mechanics via *Mathematica*. One may extend the numerical analysis of the Schroedinger equation to higher dimensions, particularly for radial potentials. Another fascinating area is the theory of scattering. Runge-Kutta solver and double-time-step (discussed in Chapter 6 under the rubric of soliton dynamics) methods can yield good plots of time-dependent quantum effects. Still other areas include path-integral techniques, spin and statistics, quantum field theory, and the complicated gauge- and group-theoretic approaches of modern particle physics.

5.3 Relativity

A good elementary example for relativity studies involves the expansion of Einstein total energy of a rest mass m moving rectilinearly with speed v:

$$E = \frac{mc^2}{(1 - v^2/c^2)^{1/2}}$$

(5.3.1)

A *Mathematica* exploration might start out thus:

(5.3.2m)

```
e[v_] := m c^2/Sqrt[1-v^2/c^2]
Series[e[v],{v,0,8}]
```

yielding the standard expansion in powers of v^2/c^2 :

```
           2        4         6           8
  2      m v      3 m v     5 m v      35 m v              9
 c   m + ---- +  ------ +  ------ +  -------  + O[v]
          2         2         4          6
                  8 c      16 c       128 c
```

Terms such as $O[v]^9$ can be removed, if desired, via the Normal[ ] function which will remove symbolic big-O errors. Note that E consists of the celebrated rest energy mc^2, followed by the Newtonian kinetic energy $mv^2/2$, followed by relativistic correction terms.

A somewhat deeper entry into relativity concepts is the following example of relativistic dynamics. The problem is not a common one to analyze, in fact the author had not analyzed it until *Mathematica* became available. Consider a relativistic dilemma that is posed in [Feynman, Leighton and Sands 1979]. Imagine as in Figure 5.3.1 that a clock is moved in some random vertical trajectory of height $h(t)$ starting from the ground at time $t = 0$, in such a way that this clock strikes the ground at time $t = 1$. Thus the only constraint on the trajectory, besides the physically reasonable ones such as differentiability, is that $h(0) = h(1) = 0$. Gravity will be treated special-relativistically in this example, that is, the full aparatus of general relativity will not be used.

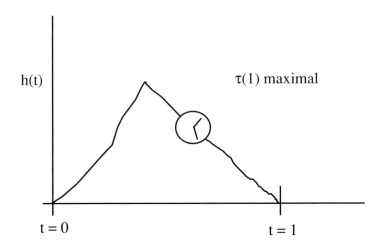

Figure 5.3.1: A relativistic clock is moved along some trajectory that connects ground level at *t*=0 and *t*=1. The question is, what trajectory maximizes the final clock reading $\tau(1)$?

The relevant question is this: what trajectory, subject to the endpoint constraints, will result in a *maximum* cumulative time reading on the clock? The clock's reading will be lower for higher trajectory speeds, due to Lorentz contraction of the time coordinate. On the other hand, higher height values $h(t)$ result in higher clock rates, because "a clock on the ceiling runs faster than a clock on the floor". Quantitatively, the clock's time will progress at a rate which is slowed by a factor $(1 - v^2/c^2)^{1/2}$, where $v = dh/dt$, but sped up by a factor of gh/c^2. This latter factor can be derived heuristically by considering that a photon of effective mass E/c^2 falling through a height h gains energy Egh/c^2. For the final clock reading to be maximal, we must find a compromise between trajectory classes for which the speed is generally too high, and those for which the height is too low. The cumulative clock reading, call it proper time $\tau(1)$, is therefore implicit in the formula:

$$mc^2(1 - \tau(1)) \; = \; \int_0^1 \left(mc^2(1 - \sqrt{1 - v^2/c^2}) \; - \; mgh \right) dt \qquad (5.3.3)$$

where mc^2, for clock rest mass m, has been multiplied through so that the ultimate dimensions of the integral signify action (energy-time). The problem thus comes down to a least action principle: we wish to minimize the integral in (5.3.3). It is a wonderful fact that the trajectory for which the action integral is a minimum is the actual dynamical path taken if you just "throw the clock" upward in such a way that this clock, under gravitational pull, meets the ground at $t = 1$. In other words, the path that maximizes the time $\tau(1)$ read on the clock (i.e., minimizes integral (5.3.3)) is the true dynamical path subject to gravity g. This problem can be couched in terms of Fermat's Principle of extremal affine time [Misner, Thorne and Wheeler 1973]. If the speed of light c were infinite, the path would turn out to be a simple parabola which for future clarity we write as:

$$h(t) \; = \; \frac{g}{8} \; - \; \frac{g}{2} \left(t - \frac{1}{2}\right)^2 \qquad (5.3.4)$$

This is the standard Newtonian ballistic trajectory satisfying $h(0) = h(1) = 0$. This result minimizes the integral (5.3.3) if we adopt the Newtonian approximation $\sqrt{(1 - v^2/c^2)} \sim 1 - v^2/2c^2$.

Now with *Mathematica* we can proceed with a somewhat delicate relativistic approximation to the solution $h(t)$.   The main idea is to use symbolic manipulation to analyze actual explicit cases of the action integral. We might assume a parabolic trajectory symmetrical around $t = 1/2$:

$$h(t) \; = \; a \; - \; 4a \left(t - \frac{1}{2}\right)^2 \qquad (5.3.5)$$

which for any a satifies the requisite endpoint conditions $h(0) = h(1) = 0$. Indeed this is a parabolic trajectory, the shape we expect only in the Newtonian limit $c \rightarrow \infty$, but in the present approximation the relativistic effect will be embodied in the final fact of $a \neq g/8$. The idea is to find the shifted parameter *a* that minimizes the action integral (5.3.3). We proceed, denoting the integrand of (5.3.3) a Lagrangian; the left-hand side itself being interpreted as an action:

(5.3.6m)

```
h[t_] := a - 4 a (t-1/2)^2
lagrangian[t_] := m c^2 (1-Sqrt[1-(D[h[t],t])^2/c^2])
                - m g h[t]
action[a_] := Integrate[lagrangian[t],{t,0,1}]
action[a]
```

```
c^2*m - ((1 - (16*a^2)/c^2)^(1/2)*c^2*m)/2 -
    (2*a*g*m)/3 + (c^3*m*ArcSin[(-4*a)/c])/(16*a) -
    (c^3*m*ArcSin[(4*a)/c])/(16*a)
```

This unwieldy expression for the relativistic action is opaque as to physical meaning. But the derivative, not the value, of the action is the important thing in these variational problems. We continue by defining the derivative of the action with respect to the parameter *a*:

(5.3.7m)

```
daction[a_] := Simplify[D[action[a],a]]
daction[a]
```

```
(8*a*m)/(1 - (16*a^2)/c^2)^(1/2) -
    (c^2*m)/(2*a*(1 - (16*a^2)/c^2)^(1/2)) -
    (2*g*m)/3 - (c^3*m*ArcSin[(-4*a)/c])/(16*a^2) +
    (c^3*m*ArcSin[(4*a)/c])/(16*a^2)
```

We want to find zeros of this derivative but the relation daction[a] = 0 is a transcendental relation in the variable *a*. One way to proceed is to do numerical analysis using FindRoot[ ] or FindMinimum[ ]. This approach is not ideal for two reasons. First, a theoretical dependence of the parameter *a* on the relativistic perturbation $1/c^2$ will not necessarily be clear from sheer numerics. Second, $1/c^2$ is so small (10^{-17} or so) in reality that round-off errors will threaten the analysis.

Are we stuck, in that closed-form exact solution is unlikely, while numerics have natural disadvantages? The answer is no, if we are content with theoretical expansions in powers of $1/c^2$. Actually, the situation is quite fortuitous, as we shall see later when the dynamical problem is *completely* solvable via another *Mathematica* route. This success will be due to the special nature of the simple potential *mgh*. Thinking in terms of perturbation expansions we look longingly at the output of (5.3.7m) and endeavor to create an approximate series whose zeros we then seek. The key operation in what follows is to approximate the ArcSin[ ] function to some finite degree:

$$\text{(5.3.8m)}$$

```
Unprotect[ArcSin]    (* Protect again at end of problem! *)
ArcSin[w_]  := w + w^3/6 + (3/40) w^5
```

The idea is to recast daction[a] in an algebraic form:

```
daction[a]
```
$$\text{(5.3.9m)}$$

```
(-8*a*m)/3 +  (8*a*m)/(1 -  (16*a^2)/c^2)^(1/2)
- (192*a^3*m)/(5*c^2)  -  (2*g*m)/3
```

This approximation is now correct to implicit perturbation order $1/c^2$. It is possible in principle to solve now daction[a] = 0 via a cumbersome quartic relation arising from (5.3.9m). But there is an interesting way to get the first perturbation terms via a symbolic form of Newton's method. Since the Newtonian limit $c \rightarrow \infty$ has $a = g/8$ from (5.3.4), we consider just one iteration

```
nexta = a - daction[a]/D[daction[a],a]
```
$$\text{(5.3.10m)}$$

```
a -  ((-8*a*m)/3 + (8*a*m)/(1 - (16*a^2)/c^2)^(1/2) -
     (192*a^3*m)/(5*c^2)  -  (2*g*m)/3)/
   ((-8*m)/3 + (8*m)/(1 - (16*a^2)/c^2)^(1/2) -
     (576*a^2*m)/(5*c^2) +
     (128*a^2*m)/((1 - (16*a^2)/c^2)^(3/2)*c^2))
```

Then we expand around $c = \infty$ and evaluate at the Newtonian zeroth-order term *g*/8 to obtain the beginning perturbation terms:

```
Series[nexta,{c,Infinity,3}] /. a->g/8
```
$$\text{(5.3.11m)}$$

```
g/8 - (3*g^3)/(320*c^2)+ O[1/c]^4
```

This result, that the next term in the $(1/c^2)$ relativistic expansion for $h(t)$ is

$$-\frac{3}{320}\frac{g^3}{c^2} \qquad (5.3.12)$$

indicates that the maximum height $h(1/2)$ is slightly *less* than its Newtonian counterpart. We shall see that the coefficient $-3/320$ is very close to the exact answer. The action formalism is correct, but the absolute minimum action is not obtained with a parabola.

We now turn to an exact solution of the moving clock problem. If L denotes the Lagrangian, i.e. the integrand of (5.3.3), then the Euler-Lagrange equation for the variational problem is

$$\frac{d}{dt}\frac{\partial L}{\partial v} - \frac{\partial L}{\partial h} = 0 \qquad (5.3.13)$$

We proceed to derive the exact solution to this differential equation, subject to the endpoint constraints $h(0) = h(1) = 0$, via *Mathematica* manipulations. The first stage is to obtain a logical expansion of the system:

$$(5.3.14m)$$

```
lagrangian = m c^2 (1-Sqrt[1-v^2/c^2]) - m g h
vmotion = LogicalExpand[
        D[lagrangian,v]== c0 + Integrate[D[lagrangian,h],t]
        ]
```

```
(m*v)/(1 - v^2/c^2)^(1/2)  == c0 - g*m*t
```

Note that we have integrated the Euler-Lagrange equation once and inserted an as yet arbitrary constant of integration $c0$. This result is equivalent to the relativistic analog of Newton's Law $dp/dt = mg$, where the relativistic momentum is

$$p = m \frac{d}{dt} \frac{v}{(1 - v^2/c^2)^{1/2}} \tag{5.3.15}$$

It should be pointed out that relativistic dynamics formalisms are problematic; even the concept of mechanical force is a dubious one. Neverthless, the present form of relativistic Newton's Law *is* a solution for the postulated action. Next we solve the output of (5.3.14m) for *v*:

(5.3.16m)

```
vsolute = Solve[vmotion,v]
```

```
{{v -> c*(1 - (c^2*m^2)/ (c0^2 + c^2*m^2 - 2*c0*g*m*t
              + g^2*m^2*t^2))^(1/2)},
 {v -> -(c*(1 - (c^2*m^2)/
              (c0^2 + c^2*m^2 - 2*c0*g*m*t + g^2*m^2*t^2))^
          (1/2))}
}
```

The two solutions correspond, in the present dynamical setting, to upward and downward going motion, respectively. It will be enough to work further with one of these solutions, so let us simplify the first of the solutions:

(5.3.17m)

```
vel = Simplify[v /. vsolute[[1]]]
(c*(c0 - g*m*t))/
   (c0^2 + c^2*m^2 - 2*c0*g*m*t + g^2*m^2*t^2)^(1/2)
```

As luck would have it, the quantity vel is the general velocity solution because it has happened fortuitously, during simplification, that the symbolic square root of a quantity x^2 is x which can have either sign. To get the exact trajectory $h(t)$, we next integrate *vel* and then resolve the constant of integration:

(5.3.18m)

```
hei = Integrate[vel,t]
hei = hei - (hei /. t->0)
```

```
(c*(c0^2 + c^2*m^2)^(1/2))/(g*m) -
   (c*(c0^2 + c^2*m^2 - 2*c0*g*m*t + g^2*m^2*t^2)^(1/2))/
   (g*m)
```

What we have done via the calculation of hei – (hei /. t–>0) is forced the height at time zero to vanish as required. Of course, we also could have introduced a second constant, say $c1$, and proceeded to solve for that constant. This is how we shall finally remove the original constant $c0$:

(5.3.19m)

```
const = Solve[(hei /. t->1) ==0, c0]
```

```
{{c0 -> (g*m)/2}}
```

The exact trajectory is finally available; we exhibit it together with checks for its endpoint constraints:

(5.3.20m)

```
Print[height = hei /. const[[1]]]
Print[height /. t->0]
Print[height /. t->1]
```

```
                    2   2
         2   2     g   m
 c Sqrt[c   m   + -----]
                    4
--------------------- -
          g m

                    2   2
         2   2     g   m      2   2       2   2   2
   c Sqrt[c   m   + ----- - g   m   t + g   m   t ]
                    4
-------------------------------------------
                  g m
0
0
```

Of course, one could also verify the Euler-Lagrange equation (5.3.13) by direct symbolic differentiation of the height quantity.

Figure 5.3.2 shows the relativistic motion (for an artificial value $c = 1$) plotted against the Newtonian case ($c = \infty$).

(5.3.21.m)

```
Plot[{height /. {m->1., g->9.8, c->1},
       (g/8 - g/2 (t-1/2)^2) /.
       {m->1., g->9.8} },
     {t,0,1}]
```

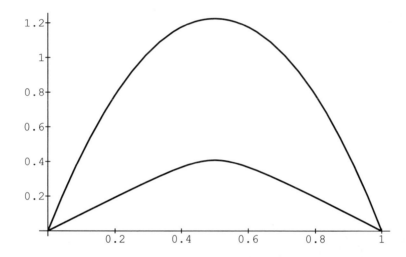

Figure 5.3.2: The problem posed in Figure 5.3.1 has a Newtonian solution
             (upper parabola) when $c = \infty$, and relativistic solutions whose shape
             depends on g and c. Note the straighter, more "light-like" upward
             and downward clock trajectories for relativistic cases.

To check the perturbation term (5.3.12) that arose from approximations to the
action, we can simultaneously expand the exact trajectory like so:

$$(5.3.22m)$$

```
Print[Series[Series[height,{t,1/2,4}],{c,Infinity,2}]]
```

```
                                       1       2
            3                    g  (-(-) + t)
  g     g            1 3         2
  -  -  ------  + O[-]    -  -------------  +
  8        2           c            2
      128  c


            3
            g          1 3     1       4        1       5
     (----  + O[-]  )  (-(-) + t)   + O[-(-) + t]
            2          c    2                2
        8  c
```

Note that this double Taylor expansion is centered around $t = 1/2$, and around $c = \infty$. The resulting exact perturbation term for height at $t = 1/2$ is read off immediately as

$$-\frac{1}{128}\frac{g^3}{c^2} \tag{5.3.23m}$$

This is the loss in maximum height with respect to the Newtonian case. The numerical agreement between $1/128$ and the value $3/320$ from (5.3.12) indicates that action approximations can be promising, especially when we cannot solve the motion in closed form.

Figure 5.3.2 shows that deep relativistic situations involve trajectories which "hug" the ground and exhibit "light-like" segments. This behavior is reminiscent of the theoretical black hole phenomenon in which particles cannot escape a sufficient gravitational pull, at least not in the absence of quantum effects. To handle these situations it is not a good idea to stay with semi-general-relativistic treatments as in the clock puzzle. Instead, one should use the full apparatus of general relativity. For example, if action principles are to be employed, one should investigate transformations of the full geodesic equation, employing Christoffel symbols, affine parameters, and the like. A sophisticated package such as *MathTensor* [Parker and Christenson 1989] has been developed to handle such profound manipulations. In *MathTensor* one may, for example, derive the Einstein field equations from an action principle. As for black hole studies, the Schwarzchild metric is analyzed in the following example project. The source below is not at all complete. It is included just to show the reader what form a large relativity project might take.

(Note: like similar research packages, the MathTensor package is generally not included in standard Mathematica issues and must be obtained separately.)

(5.3.24m)

```
============================================================
(* Here is the Schwarzschild.metric file. *)
(* Copyright 1989 Leonard Parker and Steven Christensen *)
(* SchwarzschildIn.metric *)
(* Basic input file for Components.m file. *)

Dimension = 4

x/: x[1] = r
x/: x[2] = theta
x/: x[3] = phi
x/: x[4] = t
Metricg/: Metricg[-1, -1] = (1 - (2*G*M)/r)^(-1)
Metricg/: Metricg[-2, -1] = 0
Metricg/: Metricg[-3, -1] = 0
Metricg/: Metricg[-4, -1] = 0
Metricg/: Metricg[-2, -2] = r^2
Metricg/: Metricg[-3, -2] = 0
Metricg/: Metricg[-4, -2] = 0
Metricg/: Metricg[-3, -3] = r^2*Sin[theta]^2
Metricg/: Metricg[-4, -3] = 0
Metricg/: Metricg[-4, -4] = -(1 - (2*G*M)/r)


============================================================
Please wait while the metric determinant, Detg, and the
covariant metric components are calculated.
============================================================


Here is the BlackHole.out file that is produced.
The user may read this file in at anytime if they need to use the
objects computed herein.

Dimension = 4
x/: x[1] = r
x/: x[2] = theta
x/: x[3] = phi
x/: x[4] = t
Metricg/: Metricg[i_, j_] :=
                Metricg[j, i] /; !OrderedQ[{i, j}]
Metricg/: Metricg[-1, -1] = (1 - (2*G*M)/r)^(-1)
Metricg/: Metricg[-2, -1] = 0
Metricg/: Metricg[-3, -1] = 0
Metricg/: Metricg[-4, -1] = 0
Metricg/: Metricg[-2, -2] = r^2
```

```
Metricg/: Metricg[-3, -2] = 0
Metricg/: Metricg[-4, -2] = 0
Metricg/: Metricg[-3, -3] = r^2*Sin[theta]^2
Metricg/: Metricg[-4, -3] = 0
Metricg/: Metricg[-4, -4] = -(1 - (2*G*M)/r)
Metricg/: Metricg[1, 1] = -((2*G*M - r)/r)
Metricg/: Metricg[1, 2] = 0
Metricg/: Metricg[1, 3] = 0
Metricg/: Metricg[1, 4] = 0
Metricg/: Metricg[2, 2] = r^(-2)
Metricg/: Metricg[2, 3] = 0
Metricg/: Metricg[2, 4] = 0
Metricg/: Metricg[3, 3] = 1/(r^2*Sin[theta]^2)
Metricg/: Metricg[3, 4] = 0
Metricg/: Metricg[4, 4] = -(r/(-2*G*M + r))
Metricg/: Metricg[-1, 1] = 1
Metricg/: Metricg[-1, 2] = 0
Metricg/: Metricg[-1, 3] = 0
Metricg/: Metricg[-1, 4] = 0
Metricg/: Metricg[-2, 1] = 0
Metricg/: Metricg[-2, 2] = 1
Metricg/: Metricg[-2, 3] = 0
Metricg/: Metricg[-2, 4] = 0
Metricg/: Metricg[-3, 1] = 0
Metricg/: Metricg[-3, 2] = 0
Metricg/: Metricg[-3, 3] = 1
Metricg/: Metricg[-3, 4] = 0
Metricg/: Metricg[-4, 1] = 0
Metricg/: Metricg[-4, 2] = 0
Metricg/: Metricg[-4, 3] = 0
Metricg/: Metricg[-4, 4] = 1
MatrixMetricgLower =
        {{(1 - (2*G*M)/r)^(-1), 0, 0, 0}, {0, r^2, 0, 0},
        {0, 0, r^2*Sin[theta]^2, 0},
        {0, 0, 0, -(1 - (2*G*M)/r)}}
MatrixMetricgUpper =
        {{-((2*G*M - r)/r), 0, 0, 0}, {0, r^(-2), 0, 0},
        {0, 0, 1/(r^2*Sin[theta]^2), 0},
        {0, 0, 0, -(r/(-2*G*M + r))}}
Detg = -(r^4*Sin[theta]^2)
Rmsign = 1
Rcsign = 1
AffineG/: AffineG[i_, j_, k_] := AffineG[i, k, j] /;
!OrderedQ[{j, k}]
AffineG/: AffineG[1, -1, -1] = (G*M)/((2*G*M - r)*r)
AffineG/: AffineG[1, -2, -1] = 0
AffineG/: AffineG[1, -3, -1] = 0
AffineG/: AffineG[1, -4, -1] = 0
AffineG/: AffineG[1, -2, -2] = 2*G*M - r
AffineG/: AffineG[1, -3, -2] = 0
```

```
AffineG/: AffineG[1, -4, -2] = 0
AffineG/: AffineG[1, -3, -3] = (2*G*M - r)*Sin[theta]^2
AffineG/: AffineG[1, -4, -3] = 0
AffineG/: AffineG[1, -4, -4] = -((G*M*(2*G*M - r))/r^3)
AffineG/: AffineG[2, -1, -1] = 0
AffineG/: AffineG[2, -2, -1] = r^(-1)
AffineG/: AffineG[2, -3, -1] = 0
AffineG/: AffineG[2, -4, -1] = 0
AffineG/: AffineG[2, -2, -2] = 0
AffineG/: AffineG[2, -3, -2] = 0
AffineG/: AffineG[2, -4, -2] = 0
AffineG/: AffineG[2, -3, -3] = -(Cos[theta]*Sin[theta])
AffineG/: AffineG[2, -4, -3] = 0
AffineG/: AffineG[2, -4, -4] = 0
AffineG/: AffineG[3, -1, -1] = 0
AffineG/: AffineG[3, -2, -1] = 0
AffineG/: AffineG[3, -3, -1] = r^(-1)
AffineG/: AffineG[3, -4, -1] = 0
AffineG/: AffineG[3, -2, -2] = 0
AffineG/: AffineG[3, -3, -2] = Cos[theta]/Sin[theta]
AffineG/: AffineG[3, -4, -2] = 0
AffineG/: AffineG[3, -3, -3] = 0
AffineG/: AffineG[3, -4, -3] = 0
AffineG/: AffineG[3, -4, -4] = 0
AffineG/: AffineG[4, -1, -1] = 0
AffineG/: AffineG[4, -2, -1] = 0
AffineG/: AffineG[4, -3, -1] = 0
AffineG/: AffineG[4, -4, -1] = (G*M)/(r*(-2*G*M + r))
AffineG/: AffineG[4, -2, -2] = 0
AffineG/: AffineG[4, -3, -2] = 0
AffineG/: AffineG[4, -4, -2] = 0
AffineG/: AffineG[4, -3, -3] = 0
AffineG/: AffineG[4, -4, -3] = 0
AffineG/: AffineG[4, -4, -4] = 0
RiemannR/: RiemannR[i_, j_, k_, l_] :=
      0 /; i == j || k == l
RiemannR/: RiemannR[i_, j_, k_, l_] :=
        -RiemannR[i, j, l, k] /; !OrderedQ[{k, l}]
RiemannR/: RiemannR[i_, j_, k_, l_] :=
        -RiemannR[j, i, k, l] /; !OrderedQ[{i, j}]
RiemannR/: RiemannR[i_, j_, k_, l_] :=
        RiemannR[k, l, i, j] /; !OrderedQ[{i, k}]
RiemannR/: RiemannR[i_, j_, k_, l_] :=
        RiemannR[k, l, i, j] /; i == k && !OrderedQ[{j, l}]
RiemannR/: RiemannR[-2, -1, -2, -1] = (G*M)/(2*G*M - r)
RiemannR/: RiemannR[-3, -1, -3, -1] =
      (G*M*Sin[theta]^2)/(2*G*M - r)
RiemannR/: RiemannR[-3, -2, -3, -1] = 0
RiemannR/: RiemannR[-3, -2, -3, -2] = 2*G*M*r*Sin[theta]^2
```

```
RiemannR/: RiemannR[-4, -1, -4, -1] = (-2*G*M)/r^3
RiemannR/: RiemannR[-4, -2, -4, -1] = 0
RiemannR/: RiemannR[-4, -3, -4, -1] = 0
RiemannR/: RiemannR[-4, -2, -4, -2] =
       -((G*M*(2*G*M - r))/r^2)
RiemannR/: RiemannR[-4, -3, -4, -2] = 0
RiemannR/: RiemannR[-4, -3, -4, -3] =
       -((G*M*(2*G*M - r)*Sin[theta]^2)/r^2)
RiemannR/: RiemannR[-3, -1, -2, -1] = 0
RiemannR/: RiemannR[-3, -2, -2, -1] = 0
RiemannR/: RiemannR[-4, -1, -2, -1] = 0
RiemannR/: RiemannR[-4, -2, -2, -1] = 0
RiemannR/: RiemannR[-4, -3, -2, -1] = 0
RiemannR/: RiemannR[-4, -1, -3, -1] = 0
RiemannR/: RiemannR[-4, -2, -3, -1] = 0
RiemannR/: RiemannR[-4, -3, -3, -1] = 0
RiemannR/: RiemannR[-4, -1, -3, -2] = 0
RiemannR/: RiemannR[-4, -2, -3, -2] = 0
RiemannR/: RiemannR[-4, -3, -3, -2] = 0
```

This software computes the affine connections, Riemann curvature tensor, and other constructs related to the celebrated Schwarzchild metric The black hole condition appears as the change in character in various tensor components when $1 - 2GM/r$ becomes negative, which in elementary units is when a spherically symmetric body's mass M is sufficiently great that $r \leq r_s$ where r_s = $2GM/c^2$ is the Schwarzchild radius.

The inner workings of a package such as *MathTensor* are too voluminous and intricate for this book. But the following study of elementary relativistic manipulations will give a taste of covariance principles that involve juggling of component indices, and which lead naturally to the higher reaches of tensor calculus.   We treat the celebrated problem of Compton scattering as pictorialized in Figure 5.3.3.

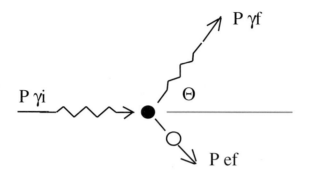

Figure 5.3.3: Compton scattering pictorial. An electron at rest is
struck by a photon of four-momentum $P_{\gamma i}$, which scatters
into four-momentum $P_{\gamma f}$, leaving the electron with P_{ef}.

A four-vector may be introduced as a construct (in *Mathematica*, a List)
envisioned as having three "spatial" parts and one "temporal" part:

$$p = \{p_x, p_y, p_z, ip_t\} \tag{5.3.25}$$

Consistent with this four-vector notation will be the rule that the list elements
of p be enumerated:

$$\text{p[[1]]} = p_x, \text{ p[[2]]} = p_y, ... \tag{5.3.26}$$

A scalar product operation is defined for four-vectors p and q by:

$$p \cdot q = p_x q_x + p_y q_y + p_z q_z - p_t q_t \tag{5.3.27}$$

which is a 4-dimensional standard dot-product, or if you wish, a 3-vector dot-
product minus the product of the imaginary parts of the temporal components.
One type of four-vector is just a space-time point $r = \{x, y, z, ict\}$. The concept
of Lorentz transformation enters when we consider multiplication of general
four-vectors by 4-by-4 matrices of a certain class. For real parameter g called
the rapidity, define the following example matrix:

$$L = \begin{matrix} \cosh g & 0 & 0 & i \sinh g \\ 0 & 1 & 0 & 0 \\ 0 & 0 & 1 & 0 \\ -i \sinh g & 0 & 0 & \cosh g \end{matrix} \qquad (5.3.28)$$

This is a so-called Lorentz x-boost because it properly transforms space-time coordinates between inertial frames that are separated by a certain x-velocity. This velocity v is given in terms of the rapidity parameter by:

$$\tanh g = v/c \qquad (5.3.29)$$

For a four-vector $r = \{x, y, z, ict\}$, first observe that its scalar product with itself is

$$r \cdot r = x^2 + y^2 + z^2 - c^2 t^2 \qquad (5.3.30)$$

It is a remarkable fact that a Lorentz transformation leaves (5.3.30) invariant. This is the central principle of relativity and we shall demonstrate the principle as follows. First we arrange for the output of the scalar product of the transformed four-vector with itself:

$$(5.3.31m)$$

```
r = {x, y, z, I c t}
lorentz = {{Cosh[g],0,0, I Sinh[g]},{0,1,0,0},{0,0,1,0},
           {- I Sinh[g],0,0,Cosh[g]}
}
(lorentz . r) . (lorentz . r)
```

```
I*c*t*(((E^(-g) + E^g)*(I/2*(E^(-g) + E^g)*c*t +
         -I/2*(-E^(-g) + E^g)*x))/2 +
    I/2*(-E^(-g) + E^g)*
      (-((-E^(-g) + E^g)*c*t)/2 + ((E^(-g) + E^g)*x)/2)) +
  x*(-I/2*(-E^(-g) + E^g)*
      (I/2*(E^(-g) + E^g)*c*t + -I/2*(-E^(-g) + E^g)*x) +
    ((E^(-g) + E^g)*(-((-E^(-g) + E^g)*c*t)/2 +
      ((E^(-g) + E^g)*x)/2))/2) + y^2 + z^2
```

Not too illuminating, except that we still have the Simplify[ ] option:

$$(5.3.32m)$$

```
Simplify[%]
```

```
-(c^2*t^2) + x^2 + y^2 + z^2
```

Which establishes the remarkable invariance property, at least for *x*-boosts. The group of physically relevant Lorentz transformations includes *x,y,z* boosts as well as pure 3-space transformations. It is not difficult to show that textbook definitions of the Lorentz group of transformations satisfy invariance principles by using *Mathematica* in this way. To see an explicit transformation, you can establish the rules:

$$(5.3.33m)$$

```
rapidityrule =
     { Exp[-g]  -> Sqrt[(1-v/c)/(1+v/c)],
              Exp[g]  -> Sqrt[(1+v/c)/(1-v/c)]}
```

and then invoke powerful *Mathematica* sequences such as matrix-vector multiplication followed by rule substitution and simplification:

$$(5.3.34m)$$

```
Simplify[lorentz . r /. rapidityrule]
```

```
{(-(t*v) + x)/((1 - v/c)^(1/2)*(1 + v/c)^(1/2)), y, z,
   (I*c^2*t + -I*v*x)/(c*(1 - v/c)^(1/2)*(1 + v/c)^(1/2))}
```

This output is precisely the textbook Lorentz transformation for *x*-boosts, velocity v. In other words, the transformed *x* coordinate is

$$x' = \frac{x - vt}{(1 - v^2/c^2)^{1/2}} \qquad (5.3.35)$$

with a similar formula for *t'*, with *y' = y* and *z' = z*. This covariance study, when applied to an energy-momentum four-vector, will yield such celebrated relations as (5.3.1). Turning to our example of Compton scattering, we need to establish nomenclature for the various four-vectors from Figure 5.3.3. An energy-momentum four-vector has the general form

$$P = \{ p_x, p_y, p_z, iE/c \} \tag{5.3.36}$$

This four-momentum has the beautiful property that its scalar product with itself is an invariant quantity. For an inertial particle of rest mass $m > 0$ there is always a rest frame in which all of the spatial momentum components vanish. Since $P \cdot P = -E^2/c^2 = -m^2c^2$ in this frame, it follows that $P' \cdot P' = -m^2c^2$ for any four-momentum P' obtained from a Lorentz transformation on P. For a photon the energy-momentum relation is $E = pc$, so that a momentum four-vector for a photon incident in the $+x$ direction will take the form

$$\{p, 0, 0, ip\} \tag{5.3.37}$$

By the de Broglie principle, the wavelength of the photon is accordingly $\lambda = h/p$ where h is Planck's constant. We may now establish nomenclature:

$$\tag{5.3.38}$$

initial photon four-vector $P_{\gamma i} = \{h/\lambda_i, 0, 0, ih/\lambda_i\}$
final photon four-vector $P_{\gamma f} = \{h/\lambda_f \cos \Theta, h/\lambda_f \sin \Theta, 0, ih/\lambda_f\}$
initial electron four-vector $P_{ei} = \{0, 0, 0, imc\}$
final electron four-vector $P_{ef} = \{p_x, p_y, 0, iE/c\}$

To use the four-vector approach efficiently, we try to remove some unknowns such as final electron momenta by exploiting invariance. Indeed, by energy and momentum conservation,

$$P_{ei} + P_{\gamma i} = P_{ef} + P_{\gamma f} \tag{5.3.39}$$

By invariance of $P_{ef} \cdot P_{ef}$ it follows that

$$(P_{ei} + P_{\gamma i} - P_{\gamma f}) \cdot (P_{ei} + P_{\gamma i} - P_{\gamma f}) = -m^2c^2 \tag{5.3.40}$$

A *Mathematica* session may now commence, with a view to a derivation of the Compton scattering relation between initial, final photon wavelengths and the scattering angle Θ of Figure 5.3.4. The strategy is to generate the left-hand side of (5.3.40) symbolically, simplify it, and infer the desired scattering identity. We start with the suppositions (5.3.38):

(5.3.41m)

```
pgi = {h/li, 0, 0, I h/li}
pgf = {h/lf Cos[t], h/lf Sin[t], 0, I h/lf}
pei = {0, 0, 0, I m c}
totsquare = (pei+pgi-pgf) . (pei+pgi-pgf)
```

```
((-I*h)/lf + (I*h)/li + I*c*m)^2 +
   (h/li - (h*Cos[t])/lf)^2 + (h^2*Sin[t]^2)/lf^2
```

Now we add m^2c^2 and work with the output which must equal zero:

(5.3.42m)

```
zero = Expand[totsquare] + m^2 c^2
```

```
-(h^2/lf^2) + (2*h^2)/(lf*li) + (2*c*h*m)/lf -
   (2*c*h*m)/li - (2*h^2*Cos[t])/(lf*li) +
   (h^2*Cos[t]^2)/lf^2 + (h^2*Sin[t]^2)/lf^2
```

(5.3.43m)

```
ru = Cos[t]^2 + Sin[t]^2 -> 1
zero = Expand[zero lf lf / h^2] /. ru
```

```
(2*lf)/li + (2*c*lf*m)/h - (2*c*lf^2*m)/(h*li) -
(2*lf*Cos[t])/li
```

(5.3.44m)

```
zero = Expand[zero * li/lf * h/(2 m c)]
```

```
-lf + li + h/(c*m) - (h*Cos[t])/(c*m)
```

This final solution to the Compton scattering problem is customarily written

$$\lambda_f - \lambda_i = \lambda_c (1 - \cos \Theta)$$ (5.3.45)

where $\lambda_c = h/mc$ is the Compton wavelength of the electron. *Mathematica* may be used in this way to support what might be called course problems in relativity, as found in references such as [Lightman, et. al. 1975].

5.4 Further explorations

E5.1) Investigate the Hamiltonian system for a perturbed two-dimensional harmonic oscillator: $H = (p_x^2 + p_y^2) / 2m + m\omega^2(x^2+y^2)/2 - k/(x^2+y^2)$. This system is exactly solvable and yields precessing closed orbits. Work out both symbolic and numerical solution approaches, far enough in each case to exhibit the precession of orbits.

E5.2) Investigate the conical pendulum, which is a mass m affixed to a ceiling-pivoted rigid rod of length L. The mass is allowed to move beyond mere planar motion; e.g. there are circular stable orbits, in which cases the rod describes a cone. Verify the result that for very small pseudo-elliptical orbits, the rate of precession of the perihelion is proportional to the ellipse's area.

E5.3) For the pendulum equation (5.1.11) it is sometimes stated informally that there can be no exact solutions. Show this presumption to be false by finding appropriate parameters a, b, c such that $\Theta(t) = a + b \arctan(e^{ct})$ is indeed an exact solution. Intepret this solution physically.

E5.4) In the tunnel effect, fix enough example parameters in order to plot the transmission probability $|t|^2$ vs. incident wave energy E, for a fixed barrier height V_0. Note that the algebra changes when E crosses the value V_0.

E5.5) Write a general numerical solver for radial Schroedinger potentials $V(r)$ in three dimensional settings. A package should find eigenstates $\Psi_{nlm}(r,\theta,\phi)$ where n = principal quantum number, l = angular quantum number, m = azimuthal quantum number. Typical potentials of interest include the inverted Gaussian $V = -Ae^{-r^2}$ and the Yukawa potential $V = -e^{-kr}/r$.

E5.6) Using four-vectors, find the minimum total energy of a fast proton such that when it hits a stationary proton, an extra proton-anti-proton pair may be produced. Hint: in a center-of-mass frame at threshold, the two original protons meet head on, resulting in a cluster of four masses hovering stationary.

E5.7) Analyze a relativistic harmonic oscillator, using the (perhaps naive) assumption that the potential appearing in the action formalism is $V(x) = kx^2/2$. Quantify, for example, the anharmonicity due to the finitude of c.

Chapter 6:
Linear and non-linear systems

6.1 Linear Oscillations

In Chapter 5 we studied dynamical trajectories for two types of oscillators: simple harmonic and perturbed (true pendulum). Instead of generalizing simple harmonic motion by introducing anharmonic terms, another way to generalize the motion is to inject new degrees of freedom. Consider the concept of coupled oscillators as exemplified in Figure 6.1.1.

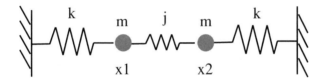

Figure 6.1.1: Coupled oscillator pictorial, giving two coupled
second-order differential equations for $x_1(t)$ and $x_2(t)$.

It is convenient to think of the respective origins of the x_i to be situated at the mass m positions of the figure, so that the $x_i(t)$ represent displacements from the pictorial equilibrium. The equations of motion for the coupled system are:

$$m\,\frac{d^2x_1}{dt^2} = -k\,x_1 - j\,(x_1 - x_2) \qquad (6.1.1)$$

$$m\,\frac{d^2x_2}{dt^2} = -k\,x_2 + j\,(x_1 - x_2)$$

We next search for normal modes, which will be oscillatory solution pairs $\{x_1, x_2\}$ having the *same* angular frequency ω, but possibly different amplitudes. Let

(6.1.2)

$$x_1 = a_1 \, e^{i\omega t}$$

$$x_2 = a_2 \, e^{i\omega t}$$

Then the equations (6.1.1) become

$$K \, \{a_1, a_2\} = \omega^2 \, \{a_1, a_2\} \tag{6.1.3}$$

where K is the matrix $(1/m) \, \{\{k+j, -j\}, \{-j, k+j\}\}$. The *Mathematica* arrangement for this matrix is lexicographic:

$(k+j)/m$	$-j/m$	(6.1.4)
$-j/m$	$(k+j)/m$	

Equation (6.1.3) mandates that the squared angular frequency ω^2 be an eigenvalue of the K matrix, while the amplitude vector $\{a_1, a_2\}$ be an eigenvector of said matrix. *Mathematica* produces the eigenvalues like so:

(6.1.5m)

```
kmat = (1/m) {{k+j,-j}, {-j,k+j}}
e = Eigenvalues[kmat]
```

```
{k/m, (2*j + k)/m}
```

Therefore the two normal mode frequencies are given by the roots $\omega_1 = \sqrt{(k/m)}$ and $\omega_2 = \sqrt{((2j+k)/m)}$. It is not easy to see at first why these two frequencies should be so important; for example why does the first eigenvalue $\sqrt{(k/m)}$ not depend on the coupling spring constant j? To answer such inquiries, we proceed to develop the eigenvectors:

(6.1.6m)

```
Eigenvectors[kmat]
```

```
{{j/((-(k/m) + (j + k)/m)*m), 1},
  {j/(((j + k)/m - (2*j + k)/m)*m), 1}}
```

This result is not yet illuminating because there are too many terms. Happily, *Mathematica* has the capacity to contract such expressions, as in this sequence:

(6.1.7m)

```
Simplify[%]
```

```
{{1, 1}, {-1, 1}}
```

Apparently the two normal modes can be written:

$$\{x_1(t), x_2(t)\} = \{1, 1\} e^{\pm i\omega_1 t}$$ (6.1.8)

and

$$\{x_1(t), x_2(t)\} = \{-1, 1\} e^{\pm i\omega_2 t}$$ (6.1.9)

where again the ω_i are the square roots of the output of (6.1.5m). It turns out that we have completely solved the system in the sense that *every* steady-state solution of the original equations of motion (6.1.1) is some superposition of modes (6.1.8), (6.1.9). The general solution has four independent constants to be determined (two for the $\pm\omega_1$ modes and two for the $\pm\omega_2$ modes). These could be fixed, for example, by knowing four natural values: the position and velocity of each mass at $t = 0$.

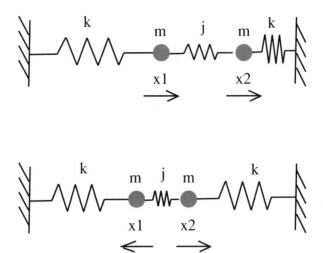

Figure 6.1.2: The two normal modes of the coupled oscillator. The
upper pictorial corresponds to eigenvector $\{1, 1\}$, frequency
ω_1, and the bottom to $\{-1, 1\}$, frequency ω_2.

Figure 6.1.2 gives credence to the eigenvalues that *Mathematica* picked out for
this problem. In the upper picture the middle coupling spring is not extended
because the masses move in phase, hence the result $\omega_1 = \sqrt{(k/m)}$ is entirely
reasonable. One superposition of the normal mode solutions that is of special
interest is the case:

$$x_1(t) = \cos \omega_1 t - \cos \omega_2 t \qquad\qquad (6.1.10)$$
$$x_2(t) = \cos \omega_1 t + \cos \omega_2 t$$

This solution is a mixture of the real parts of the two modes (6.1.8), (6.1.9) with
equal weighting. A sequence that shows the explicit time-dependent motion is
the following:

$$(6.1.11m)$$

```
k = 1.; m = 1.; j = 0.1
w1 = Sqrt[e[[1]]]
```

```
w2 = Sqrt[e[[2]]]
x1[t_] := Cos[w1 t] - Cos[w2 t]
x2[t_] := Cos[w1 t] + Cos[w2 t]
Plot[x1[t],{t,0,200}]
Plot[x2[t],{t,0,200}]
```

which results in a plot of the "sloshing" phenomenon of Figure 6.1.3. The kinetic energy sloshes from one mass to the other. One imagines that one of the masses is set into oscillatory motion. Because the coupling j is relatively weak, it takes some time for the other mass to respond, but when it does it becomes the more energetic body.

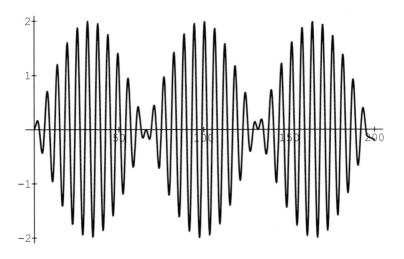

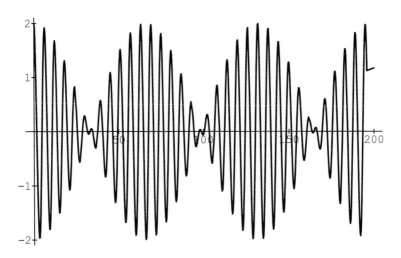

Figure 6.1.3: A particular coupled oscillator solution: the equal
mixture of normal modes. The top plot is $x_1(t)$, the
bottom $x_2(t)$. The energy sloshes between the masses
at a rate determined by the coupling constant j.

These methods may be applied to more profound cases. If there be N mass coordinates coupled in one dimension by equal spring constants k, then an N-by-N matrix with values $2k$ along the diagonal, and $-k$ values on the off-diagonals will arise. One may analyze such systems to obtain celebrated classical results as pertain to solid-state physics and wave mechanics.

As a second example of linear vibration studies we turn to the problem of the circular acoustic planar membrane. The wave equation for the z-displacement of a the membrane in polar coordinates (r, Θ) and time t is taken to be

$$\frac{1}{v^2} \frac{\partial^2 z}{\partial t^2} - \frac{1}{r} \frac{\partial}{\partial r} \left(r \frac{\partial}{\partial r} \right) z - \frac{1}{r^2} \frac{\partial^2 z}{\partial \Theta^2} = 0 \qquad (6.1.12)$$

where v is the acoustic speed. The normal procedure is to posit an eigensolution

$$z(r, \Theta, t) = Z(r, \Theta) e^{i\omega t} \qquad (6.1.13)$$

in which case the solutions that are finite at the origin can be indexed by integers n = 0, 1, 2, ...:

$$Z(r, \Theta) = J_n(\omega r/v) e^{in\Theta} \qquad (6.1.14)$$

with J_n denoting the Bessel function of order n. Interesting solutions obtain when we assume natural boundary conditions, such as $Z(a, \Theta) = 0$ for all angles Θ; corresponding to a membrane clamped at radius a. This constraint pertains to a drum membrane with a rigid circular boundary. Let us analyze the example eigensolution for $n = 2$. This vibrational mode requires that $\omega a/v$ be a zero of J_2. One could look up such zeros, but we have *Mathematica* at hand. A numerical zero of the Bessel function J_2 may be found via the observation that [Abramowitz and Stegun, eds. 1970]

$$J_2' = (J_1 - J_3) / 2 \qquad (6.1.15)$$

A zero of J_2 may therefore be converged upon via Newton's method iteration:

$$(6.1.16m)$$

```
root[x_] := N[x - 2 BesselJ[2,x]/
            (BesselJ[1,x] - BesselJ[3,x]),20
        ]
NestList[root,5,4] // TableForm
```

```
5
5.134501499157092
5.135622179927338
5.135622301840681
5.135622301840683
```

The zero may also be approximated via a *Mathematica* function such as:

$$(6.1.17.m)$$

```
FindRoot[BesselJ[2,x]==0,{x,{4,5}}]
```

```
{x -> 5.135622171088557}
```

The former method (6.1.16m), though it involves writing of a program instead of a simple function call, is sometimes the superior approach. There is often advantage in using a symbolic derivative such as (6.1.15), which provides extra information that *Mathematica* may not know about. Indeed the output of (6.1.17m) is less accurate than that of (6.1.16m).

One is motivated to animate the plot in order to see real-time vibration of the membrane eigenfunction. For this purpose we plot the membrane height $J_2(r)$ $\sin(2\Theta) \cos t$, in succesive frames:

$$(6.1.18m)$$

```
z = 5.13562^2
Do[Plot3D[-BesselJ[2,Sqrt[x^2+y^2]]*x*y/(x^2+y^2)*
        Cos[t]*(1+Sign[z-x^2-y^2])-0.1(1-Sign[z-x^2-y^2]),
        {x,-6.5001,6.5},{y,-6.5001,6.5},
        PlotRange->{-0.46,0.46}, PlotPoints->25
    ],
    {t,0,6}
]
```

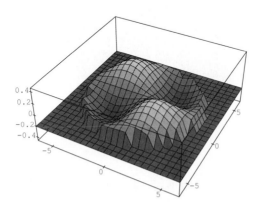

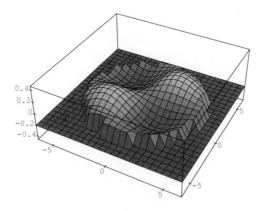

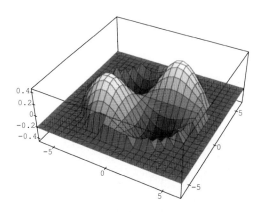

Figure 6.1.4: Animated frames of a drum membrane eigenstate. The
state $z = J_2(r) \sin 2\theta \cos t$ is plotted at various times t.

Note that these plots have been given a negative ambient level for r greater than
the zero of J_2, so that the circular boundary condition be visible.

We turn to a fundamental system: the forced, damped harmonic oscillator.
Concepts of resonance and phase shift are well exemplified in this oscillator,
whose equation of motion for displacement $x(t)$ is taken to be:

$$m \frac{d^2x}{dt^2} + 2m\gamma \frac{dx}{dt} + m\omega_0^2 x = F e^{i\omega t} \qquad (6.1.19)$$

where m is the mass, γ is a damping constant, $m\omega_0^2$ is the spring constant, and
the right-hand side is a periodic force of constant amplitude F. On the idea that
steady-state motion will be sinusoidal, at the driving frequency ω, we solve for
the complex amplitude A in the *ansatz*:

$$x(t) = A\, e^{i\omega t} \qquad (6.1.20)$$

as follows:

(6.1.21m)

```
x[t_] := A Exp[I w t]
sol = Solve[m D[x[t],{t,2}] + 2 m g D[x[t],t] +
            m w0^2 x[t] == f Exp[I w t],
        {A}
      ]
A = A /. sol [[1]]
A = Cancel[A]
```

```
                 f
------------------------
              2       2
2 I g m w - m w  + m w0
```

This amplitude *A* can be thought of as an absolute amplitude response times a phase term:

$$A = |A| \, e^{i\phi}$$

(6.1.22)

The response |A| will generally peak near the natural resonance frequency ω_0. A typical plot of amplitude response versus driving frequency ω looks like so:

(6.1.23m)

```
rule = {m->1, f->1, w0->10, g->0.3}
Plot[Abs[A /. rule], {w,0,15}]
```

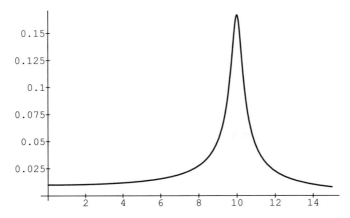

Figure 6.1.5: Typical resonance curve for a forced, damped harmonic
oscillator.

Note that the maximum response |A| occurs near the natural frequency $\omega_0 = 10$
in this plot. The associated phase plot is obtained by:

(6.1.24m)

```
Plot[ArcTan[Im[A]/Re[A] /. rule], {w,0,14.5}]
```

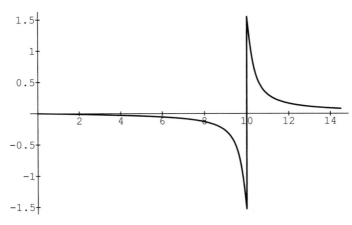

Figure 6.1.6: Typical phase (vertical, radians) versus frequency for a
forced, damped oscillator of natural frequency = 10.

It is interesting to seek the exact driving frequency for which the amplitude $|A|$ is maximum. It is a rule-of-thumb that damping *lowers* this frequency somewhat below the natural value ω_0. Observe that, from the output of (6.1.21m), the complex conjugate of the denominator of A is obtained via $\omega \rightarrow -\omega$, so that the minimization of the denominator of $A(\omega)A(-\omega)$ will provide the maximum amplitude:

$$(6.1.25m)$$

```
d = Denominator[A]
e = Expand[d * (d /. w -> -w)]
```

```
     2  2  2     2  4        2  2   2      2   4
4 g  m  w  + m   w   - 2 m   w   w0  + m   w0
```

and we solve for the minimum absolute square of the denominator:

$$(6.1.26m)$$

```
Solve[D[e,w] ==0, w]
```

```
              2      2                      2      2
{{w -> Sqrt[-2 g  + w0 ]}, {w -> -Sqrt[-2 g  + w0 ]},

  {w -> 0}}
```

This result shows that the driving frequency ω_m for maximum response is indeed lowered by the damping effect:

$$\omega_m = \sqrt{\omega_0{}^2 - 2\gamma^2} \qquad\qquad (6.1.27)$$

A numerical result consistent with Figure 6.1.5 and with the theoretical result (6.1.27) is obtained via:

$$(6.1.28m)$$

```
FindMinimum[N[Abs[d/. rule]], {w,{8,9}}]
```

{35.96759999999972, {w -> 9.990995945422}}

showing that the effective resonant frequency has been shifted below $\omega_0 = 10$. Indeed, Sqrt[10^2 – 2(0.3)^2] ~ 9.991. One instructive continuation of this study is to apply the Runge-Kutta solver methods of Section 5.1 to the problem of transients for the differential equation (6.1.19).

6.2 Solitons

Solitons are loosely defined as coherent non-linear wave equation solutions (i.e., solitary waves) that also preserve their shape even after certain collisions (with other solitons for example). Solitary waves and/or solitons can take the form of pulses, globules, or even vortices in fluid flow [Aref and Flinchem 1984]. In one dimensional space, a soliton $u(x,t)$ running free, without collisions, maintains its shape forever in that $u(x,t) = f(x - vt)$ for some velocity parameter v. A classic non-linear wave equation that gives rise to solitons is the Korteweg–de Vries (KdV) equation:

$$\frac{\partial u}{\partial t} = 6u \frac{\partial u}{\partial x} - \frac{\partial^3 u}{\partial x^3} \qquad (6.2.1)$$

This equation is an approximate description of water waves that move in the $+x$ direction, in the sense that the quantity $-u(x,t)$ is the wave displacement above the equilibrium water level. The KdV equation can be derived from first principles of irrotational, incompressible, inviscid flow with certain boundary conditions [Drazin and Johnson 1989]. Liquid surface tension, acceleration of gravity, and so on are involved in the complete theory; but it is customary to scale in such a way that the dimensionless form (6.2.1) results. A standard soliton solution of (6.2.1) is

$$u(x,t) = -2 \operatorname{sech}^2(x - 4t) \qquad (6.2.2)$$

which moves in the $+x$ direction with speed 4. Let us verify that this soliton is an exact solution of the KdV equation:

(6.2.3m)

```
u = -2 Sech[x-4 t]^2
LogicalExpand[D[u,t] -6 u D[u,x] + D[u,{x,3}]==0]
```

```
       4 t - x     -4 t + x
768 (-E         + E        )
-------------------------- +
    4 t - x    -4 t + x 5
  (E        + E        )


          4 t - x    -4 t + x 3
  192 (-E         + E         )
  --------------------------- +
      4 t - x    -4 t + x 5
    (E        + E         )


         4 t - x      -4 t + x
 16 (4 E         - 4 E        )
 ------------------------------ -
     4 t - x    -4 t + x 3
   (E        + E         )


        4 t - x    -4 t + x
 128 (-E        + E        )
 -------------------------- == 0
     4 t - x    -4 t + x 3
   (E        + E         )
```

This output expression is not as bad as it looks, for:

(6.2.4m)

```
Simplify[%]
```

```
True
```

Proving that (6.2.2) is an exact solution.
It is instructive to endeavor to solve the KdV equation numerically for given

initial data $u(x,0)$. To this end, a simple approach (which does not work out as well as do other approaches) is to write out a difference approximation to (6.2.1). For some fixed, finite increments dx, dt let $u_j(k)$ denote $-u(k\,dx, j\,dt)$, where we changed sign so that the negative KdV soliton pulses will appear plotted as upward pulses. Then one is tempted to approximate by:

$$(6.2.5)$$

$$(u_{j+1}(k) - u_j(k))/dt \quad \sim \quad -6\,u_j(k)(\,u_j(k+1) - u_j(k))/dx \,-$$
$$(\,u_j(k+2) - 3u_j(k+1) + 3u_j(k) - u_j(k-1))/dx^3$$

This leads easily to an expression for $u_{j+1}(k)$ in terms of various past quantities, i.e. quantities with no subscript as large as j+1. It is interesting to see this difference approximation fail. Let us try the initial data $u(x,0) = -6$ sech$^2 x$:

$$(6.2.6m)$$

```
(* Soliton solver, straightforward,
      but not a robust numerical method! *)
dx = 0.2
dt = 0.002
max = 64
uPast = Table[6 Sech[(k-max/2) dx]^2,{k,1,max}]
uPres = uPast
Do[
  Do[
      uPres[[j]] = uPast[[j]] +
          dt (-6 uPast[[j]] (uPast[[j+1]]-uPast[[j]])/(dx)
          - (uPast[[j+2]] - 3 uPast[[j+1]] + 3 uPast[[j]]
                            - uPast[[j-1]])/(dx^3)),
      {j,2,max-2}
  ];
  uPast = uPres;
  If[Mod[n,30]==0,
    a = ListPlot[uPres, PlotRange->{-0.5,15},
                PlotJoined->True]
  ],
  {n,0,30}
]
```

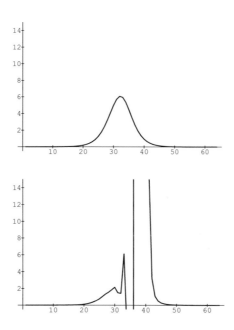

Figure 6.2.1: The Korteweg–deVries equation is solved, by a non-optimal
but straightforward numerical method. The initial data $-u(x,0) =$
$6 \operatorname{sech}^2 x$ (upper plot) degenerates after a certain time (lower plot).

It turns out that two substantial improvements to (6.2.6m) result in a much
more useful solver. First, it proves advantageous to approximate the first and
third derivatives more symmetrically, e.g.

$$(6.2.7)$$

$$\partial^3 u / \partial x^3 \ \sim \ (u(x+2dx) - 2u(x+dx) + 2u(x-dx) - u(x-2dx))/(2\ dx^3)$$

A second improvement is to use a "double-time-step" method on the KdV
equation, as suggested by [Goldberg, et. al. 1967] for the time-dependent
Schroedinger equation. The latter equation is admittedly linear, but the method
still works reasonably well for the former. Certain stability criteria for the
double-time-step approach (on linear systems) are well known in the theory of
related Crank-Nicholson methods [Press, et. al. 1988]. The idea is to keep track
of three wave functions instead of two. We use an improved version of (6.2.5):

$$(6.2.8)$$

$$(u_{j+1}(k) - u_{j-1}(k))/(2dt) \quad \sim \quad -6\, u_j(k)(\, u_j(k+1) - u_j(k-1))/(2dx) \,-$$
$$(\, u_j(k+2) - 2u_j(k+1) + 2u_j(k-1) - u_j(k-2))/(2dx^3)$$

Here are the algorithm steps:

1) Assume initial data $u_{past}(x)$.
2) Use just one Euler integration ((6.2.5) or similar one-time-step method) to obtain the next iteration of the wave as $u_{present}(x)$.
3) Use the improved evolution approximation (6.2.8) to obtain $u_{future}(x)$, by writing the left-hand side as $(u_{future}(x) - u_{past}(x))/(2\,dt)$.
4) Update the waves: $u_{past} := u_{present}$, $u_{present} := u_{future}$.
5) Loop back to step (3).

Next we test this approach on the initial data $u(x,0) = -6\,\mathrm{sech}^2 x$:

$$(6.2.9m)$$

```
dx = 0.2
dt = 0.002
max = 64
uPast = Table[6 Sech[(k-max/2) dx]^2,{k,1,max}]
uPres = uPast
uFutu = uPres
Do[uPres[[j]] = uPast[[j]] +
    dt (-6 uPast[[j]] (uPast[[j+1]]-uPast[[j-1]])/(2 dx)
    - (uPast[[j+2]] - 2 uPast[[j+1]] + 2 uPast[[j-1]]
    - uPast[[j-2]])/(2 dx^3)),
    {j,3,max-2}
]
Do[
  Do[
  uFutu[[j]] = uPast[[j]] +
    2 dt (-6 uPres[[j]] (uPres[[j+1]]-uPres[[j-1]])/(2 dx)
    - (uPres[[j+2]] - 2 uPres[[j+1]] + 2 uPres[[j-1]]
    - uPres[[j-2]])/(2 dx^3)),
    {j,3,max-2}
  ];
  uPast = uPres;
  uPres = uFutu;
  If[Mod[n,40]==0,
    a = ListPlot[uFutu, PlotRange->{-0.5,9},
```

```
                               PlotJoined->True
                  ]
       ],
       {n,0,120}
    ]
```

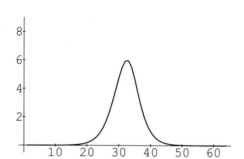

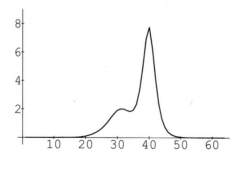

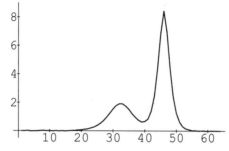

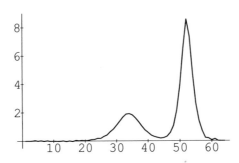

Figure 6.2.2: A more successful, double-time-step, symmetrized method propagates the initial data $-u(x,0) = 6 \operatorname{sech}^2 x$ correctly into two solitons.

This last output sequence verifies a wonderful fact about solitons: the number of independent solitons that eventually emerge from initial data $u(x,0)$ is the number of bound states for the appropriate Schroedinger equation with potential $u(x,0)$ [Drazin and Johnson 1989]. In fact, the Schroedinger potential $V(x) = -N(N+1) \operatorname{sech}^2 x$ for positive integers N has N bound states, which explains why we see two solitons emerge in Figure 6.2.2 in our case $N = 2$.

Actually an *exact* solution for the initial data $u(x,0) = -6 \operatorname{sech}^2 x$ can be written out as a fraction involving cosh functions. It is informative to plot the exact solution directly:

$$(6.2.10m)$$

```
Plot3D[12 (4*Cosh[2 x-8 T]+Cosh[4 x-64 T]+3)/
       (3Cosh[x-28 T]+Cosh[3 x-36 T])^2,{x,-5,5},
       {T,-0.2,0.2},
       PlotRange->{0,9},PlotPoints->50
]
```

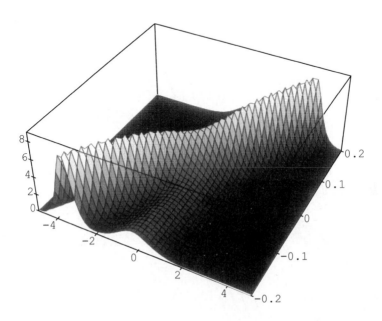

Figure 6.2.3: The two-soliton KdV solution plotted in space-time-amplitude.
Time runs southwest to northeast; i.e. from –0.2 to 0.2. Note the
decrease in amplitude of at least the faster soliton during collision.

The output Figure 6.2.3 shows clearly the difference in speed of the two
solitons, as well as amplitude fluctuations. Another interesting plotting mode
for the two-soliton solution is contour mode:

$$(6.2.11m)$$

```
ContourPlot[(4*Cosh[2x-8T]+Cosh[4x-64T]+3)/
     (3Cosh[x-28T]+Cosh[3x-36T])^2,{x,-10,10},
     {T,-1,1},   Axes->None, PlotRange->{0,0.7},
     PlotPoints->100
]
```

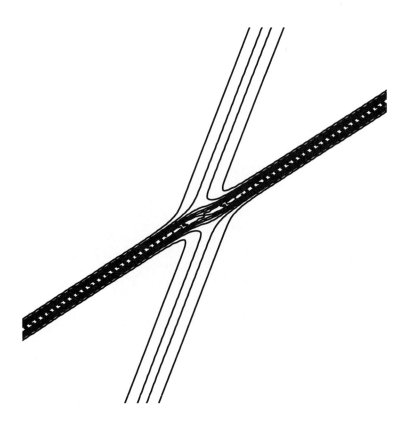

Figure 6.2.4: The two-soliton KdV solution plotted in contour mode. Time
is the vertical axis. One easily sees that the thinner soliton moves
faster and is taller. Note the interesting phase shifts during collision.

Figure 6.2.4 reveals yet more phenomena, such as a sharp phase shift, stronger for the squatter soliton.

The exact two-soliton solution plotted in (6.2.10m) and (6.2.11m) can be analyzed asymptotically via *Mathematica*. It turns out that the velocity of the faster, taller soliton is $v = 16$. This can be derived in a clear way, but let us just assume such a velocity for the moment. The question is, in a frame of reference moving with velocity +16, what is the limiting shape of the two-soliton solution? To answer this, we take an infinite time limit as follows:

(6.2.12m)

```
u = -12(4*Cosh[2x-8T]+Cosh[4x-64T]+3)/
           (3Cosh[x-28T]+Cosh[3x-36T])^2
u = u/. x -> w+16 T
timeLimit = Limit[Expand[u],T->Infinity]
```

```
        4 w
  -96 E
  -----------
        4 w 2
  (3 + E   )
```

This output is the shape of the solution in the variable $w = x - 16t$, as $t \to \infty$. The exact large-t behavior is claimed to be [Drazin and Johnson 1989]:

$$u(w + 16t, t) \quad \sim \quad -8 \operatorname{sech}^2(2w - (\log 3)/2) \qquad (6.2.13)$$

which shows an overall asymptotic phase shift. We are in a position to prove this in a quick pass:

(6.2.14m)

```
Simplify[-8 Sech[2 w - (1/2) Log[3]]^2]
```

```
        4 w
  -96 E
  -----------
        4 w 2
  (3 + E   )
```

which is precisely the output of (6.2.12m). Similar asymptotic formulae apply to the slower, squatter soliton.

Mathematica has sufficient symbolic power that one may generate an N-soliton solution in an exact way, in principle for any N. The theoretical analysis here follows [Drazin and Johnson 1989]. Let the KdV equation (6.2.1) be assumed, for initial data

$$u(x,0) = -N(N+1) \operatorname{sech}^2 x \qquad (6.2.15)$$

We have already mentioned that if this is interpreted as a Schroedinger potential, then N bound states exist. The actual Schroedinger states are indexed, say, by $m = 1,...,N$ as:

$$\Psi_m(x) = c_m P^m{}_N (\tanh x) \qquad (6.2.16)$$

where P is the associated Legendre polynomial and c_m is a normalization coefficient such that the integral of $| \Psi |^2$ over the x-axis is unity. The next step (much modern theory is required to get there; we'll just state the recipe) is to form the N-by-N matrix A whose components are:

$$A_{jk} = \delta_{jk} + (c_j^2/(j+k)) \, e^{8j^3 t \, - \, (j+k)x} \qquad (6.2.17)$$

Then the *exact* solution to the KdV equation subject to initial data (6.2.15) is given by:

$$u(x,t) = -2 \frac{\partial^2}{\partial x^2} \log \det A \qquad (6.2.18)$$

The first stanza of our *Mathematica* tour of N-soliton solutions starts from (6.2.18) for the trial value $N = 4$. We construct the associated Legendre polynomials for (6.2.16):

$$(6.2.19m)$$

```
n = 4
f[x_,m_]  := Simplify[LegendreP[n,m,Tanh[x]]]
norm[m_]  := Sqrt[Integrate[f[x,m]^2,
                  {x,-Infinity,Infinity}]]
psi[x_,m_]  := f[x,m]/norm[m]
psi[x,1]
```

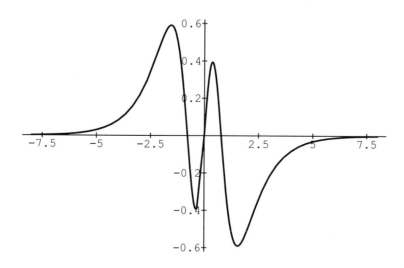

Figure 6.2.5: An exact four-soliton solution involves Schroedinger wave functions, such as this highest bound state for $V(x) = -20 \operatorname{sech}^2 x$.

Next we find the normalization constants explicitly:

$$(6.2.20m)$$

```
Do[c[j]  =  Limit[Expand[psi[x,j] E^(j x)], x->Infinity];
    Print[c[j]],
      {j,n}
]
```

```
  -10
 -------
 Sqrt[5]

   30
 -------
 Sqrt[5]

  -210
 ---------
 Sqrt[105]
```

```
  140
--------
Sqrt[70]
```

These normalization constants in turn give us the *A* matrix according to (6.2.17):

(6.2.21m)

```
a = IdentityMatrix[n] +
        Table[(c[i]^2)/(i+k) Exp[8 i^3 t - (i+k) x],
              {i,1,n},{k,1,n}
        ]
d = Det[a]
```

```
      800 t - 20 x            792 t - 18 x             736 t - 16 x
1 + E                   + 10 E                   + 45 E                    +

      584 t - 14 x            728 t - 14 x             288 t - 12 x
 70 E                   + 50 E                   + 35 E                    +

       576 t - 12 x            280 t - 10 x
175 E                   + 126 E                   +

       520 t - 10 x            224 t - 8 x             512 t - 8 x
126 E                   + 175 E                   + 35 E                    +

      72 t - 6 x             216 t - 6 x             64 t - 4 x
 50 E                   + 70 E                   + 45 E                    +

       8 t - 2 x
 10 E
```

The trick to taking the second derivative in (6.2.18) is to observe that (log *A*)''
= (*A*'/*A*)'. We thus arrive at the four-soliton solution:

(6.2.22m)

```
u = -2 D[D[d,x]/d,x]
```

```
               800 t - 20 x            792 t - 18 x
-2 (-(Power[-20 E             - 180 E              -

              736 t - 16 x            584 t - 14 x
        720 E             - 980 E              -
```

$$700\,E^{728\,t\,-\,14\,x}\,-\,420\,E^{288\,t\,-\,12\,x}\,-$$

$$2100\,E^{576\,t\,-\,12\,x}\,-\,1260\,E^{280\,t\,-\,10\,x}\,-$$

$$1260\,E^{520\,t\,-\,10\,x}\,-\,1400\,E^{224\,t\,-\,8\,x}\,-$$

$$280\,E^{512\,t\,-\,8\,x}\,-\,300\,E^{72\,t\,-\,6\,x}\,-$$

$$420\,E^{216\,t\,-\,6\,x}\,-\,180\,E^{64\,t\,-\,4\,x}\,-\,20\,E^{8\,t\,-\,2x}$$

, 2] /

$$\text{Power}[1\,+\,E^{800\,t\,-\,20\,x}\,+\,10\,E^{792\,t\,-\,18\,x}\,+$$

$$45\,E^{736\,t\,-\,16\,x}\,+\,70\,E^{584\,t\,-\,14\,x}\,+$$

$$50\,E^{728\,t\,-\,14\,x}\,+\,35\,E^{288\,t\,-\,12\,x}\,+$$

$$175\,E^{576\,t\,-\,12\,x}\,+\,126\,E^{280\,t\,-\,10\,x}\,+$$

$$126\,E^{520\,t\,-\,10\,x}\,+\,175\,E^{224\,t\,-\,8\,x}\,+$$

$$35\,E^{512\,t\,-\,8\,x}\,+\,50\,E^{72\,t\,-\,6\,x}\,+$$

$$70\,E^{216\,t\,-\,6\,x}\,+\,45\,E^{64\,t\,-\,4\,x}\,+\,10\,E^{8\,t\,-\,2\,x},$$

2]) + $$(400\,E^{800\,t\,-\,20\,x}\,+\,3240\,E^{792\,t\,-\,18\,x}\,+$$

$$11520\,E^{736\,t\,-\,16\,x}\,+\,13720\,E^{584\,t\,-\,14\,x}\,+$$

$$9800\,E^{728\,t\,-\,14\,x}\,+\,5040\,E^{288\,t\,-\,12\,x}\,+$$

$$25200\,E^{576\,t\,-\,12\,x}\,+\,12600\,E^{280\,t\,-\,10\,x}\,+$$

$$12600\,E^{520\,t\,-\,10\,x}\,+\,11200\,E^{224\,t\,-\,8\,x}\,+$$

$$2240\,E^{512\,t\,-\,8\,x}\,+\,1800\,E^{72\,t\,-\,6\,x}\,+$$

$$2520\,E^{216\,t\,-\,6\,x}\,+\,720\,E^{64\,t\,-\,4\,x}\,+\,40\,E^{8\,t\,-\,2\,x}\,)$$

$$/\,(1\,+\,E^{800\,t\,-\,20\,x}\,+\,10\,E^{792\,t\,-\,18\,x}\,+$$

$$45\,E^{736\,t\,-\,16\,x}\,+\,70\,E^{584\,t\,-\,14\,x}\,+$$

$$50\,E^{728\,t\,-\,14\,x}\,+\,35\,E^{288\,t\,-\,12\,x}\,+$$

$$175\,E^{576\,t\,-\,12\,x}\,+\,126\,E^{280\,t\,-\,10\,x}\,+$$

$$126\ E^{520\ t\ -\ 10\ x} + 175\ E^{224\ t\ -\ 8\ x} +$$

$$35\ E^{512\ t\ -\ 8\ x} + 50\ E^{72\ t\ -\ 6\ x} +$$

$$70\ E^{216\ t\ -\ 6\ x} + 45\ E^{64\ t\ -\ 4\ x} + 10\ E^{8\ t\ -\ 2\ x}))$$

Note that the hardest part of this derivation was to obtain the normalization factors c_m. This is why it is good to have handy in wave studies of any sort the orthogonal functions, such as the associated Legendre polynomials, as well as good symbolic integration.

The four-soliton solution may now be plotted using the exact expression, the output of (6.2.22m):

(6.2.23m)

```
For[t = -0.15, t<0.15, t+= 0.05,
      Plot[-N[u],{x,-10,10},
              PlotRange->{0,2(n^2+n)}
      ]
]
```

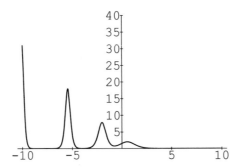

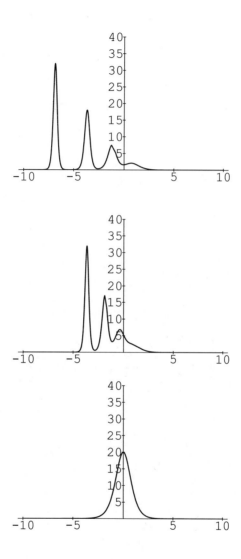

Figure 6.2.6: *Mathematica* successfully derives an exact four-soliton solution
via symbolic manipulation of special functions and integrals. The
solution continues to the right as *t* advances; eventually four
independent solitons will emerge as separate entities once again.

There would seem to be no end to the applications of *Mathematica* in non-linear wave theory. We have used the KdV equation as a centerpiece. One may equally well study such as the "sine-Gordon" equation, fluid vortices, the Toda lattice, general-relativistic solitons, and so on.

6.3 Chaos and fractals

In this chapter we have investigated regular phenomena: pure linear oscillations and coherent pulses (solitons). But non-linearity can give rise to chaos. Loosely interpreted, this chaos is essentially just unpredictable behavior. Examples of chaos include certain instances of shock waves, turbulence, strange attractors, spurious oscillations, bifurcation and the like. Closely related to chaos is the world of fractals, especially in that some chaotic phenomena exhibit distinct self-similarity, in either the spatial or the time domain. One thing that chaos and fractal phenomena have in common is that tremendous complexity is involved. For this reason, extra care need be taken in graphics operations.

A good starting example of chaos study is a *Mathematica* tour of bifurcation in iterative maps. Consider the map

$$x := x^2 - c \qquad\qquad\qquad\qquad (6.3.1)$$

where for the moment c, x are restricted to real values. It is a fascinating fact that for many values of c the x values obtained during this iteration cluster around certain attraction points. Let us take the value $c = 1.23$ as a specific case:

$$(6.3.2m)$$

```
c = 1.23
x = 0
ListPlot[NestList[(#^2-c)&,x,50]]
```

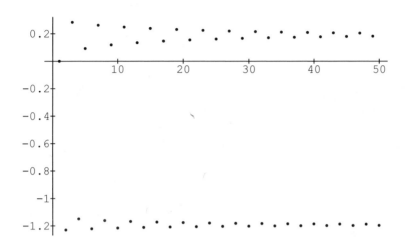

Figure 6.3.1: The map $x = x^2 - c$ is plotted for $c = 1.23$, starting with $x = 0$. The x values (vertical axis) tend to two attraction points.

It turns out that as c increases the attraction values of x generally increase in number. A full bifurcation diagram may be obtained by plotting the x attraction points vs. c values. It is customary for the generation of bifurcation plots to omit some number, say the first one hundred, of x values, so that the attraction points be clearer. To this end we plot a diagram of the iterative map by creating, for each c value, a list of points reached by iterated x values *after* the first hundred iteration. This approach saves compute time since the lists of orbit points will, at least for the orderly regions of Figure 6.3.1, be kept to minimum length:

$$(6.3.3m)$$

```
list = {}
For[c=0.5,c<2,c+= 0.005,
    x = 0;
    Do[x = x^2-c, {j,100}];
    y = {};
    Do[x = x^2-c;
        yv = N[Round[300*x]/300.0];
        If[MemberQ[y,{c,yv}]==False,
            AppendTo[y,{c,yv}];
            AppendTo[list,{c,yv}];
        ],
        {j,100}
    ];
];
```

```
];
ListPlot[list, Axes->None]
```

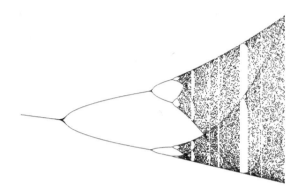

Figure 6.3.2: Bifurcation diagram of the map $x = x^2 - c$, for $c = 0.5$ to 2.0
(horizontal axis). The value $c = 1.23$ is just to the left of center;
the two vertical intercepts for this c value being the two branches
of Figure 6.3.1.

In essentially the left half of Figure 6.3.2 one sees a progression of branch points c_k, $k = 1,2,3,...$ at which the orbit of x values splits into a total of 2^k distinct parts. This "period doubling" sequence of c_k values can be used to define a universal constant in chaos studies–the Feigenbaum Constant. This number F is the asymptotic value [Holden ed. 1986]:

$$\frac{c_{k+1} - c_k}{c_{k+2} - c_{k+1}} \sim F = 4.6992016091029909... \qquad (6.3.4)$$

It is instructive to estimate the Feigenbaum constant numerically by finding approximate locations for the branch points:

$$(6.3.5m)$$

```
list = {}
clow = 1.2
chigh = 1.3
While[True,
    c = (clow+chigh)/2.0;
      x = 0;
      Do[x = x^2-c, {j,50}];
```

```
        y = {};
        Do[x = x^2-c;
            yv = N[Round[300*x]/300.0];
            If[MemberQ[y,{c,yv}]==False,
                y = Append[y,{c,yv}];
            ],
          {j,100}
        ];
        Print[c," ",Length[y]];
        If[Length[y]<=2,clow=c,chigh=c];
];
```

```
1.25 4
1.225 2
1.2375 2
1.24375 2
1.24687 2
1.24844 2
1.24922 2
1.24961 2
1.2498 3
```

The technique of binary searching has settled on the point $c_2 = 1.249$ as the c value where the second bifurcation occurs, that is, two branches turn into four. This result is visually consistent with Figure 6.3.1. Similar runs result in a table:

$$c_1 = 0.7500 \qquad\qquad (6.3.6)$$
$$c_2 = 1.2498$$
$$c_3 = 1.3680$$
$$c_4 = 1.39403$$
$$c_5 = 1.39960$$

From which we compute approximations to the universal F as 4.23, 4.54, 4.67 respectively; in agreement with the numerical claim (6.3.4).

In the complex plane a quadratic iterative map will generally give rise to the celebrated Mandelbrot set. For a complex number c, one iterates the relation

$$z := z^2 + c \qquad\qquad (6.3.7)$$

starting with $z = 0 + 0i$. If $|z|$ is forever bounded, then c is a member of the set. It can be shown that if ever $|z| > 2$, then c is not in the set. It is customary to plot the set by coloring the point z according to how many iterations of (6.3.7) are required to throw the absolute value of z to a value greater than 2. One way to exhibit the Mandelbrot set via *Mathematica* is as follows:

$$(6.3.8m)$$

```
iter[x_, y_, lim_] := Block[{c, z, ct},
                c = x + I y;
                z = c;
                ct = 0;
                While[(Abs[z]<2.0) && (ct<lim),
                        ++ct;
                        z = z*z + c;
                ];
                Return[ct];
        ]
DensityPlot[-iter[x,y,50], {x,-2.0,1.0}, {y,-1.5,1.5},
        PlotPoints->120, Mesh->False
]
```

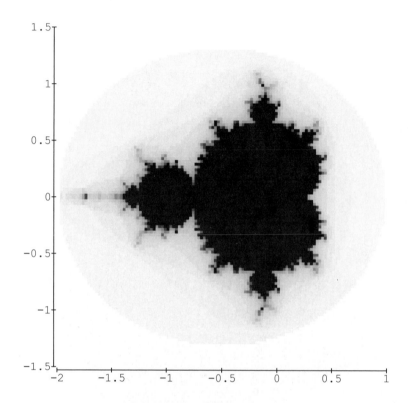

Figure 6.3.3: Density plot of the Mandelbrot set. For c values with
real (horizontal) and imaginary (vertical) parts, the gray level
corresponds inversely to the number of iterations required
for z to escape magnitude 2.

It is interesting to apply *Mathematica* graphics in other modes for special
regions of the complex plane. Note the area in Figure 6.3.3 near the complex
point $0 - i$. One may plot a "mountain range" in density mode as follows:

(6.3.9m)

```
Plot3D[iter[x,y,50], {x,-0.4,0.4}, {y,-1.2,-0.4},
    PlotPoints->120, Mesh->False, PlotRange->{0,50},
    Boxed->False
]
```

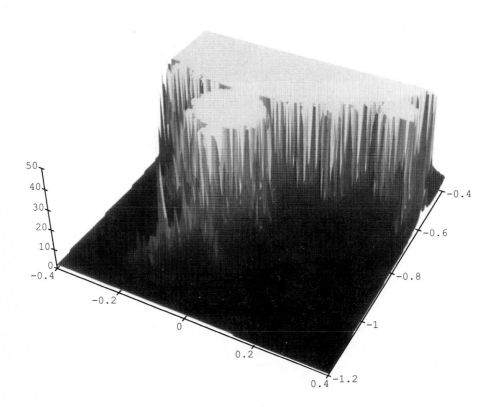

Figure 6.3.4: Height plot of the Mandelbrot escape values over the region
$-0.4 < Re(c) < 0.4$, $-1.2 < Im(c) < -0.4$.

It is interesting to compare the bifurcation diagram Figure 6.3.2 with the
Mandelbrot plot Figure 6.3.3. It has been observed that if you turn the former
figure around left-right, then the qualitative changes in that bifurcation diagram
correspond to changes in the character of the Mandelbrot set. Indeed the triple
bifurcation region in Figure 6.3.2 occuring at about $c = 1.7$ corresponds to the
bulge at $c \sim -1.7$ in the set, Figure 6.3.3 [Devaney 1990].

Chaos studies lead naturally to studies of fractal phenomena. Generally, fractal means "fractured". The fractal label is used also to indicate self-similarity [Devaney 1986] or fractional dimension. Consider the triangle defined by three points in the plane: (0,0), (0,1), (1,0). For some initial point (m, n) we define the next iterative point (m', n') as the midpoint between (m, n) and a random vertex of said triangle. Continuing this algorithm on successive pairs (m', n'), one may plot orbits, where, as with the previous bifurcation study, a certain amount of initial iterations are bypassed. Let us take the random initial point $(m, n) = (0.7, 0.4)$ and iterate against random vertices:

(6.3.10m)

```
grid = 200.0
aging = 1000
m = 0.7
n = 0.4
lis = {}
Do[ If[i>aging,
             mm = N[Round[grid*m]/grid];
             nn = N[Round[grid*n]/grid];
             If[MemberQ[lis,{mm,1.0-nn}]==False,
                 AppendTo[lis,{mm,1.0-nn}]
                 ];
      ];
      q = Floor[3 Random[]];
      If[q<1,
          m = m/2.0;
          n = n/2.0;
          Continue[];
      ];
      If[q<2,
          m = m/2.0;
          n = (1+n)/2.0;
          Continue[];
      ];
      m = (1+m)/2.0;
      n = (1+n)/2.0,
      {i,grid*grid/2+aging}
]
Print[Length[lis]]
ListPlot[lis,AspectRatio->Automatic]
```

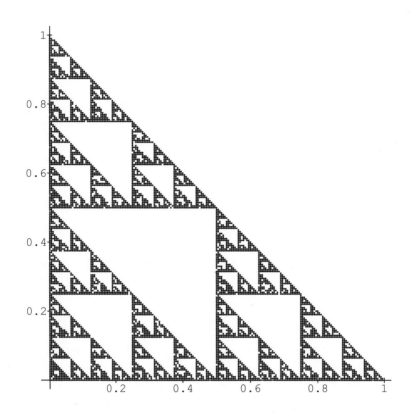

Figure 6.3.5: Fractal pattern obtained from a random-vertex algorithm.
20000 iterated points are plotted (as black) on a basic grid of 20000.
The fractal nature of the plot is manifest in the mere number 6154
of distinct black points.

It is interesting that a plot very similar to Figure 6.3.5 results from virtually *any* initial seed point Note for the moment that in the program (6.3.10m) a 200-by-200 grid is used, so the whole triangle has 20000 grid points. That only 6154 distinct points are plotted signals the fractal nature of the plot. Let us turn to an analysis of the fractional dimension for this structure.

The figure is a type of Sierpinski gasket and can be constructed via a direct removal process, with the black regions of Figure 6.3.5 corresponding to remaining points. The amazing fact is that the ultimate area remaining is a fraction *zero* of the whole triangle. This must be so since the Sierpinski construction may be thought of as the removal of the large central white area, which is 1/4 of the whole triangle, followed by 3 removals of 1/16 area, 9 removals of 1/64 area, and so on. The ultimate fraction of area removed, i.e. the ultimate relative area of white, should be:

$$1/4 + 3/16 + 3^2/64 + \ldots = 1 \qquad (6.3.11)$$

leaving nothing for black area. The black regions of the full Sierpinski gasket, of which Figure 6.3.5 provides an approximate picture, can therefore be thought of as a kind of fractal "dust". Within our randomization model for this fractal, another way to say this is that a random point will ultimately be thrown out of any fixed positive area region with probability one, so our plot will, in the limit of infinite grid size, become white almost everywhere.

The Sierpinski gasket shows up in some appealing guises. One way such a fractal appears in computer science is in connection with recursive procedures. Whereas the grammar-school method of squaring a large number takes $O(N^2)$ basic multiply operations, where N is the number of digits; the squaring can be done in $O(N^d)$ steps where $d<2$ is the gasket's fractal dimension. One way to so lower the "dimension" of the squaring problem's difficulty is to let a general x with N digits be represented by $x = uB + v$, where B is "1" followed by $N/2$ zeros in the prevailing base. Using the formula

$$x^2 = u^2(B^2 + B) - (u - v)^2 B + v^2(B + 1) \qquad (6.3.12)$$

we can square x by calling three smaller squarings each having about $N/2$ digits (the additions, subtractions, and shifts are considered negligible work). Each of these smaller squarings may call three more even smaller ones, and so on recursively. Since "grammar-school" squaring of an $N/2$-digit number is only *one-fourth* the work of squaring an N-digit number, and since (6.3.12) involves *three* small squarings, it is easy to see that via recursion of this type we can obtain x^2 in somewhat fewer than N^2 basic multiplies. The Sierpinski gasket is obtained if you represent the computational effort for the grammar-school N^2 method by the area of the square circumscribing the gasket, then proceed to remove the upper-right quadrant leaving three connected square areas, then removing the upper-right quadrants of the three smaller squares, and so on. This fractal nature for recursive squaring is described in [Riesel 1985], and the overall computational cost turns out to be roughly $N^{1.5\cdots}$ as we discuss next.

Measurement of fractional dimension is a fascinating, sometimes difficult endeavor. It is instructive to see first how dimension measurement would work for standard, integer dimensions. Say we were to plot not the Sierpinski fractal, but something more trivial, such as a checkerboard of black and white points over a triangular grid of $N^2/2$ points (i.e., about N grid points on a side). Now consider the interesting ratio log #/log N, where # denotes the number of black points in the checkerboard. If # behaves as N^d for some d, then the logarithm ratio is d, which in some formalisms is then the "dimension" of the fractal. In the limit of large N we would have for the checkerboard:

$$\frac{\log \#}{\log N} = \frac{\log \dfrac{N^2}{4}}{\log N} \rightarrow 2 \qquad (6.3.13)$$

Giving dimension 2 for the set of black cheques of the checkerboard. This makes sense because the black set of a trivial checkboard, no matter how small be the squares, is clearly just a disjoint union of the 2-dimensional black squares.

But for our gasket the ratios in (6.3.13) behave in a non-trivial way. After doing a run as in (6.3.10m) one may print out #, the number of *distinct* black grid points together with an estimate for the fractal dimension like so:

(6.3.14m)

```
Print[Length[lis], " ",
      Log[N[Length[lis]]]/Log[grid]]
```

from which tables like the following can be consructed:

grid (N)	grid pts.	# = Length[lis]	d = log # / log N
10	50	38	1.580
20	200	117	1.589
50	1250	579	1.626
60	1800	775	1.625

This data is not too accurate; in fact convergence appears problematic. The author has intenionally included this study to show what difficulties may accrue from a statistical treatment of fractals. The exact dimension of a Sierpinski gasket fractal is:

$$\log 3 \, / \log 2 \; = \; 1.58496... \tag{6.3.15}$$

We can verify this exact result by visual inspection of Figure 6.3.5. Appealing to self-similarity of the (exact, ultimate) fractal dust, we note that whenever the scale is halved, we cut the black point count down by a factor of three. For example, the triangular subsection of Figure 6.3.5 defined by vertices (0,0), (0,1/2), (1/2,0) should have by symmetry 1/3 the total black points. The self-similarity thus means that if $\# \sim N^d$, then $(2N)^d \sim 3(N^d)$, so that $d = \log 3 \, / \log 2$. Our tabulated numerical data above are only in rough agreement with this dimension. It appears that convergence to $\log 3 \, / \log 2$, if it happens at all, is certainly slow. It is not clear how to show rigorously that such tabulations should approach exact dimensions. It is not clear how the aging constant, for example, affects the tabulation. Furthermore, one can find in the literature more efficient ways to calculate dimensional approximations for fractals [Holden ed. 1986] [Buchler, et. al., ed., 1985].

6.4 Further explorations

E6.1) Let an n-by-n matrix m have diagonal elements all equal to 2 cos z, with off-diagonal elements all equal to -1, and all other elements zero. Prove, or at least verify by cases, that det $m = \sin((n+1)z)/\sin(z)$. Find a closed-form expression that produces all the eigenvalues.

E6.2) Analyze a linear chain of N springs, all with the same spring constants k, connecting $(N–1)$ masses m in the style of Figure 6.1.1. Show that for large N the eigenvalues approach a smooth curve when plotted against the appropriate index. Exploration E6.1 is a key to this analysis.

E6.3) Four equal masses m sit in equilibrium as vertices of a regular tetrahedron, connected by six springs of equal constant k; these springs forming the edges of the tetrahedron. What are the normal mode frequencies?

E6.4) Let an annular membrane, acoustic speed v, be clamped to zero amplitude at radii $r = a$ and $r = b$. Find and plot some normal modes for membrane vibration. Note: because the origin is not included, both J_n and the Neumann functions Y_n must be considered.

E6.5) Solve the damped harmonic oscillator (6.1.19) with a Runge-Kutta technique as described in Section 5.1, assuming a force function on the right-hand side to be a pulse of unit height, starting at time $t = 0$, of duration τ. The initial conditions should be $x(0) = dx/dt(0) = 0$, corresponding to a quiescent oscillator suddenly hit by the force pulse.

E6.6) Work out a Schroedinger scattering package that uses the double-time step method to plot, for example, a Gaussian packet incident on a potential.

E6.7) Plot such beautiful creatures as Julia sets, or Newton's method fractal sets [Schroeder 1986].

E6.8) Analyze the fractal nature of signals $S(t) = \sum_k e^{i\omega^k t}$. For long enough finite sequences of consecutive integers k, the signal is virtually self-similar: $S(t) \sim S(\omega t)$. Recordings of such (sound) signals can actually "seem" higher-pitched when played back slowly [Schroeder 1986].

Chapter 7:
Chemistry and biology

7.1 Reactions

A good elementary example for chemical studies involves the use of *Mathematica* Lists to represent chemical species. Consider reactions such as this burning of methane:

$$CH_4 + O_2 \rightarrow CO_2 + H_2O \qquad \text{(unbalanced)} \qquad (7.1.1)$$

The problem is to balance the reaction by insertion of proper coefficients. Often this can be done by hand, with adroit guesswork or systematic manual algebra, to yield such as:

$$CH_4 + 2O_2 \rightarrow CO_2 + 2H_2O \qquad \text{(balanced)} \qquad (7.1.2)$$

It is interesting that, via *Mathematica* list representation of each molecule, an automated equation balancer can be effected. In this reaction we may, for example, represent the chemical species by:

$$(7.1.3)$$

$$\text{reactants} = \{\{c,1,h,4\},\{o,2\}\}$$
$$\text{products} = \{\{c,1,o,2\},\{h,2,o,1\}\}$$

It is a straightforward matter to pick apart such lists and perform the requisite algebra, like so:

$$(7.1.4m)$$

```
reactants = {{c,1,h,4},{o,2}}
products = {{c,1,o,2},{h,2,o,1}}
atoms = {}
lexp = 0
numvars = 1
Do[m = reactants[[r]];
    Do[atom = m[[j]];
        If[!MemberQ[atoms,atom],
```

```
                    AppendTo[atoms,atom]
        ];
            lexp += a[numvars] m[[j+1]] atom,
        {j,1,Length[m],2}
    ];
    ++numvars,
    {r,Length[reactants]}
]
rexp = 0
Do[m = products[[r]];
    Do[rexp += a[numvars] m[[j+1]] m[[j]],
            {j,1,Length[m],2}
    ];
    ++numvars,
    {r,Length[products]}
]
--numvars
varlist = {}
Do[Append[varlist,a[j]], {j,2,numvars}]
exp = True
Do[exp = exp &&
                (D[lexp,atoms[[j]]] == D[rexp,atoms[[j]]]),
    {j,Length[atoms]}
]
a[1] = 1
sol = Solve[exp, varlist]
Print[atoms]
Print[lexp]
Print[rexp]
Print[exp]
Print[sol]
```

```
{c, h, o}
c + 4 h + 2 o a[2]
c a[3] + 2 o a[3] + 2 h a[4] + o a[4]
1 == a[3] && 4 == 2 a[4] && 2 a[2] == 2 a[3] + a[4]
{{a[2] -> 2, a[3] -> 1, a[4] -> 2}}
```

The output shows first that atoms C, H, O were detected. Then the relevant algebraic relations follow, eventually yielding the coefficients in the balanced reaction:

$$a[1]\, CH_4 + a[2]\, O_2 \rightarrow a[3]\, CO_2 + a[4]\, H_2O \qquad (7.1.5)$$

Note that, without loss of generality, we fix $a[1] = 1$. If we wish to avoid fractional coefficients, we can invoke least-common-multiple arithmetic as follows:

$$(7.1.6m)$$

```
den = 1
Do[k = a[j] /. sol[[1]];
   If[!IntegerQ[k], den = LCM[den,Denominator[k]]],
   {j,2,numvars}
]
Do[a[j] = (a[j] /. sol[[1]]) den;
   Print[j," ",a[j]],
   {j,numvars}
]
```

```
1 1
2 2
3 1
4 2
```

The result is the same, but if the balancing had involved a coefficient such as 2/3, then the sequence (7.1.6m) would have removed the appropriate denominator. When the LCM procedure is applied to the reaction

$$(7.1.7)$$
$$Ca(OH)_2 + H_3PO_4 \rightarrow Ca_3(PO_4)_2 + H_2O \quad \text{(unbalanced)}$$

we find that the initializations

$$(7.1.8m)$$

```
reactants = {{ca,1,o,2,h,2},{h,3,p,1,o,4}}
products = {{ca,3,p,2,o,8},{h,2,o,1}}
```

lead eventually, through the LCM arithmetic of (7.1.6m), to the correct result:

$$3Ca(OH)_2 + 2H_3PO_4 \rightarrow Ca_3(PO_4)_2 + 6H_2O \qquad (7.1.9)$$

These ideas may readily be extended to stoichiometry, whereby through a little more algebra one may solve for the masses and concentrations pertaining to a particular reaction.

As a second example we investigate equilibrium chemistry. For the abstract reaction

$$A + B \ \ -> \ C + D \qquad (7.1.10)$$

The classical relation for the equilibrium constant K is:

$$K = \frac{[C]_e \, [D]_e}{[A]_e \, [B]_e} \qquad (7.1.11)$$

where $[X]_e$ generally represents the equilbrium concentration of species X. Denote by $[X]_0$ the initial concentration of species X. Then, if x is the total amount of species A that is converted at equilibrium, we have:

$$(7.1.12)$$

$$[A]_e = [A]_0 - x$$

$$[B]_e = [B]_0 - x$$

$$[C]_e = [C]_0 + x$$

$$[D]_e = [D]_0 + x$$

When the constant K and the initial concentrations $[X]_0$ are given, we may solve via (7.1.11) and (7.1.12) for the conversion variable x:

$$(7.1.13m)$$

```
ae = a0 - x
be = b0 - x
ce = c0 + x
de = d0 + x
sol = Solve[k == (ce de)/(ae be),x]
```

```
                                       a0       b0        c0
{{x -> (a0 + b0 + Sqrt[(-a0 - b0 + ----- + ----- + ----- +
                                   1 - k   1 - k   1 - k

         d0    2            a0 b0   c0 d0       a0
        -----)   - 4 (a0 b0 - ----- + -----)] - ----- -
         1 - k                 1 - k   1 - k      1 - k

    b0      c0       d0
   ----- - ----- - -----) / 2},
   1 - k   1 - k   1 - k

                                       a0       b0
    {x -> (a0 + b0 - Sqrt[(-a0 - b0 + ----- + ----- +
                                      1 - k   1 - k

      c0      d0    2            a0 b0   c0 d0
     ----- + -----)   - 4 (a0 b0 - ----- + -----)] -
     1 - k   1 - k                 1 - k   1 - k

    a0      b0      c0      d0
   ----- - ----- - ----- - -----) / 2}}
   1 - k   1 - k   1 - k   1 - k
```

This result is completely general for reactions $A + B \rightarrow C + D$, except that the only chemically meaningful solution is the first of the two quadratic roots. Following the interesting treatment of [Atkinson, et. al. 1987] we analyze next a specific chemical engineering scenario. To quote these authors:

> "Your cousin Joe works as a laboratory technician for a local chemical company. He has been assigned the task of synthesizing Superzap, a critical compound in the manufacture of a profitable hygiene product. Superzap is synthesized from Zap and Reagant B via the reaction:
>
> Zap + Reagant B ->   Superzap + Reagant D
>
> Zap is much more expensive than Reagent B.
> The equilibrium constant for the reaction is small ($K = 0.01$),

and so the yield of Superzap in Joe's first run is very low. He
intends to overcome this problem by increasing the concentration of
Zap and doesn't believe you when you tell him he's only going
to make matters worse."

Continuation from (7.1.13m) will answer in part the implied question of the
authors. We let the initial concentration of species A (Zap) run through various
values, with $[B]_0$ held constant; and both C and D start with zero concentration:

(7.1.14m)

```
b0 = 1; c0 = 0; d0 = 0
k = 0.01
Print["[Zap]0\t\t[B]0\t\t[Fraction converted]"]
Do[Print[a0,"\t\t\t",b0,"\t\t\t",
     N[(x /. sol[[1]][[1]])/a0]],
   {a0,25,100,25}
]
```

[Zap]0	[B]0	[Fraction converted]
25	1	0.0155232
50	1	0.00996663
75	1	0.00756571
100	1	0.00616977

Indeed, the higher the initial concentration of Zap, the lower the fractional
yield. The authors go on to say:

"When you tell Joe that he can solve his problem by increasing
the concentration of Reagent B, he is delighted...but skeptical...
show him how to obtain higher yields of Superzap from Zap."

For this problem we hold $[A]_0$, the initial concentration of Zap, constant; while
the initial value $[B]_0$ varies:

(7.1.15m)

```
a0 = 1; c0 = 0; d0 = 0
k = 0.01
Print["[Zap]0\t\t[B]0\t\t[Fraction converted]"]
```

```
Do[Print[a0,"\t\t\t",b0,"\t\t\t",
    N[(x /. sol[[1]][[1]])/a0]],
  {b0,25,100,25}
]
```

[Zap]0	[B]0	[Fraction converted]
	0	0
1	25	0.388079
1	50	0.498331
1	75	0.567428
1	100	0.616977

These results are all consistent with the very effective spread-sheet approach of [Atkinson, et. al. 1987]. These authors go on to much more complex chemistry, such as enzyme kinematics and buffer pH calculations. One may have confidence though that anything a spread-sheet can tackle is fair game for *Mathematica*.

7.2 Quantum chemistry

Approaches abound for *Mathematica* application of quantum theory to the problems of atomic and molecular structure. To study such structure one may invoke various tried and true methods; to name a few: molecular-orbital program packages, Monte Carlo integrals, self-consistent Hartree-Fock methods, finite element calculations, semi-classical path integral methods, or variational techniques [Truhlar, ed. 1988][Koonin and Meredith 1986]. Here we present two examples: finite elements (for the hydrogen atom) and variational principles (for the helium atom).

Demonstrative finite element calculations for the hydrogen system have been worked out by [Ram-Mohan, et. al. 1990]. To follow this treatment, we begin by demanding that the hydrogenic wave function $\Psi(r)$ satisfy:

$$(-\frac{d^2}{dr^2} - \frac{2}{r}\frac{d}{dr} - \frac{2}{r}) \Psi = E \Psi \qquad (7.2.1)$$

We adopt a finite-element approximation to the true wave function by taking piecewise linear segments as shown in Figure 7.2.1.

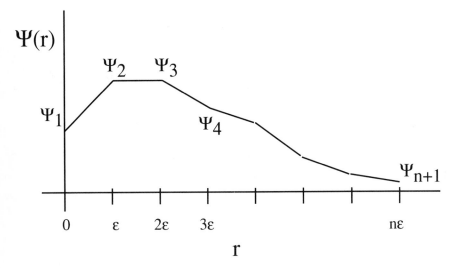

Figure 7.2.1: Setting for finite-element approximation to the hydrogenic
wave function. Segments are linear between successive r values
$(j\varepsilon, (j+1)\varepsilon)$.

The precise definition of the finite-element approximation is that for $j\varepsilon \leq r < (j+1)\varepsilon$,

$$\Psi(r) = (1-y)\,\Psi_{j+1} \; + \; y\,\Psi_{j+2} \tag{7.2.2}$$

where the auxiliary variable $y = (r - j\varepsilon)/\varepsilon$ runs from 0 to 1 on any one interval. Thus the wave function approximation is parameterized by $(n+1)$ numbers Ψ_{j+1}, $j = 0,1,2,...,n$. Next we multiply the Schroedinger equation (7.2.1) on both sides by Ψ^{*} ($= \Psi$ in this case since we may assume a real-valued solution) and integrate by parts to obtain:

$$\int_{0}^{\infty} r^2 \left(\Psi'^{2} - \frac{2}{r}\,\Psi^2 \right) dr \; = \; E \int_{0}^{\infty} r^2 \Psi^2 \, dr \tag{7.2.3}$$

This integral relation can be thought of as an identity involving energy expectations. But when we substitute the finite-element form (7.2.2) into the integral relation, and change "∞" to the finite endpoint $n\varepsilon$, we obtain a rather complicated matrix relation involving the $(n+1)$-component column vector $C = \{\Psi_{j+1}\}$. For example, the right-hand side of (7.2.3) becomes:

$$(7.2.4)$$

$$\varepsilon^3 E \sum_{j=0}^{n-1} \int_0^1 (y+j)^2 \, ((1-y)\,\Psi_{j+1} + y\,\Psi_{j+2})^2 \; dy$$

which can be written in the form $E\,C^T U C$ for an appropriate matrix U. The left-hand side of (7.2.3) can be written similarly as $C^T H C$. Note that the single-element integrals such as (7.2.4) may themselves be evaluated via *Mathematica*. Such labors result in a complete description of the matrices H and U, whence it suffices to solve an $(n+1)$-dimensional eigenvalue equation:

$$HC = EUC \qquad\qquad (7.2.5)$$

for the energy eigenvalues E and, if desired, the wave function eigenvector $C = \{\Psi_1, ..., \Psi_{n+1}\}$.

A *Mathematica* sequence to derive in this way approximate hydrogenic wave functions and energies runs like the following. Note that the cascades of If[] statements could be performed a little more efficiently by Which[] statements (the author prefers the If[] structure for ease in translation to other languages):

$$(7.2.6m)$$

```
eps = 0.5
n = 40
h11[m_] := eps (m^2 - m + 1/3) + eps^2 (1/2 - 2 m/3)
h12[m_] := -eps (m^2 - m + 1/3) + eps^2 (1/6 - m/3)
h22[m_] := eps (m^2 - m + 1/3) + eps^2 (1/6 - 2 m/3)
u11[m_] := eps^3 (m^2/3 - m/2 + 1/5)
u12[m_] := eps^3 (m^2/6 - m/6 + 1/20)
u22[m_] := eps^3 (m^2/3 - m/6 + 1/30)
hterm[a_, b_] := Block[{},
                  If[(a==1)&&(b==1), Return[h11[a]]];
                  If[(a==n+1)&&(b==n+1),Return[h22[a-1]]];
                  If[(a==b), Return[h22[a-1] + h11[a]]];
                  If[Abs[a-b]==1, Return[h12[Min[a,b]]]];
```

```
                           Return[0];
                           ]
uterm[a_, b_] := Block[{},
                    If[(a==1)&&(b==1), Return[u11[a]]];
                    If[(a==n+1)&&(b==n+1),Return[u22[a-1]]];
                    If[(a==b), Return[u22[a-1] + u11[a]]];
                    If[Abs[a-b]==1, Return[u12[Min[a,b]]]];
                         Return[0];
                    ]
h = Table[hterm[i,j], {i,n+1}, {j,n+1}]
u = Table[uterm[i,j], {i,n+1}, {j,n+1}]
v = Inverse[u] . h
energies = Eigenvalues[v]
wavefunctions = Eigenvectors[v]
Do[If[energies[[k]]<0,
          Print["Energy = ",energies[[k]]];
          ListPlot[wavefunctions[[k]],PlotJoined->True];
    ],
    {k,n+1}
]
```

```
Energy = -0.981594
Energy = -0.246476
Energy = -0.122469
Energy = -0.0424562
```

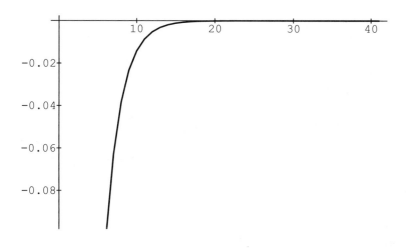

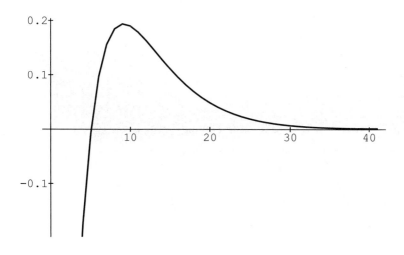

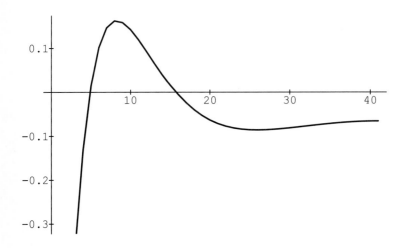

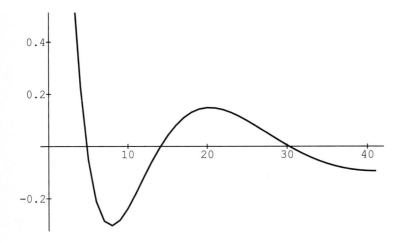

Figure 7.2.2: Bound state hydrogenic wave functions resulting from
a finite element method with $n = 40$ elements, radial step size
$\varepsilon = 0.5$. Horizontal axis is r, vertical axis is Ψ.

The energies printed out may be compared with the theoretical Bohr levels: E_m
$= -1/m^2$ for principal quantum number m:

(7.2.7)

m	Approx. E_m	Exact E_m
0	−0.981594	−1.000000
1	−0.246476	−0.250000
2	−0.122469	−0.1111111
3	−0.0424562	−0.0625000

These energies are off by 2, 4, 10, and 50 per cent respectively. Naturally this discrepancy can be improved by taking higher numbers of finite elements.

We turn next to a variational treatment of the helium atom. Let coordinates r_1, r_2, r_{12}, Θ be defined as in Figure 7.2.3. On the space of symmetrical, separable, real trial wave functions

$$\Psi = f(r_1)f(r_2) \qquad\qquad (7.2.8)$$

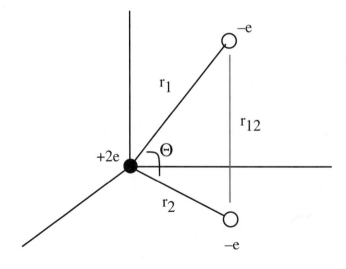

Figure 7.2.3: Coordinate definitions for a variational treatment of the helium atom.

The Hamiltonian in atomic units ($h = 2\pi$, $m = 1$) can be taken to be

$$(7.2.9)$$

$$H = -\frac{1}{2}\frac{1}{r_1^2}\frac{\partial}{\partial r_1}\left(r_1^2\frac{\partial}{\partial r_1}\right) - \frac{1}{2}\frac{1}{r_2^2}\frac{\partial}{\partial r_2}\left(r_2^2\frac{\partial}{\partial r_2}\right) - \frac{2}{r_1} - \frac{2}{r_2} + \frac{1}{r_{12}}$$

It is well known that the ground state energy of an atomic system is generally bounded above by the expectation of this Hamiltonian with respect to a real trial wave function such as (7.2.8) [Schiff 1968]. In the present case, the ground state energy E therefore satisfies:

$$E \leq <H> = \frac{1}{N}\int \Psi H \Psi \, dv \qquad (7.2.10)$$

where N is a normalization integral defined below, and the volume differential is

$$dv = 8\pi^2 \, r_1^2 \, r_2^2 \, dr_1 \, dr_2 \, d\cos\Theta \qquad (7.2.11)$$

Note that any prefactors such as this $8\pi^2$ will cancel in the expectation calculation. Now we posit an explicit trial wave function in the form of a simple product of hydrogen-like ground state functions:

$$\Psi(r_1, r_2) = e^{-Zr_1} e^{-Zr_2} \qquad (7.2.12)$$

where the "effective nuclear charge" Z is a variational parameter. The idea is to minimize $<H>$ with respect to Z; this should give a good (upper) approximation to the ground state energy.

It turns out to be quite convenient before performing the relevant *Mathematica* integrals to effect scaling of integrands as early in the game as possible. It is a straightforward task to see that, subject to the substitutions

$$u_1 = Zr_1$$
$$u_2 = Zr_2$$

(7.2.13)

and the definition

$$du = u_1{}^2 u_2{}^2 \, du_1 \, du_2$$

(7.2.14)

the expectation (7.2.10) is given exactly by:

$$<H> = (-Z^2K - 4ZA + ZR) / N$$

(7.2.15)

where K is the "kinetic" term:

$$K = \int \int \Psi \, \frac{1}{u_1{}^2} \, \frac{\partial}{\partial u_1} \left(u_1{}^2 \, \frac{\partial}{\partial u_1} \right) \Psi \, du$$

(7.2.16)

A is the "attraction" term:

$$A = \int \int \Psi \, \frac{1}{u_1} \, \Psi \, du$$

(7.2.17)

and R is the "repulsion" term:

(7.2.18)

$$R = \int_0^\infty du_2 \left\{ \int_0^{u_2} u_1{}^2 \Psi^2 \, du_1 + \int_{u_2}^\infty u_1 u_2 \Psi^2 \, du_1 \right\}$$

Finally, the normalizer is

$$N = \int \int \Psi \Psi \, du \qquad\qquad (7.2.19)$$

The following *Mathematica* sequence completes this helium calculation. Note that the double integrals could have been done each with one Integrate[] call over two variables of integration (the author prefers writing out the nested integrals for reasons of analogy with blackboard work):

(7.2.20m)

```
psi[u1_,u2_] := Exp[-u1-u2]
laplacian1[u1_,u2_] := 1/u1^2 D[u1^2 D[psi[u1,u2],u1],u1]
normalizer = Integrate[Integrate[u1^2 u2^2 psi[u1,u2]^2,
                           {u1,0,Infinity}],{u2,0,Infinity}]
attraction = Integrate[Integrate[u1^1 u2^2 psi[u1,u2]^2,
                           {u1,0,Infinity}],{u2,0,Infinity}]
kinetic = Integrate[Integrate[u1^2 u2^2 psi[u1,u2]
                           laplacian1[u1,u2],
                           {u1,0,Infinity}],{u2,0,Infinity}]
repulsion = Integrate[
               (Integrate[psi[u1,u2]^2 u1^2,{u1,0,u2}] +
                Integrate[psi[u1,u2]^2u1 u2,
                    {u1,u2,Infinity}
                   ]) u2,{u2,0,Infinity}
               ]
expect = (-z^2 kinetic - 4 z attraction + z repulsion)/
               normalizer
```

```
          2
    -27 z   z
16 (----- + --)
     128    16
```

This result is the precise expectation of the Hamiltonian for the state defined by (7.2.12). We are still at liberty to minimize this energy with respect to *Z*. One of several ways to do this is:

(7.2.21m)

```
zsol = Solve[D[expect,z]==0,z]
```

```
{{z -> 27/16}}
```

This interesting result says in effect that the "ideal" nuclear charge parameter is less than 2. The physical interpretation of such a result is that each electron sees somewhat less than a full +2 nuclear charge, due to average screening by the other electron. The actual expectation for this ideal Z is obtained by:

(7.2.22m)

```
expect /. zsol[[1]]
```

```
-729/256
```

which has the numerical value –2.84766. Converting to physically meaningful units we find that our approximation is $E = -77.4$ ev, which is only 2 per cent higher than the experimental value –78.9 ev [Schiff 1968].

7.3 Genetics and population biology

Genetics problems can sometimes be treated rigorously, as when manipulation of genetic symbols is called for. But usually it is preferable to invoke methods that take into account experimental error. Consider the following problem posed in [Russell 1986]:

(7.3.1)

"Use the following two-point recombination data to map the genes concerned:

Gene loci	%recombination
a,b	50
a,c	15
a,d	38
a,e	8
b,c	50
b,d	13
b,e	50
c,d	50
c,e	7
d,e	45

Show the order and length of the shortest intervals."

Let us define a much simpler, analogous problem first; in so doing we shall also indicate the relation between recombination percentage and interval length. Pretend that the data set is instead:

(7.3.2)

Gene loci	%recombination
a,b	10
a,c	5
b,c	15

The idea is to find some permutation of loci coordinates $\{a,b,c\}$ such that:

$$|a - b| = 10$$ (7.3.3)
$$|a - c| = 5$$
$$|b - c| = 15$$

That is, the recombination percentage corresponds to an absolute distance between the relevant gene loci. In this idealized trivial case it is not hard to find an answer by inspection. Figure 7.3.1 shows a solution which is, in fact, not unique: one may swap the positions of c and b to get another solution. The entire issue of these allowed symmetries, coupled with the issue of solving the non-linear percentage-distance relations, comprises a generally formidable analytical dilemma.

Figure 7.3.1: Exact solution to an ideal recombination data set.

But *Mathematica* multivariate solver techniques can often give useful numerical results on such problems. Let us turn to the original data set (7.3.1), noting first that there is no exact solution. This lack of exact solution is easy to infer, for example the conditions:

$$(7.3.4)$$

$$|a - b| = 50$$
$$|a - d| = 38$$
$$|b - d| = 13$$

are mutually incompatible (translate with $a = 0$, in which case $b = \pm50$, $d = \pm38$ whence $|b - d| = 13$ cannot hold). But, as explained in [Russell 1986], *the data for the shorter lengths is more reliable.* This is why we must analyze the data set (7.3.1) in some statistical fashion. One approach is simply to strike out the larger percentages and work only with the smaller ones, for example the five smallest. But a more unified approach is to somehow weight the smaller distances preferentially. To this end, we use the nomenclature:

$$| g_i - g_j | \sim \%_{ij} \qquad (7.3.5)$$

to represent the distance-percentage relation for genes g_i, g_j, $i \neq j$. We use a particular metric of error for a choice of coordinates $\{g_1, g_2, ...\}$:

$$error = \sum_{i \neq j} \frac{((g_i - g_j)^2 - \%_{ij}^2)^2}{\%_{ij}^4} \qquad (7.3.6)$$

This error metric has two good properties. First, if a coordinate solution (7.3.5) is exact, the error is zero. Second, shorter distances (percentages) enter with greater weight. The following *Mathematica* sequence computes the error (7.3.6) and attempts to minimize same over the 4-dimensional space of coordinates $\{b, c, d, e\}$, where without loss of generality we force $a = 0$:

$$(7.3.7m)$$

```
s[d_,p_] := ((d/p)^2-1)^2
err = s[a-b,50] + s[a-c,15] + s[a-d,38] + s[a-e,8] +
      s[b-c,50] + s[b-d,13] + s[b-e,50] + s[c-d,50] +
      s[c-e,7] + s[d-e,45]
a = 0
FindMinimum[err,{b,20},{c,-10},{d,10},{e,-10}]
```

```
{0.3559124966455703, {b -> 45.3647425125615,
    c -> -14.65858077501916, d -> 33.32900076460574,
    e -> -7.814286685499391}}
```

Note that some fortuitous choice of initial values of $\{b, c, d, e\}$ is necessary; after all we are minimizing a complicated quadratic expression in a fair number of dimensions. In general, one may use various *Mathematica* options to terminate the FindMinimum[] iterations for "bad" initial choices. The result of the session (7.3.7m) is depicted in Figure 7.3.2.

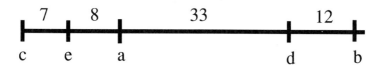

Figure 7.3.2: *Mathematica* solution to a genetic mapping problem.

Next we turn to the population biology setting: a statistical investigation of time-to-termination. Consider a one gene locus, two allele model of genetic drift [Kaplan 1989]. The aim is to investigate random population walks that terminate in extinction of some allele. The input parameters are:

$$(7.3.8)$$

n = constant number of individuals (aa, aA, Aa, or AA)
fA = frequency of allele A
fa = frequency of allele $a = 1 - fA$

For initial values of fA, we draw, for each of n individuals, two gametes from a pool, with fA weighting for A gametes and fa weighting for a gametes; continuing to update fA according to the new A frequency. On each draw we may find combinations aa, aA, Aa, or AA. On each subsequent generation (of n draws) we update the A frequency according to:

$$(7.3.9)$$

$$fA \; = \; \frac{\text{number of } AA}{n} \; + \; \frac{\text{number of } Aa}{2n} \; + \; \frac{\text{number of } aA}{2n}$$

We continue this iteration until one gamete is extinct; i.e. until $fA = 0$ or $fA = 1$:

(7.3.10m)

```
n = 30
fA = 0.5
freqList = {}
While[(fA>0) && (fA<1),
          AppendTo[freqList, N[fA]];
          numA = 0;
          Do[If[Random[]<fA, ++numA];
             If[Random[]<fA, ++numA],
             {j,n}
          ];
          fA = numA/(2 n);
]
ListPlot[freqList, PlotJoined->True, PlotRange->{0,1}]
```

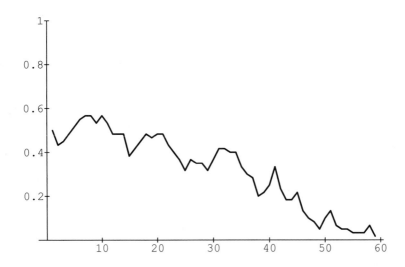

Figure 7.3.3: Typical genetic drift. Allele A, though starting at equal
odds $fA = 1/2$, becomes by chance extinct in 59 generations.
We say the time to termination is 59.

An interesting study pertains to the average number of generations to extinction
of some gamete. For various initial values of fA, we count generations (each
generation amounting to the combination of n individuals according to current
weighting) up to the extinction of one or the other gamete. The resulting plot

of average-generations-to-termination vs. initial *A* frequency conveys an idea of
how extinction time varies with initial conditions. In the following session we
take *n* = 30 individuals, and for various initial values of *fA* we average, over 20
independent trials, how many generations elapse prior to extinction of some
allele:

$$(7.3.11m)$$

```
n = 30
trials = 20
extinctionList = {}
For[fAinit = 1/n, fAinit<1, fAinit += 1/n,
   genAverage = 0;
   Do[  fA = fAinit;
        generation = 0;
        While[(fA>0) && (fA<1),
             numA = 0;
             Do[  (* Assemble the gametes. *)
                  If[Random[]<fA, ++numA];
                  If[Random[]<fA, ++numA],
                  {j,n}
             ];
             fA = numA/(2 n);
             ++generation;
          ];
          genAverage += generation,
          {k,trials}
      ];
   genAverage = genAverage/trials;
   extinctionList =
          Append[extinctionList, {fAinit,genAverage}];
]
ListPlot[extinctionList, PlotJoined->True]
```

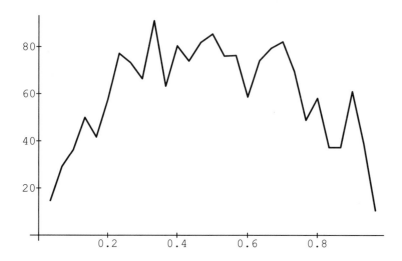

Figure 7.3.4: Average termination time (vertical axis) required to
reach extinction of some allele, vs. initial frequency of allele A
(horizontal axis). There are 30 individuals each generation and
the average is taken over 20 trials for each initial fA.

The result of this time-to-termination averaging as shown in Figure 7.3.4
reveals certain intuitive aspects of such expectation problems. For one thing,
the time to termination is generally largest for the values $fA \sim 1/2$, because the
system takes longest to "decide" on which allele to favor if the alleles start out
on equal footing. For another, the time is fairly symmetrical about $fA = 1/2$,
because in the present setting the evolution for fA should be statistically
identical to the evolution for $fa = 1 - fA$. It is possible, using the theory of
Markov chains, to derive exact expectations for time-to-termination, sometimes
called time-to-absorption [Dudman 1990]. Let us simplify the problem in order
to concentrate on the combinatorical details. Assume that

$$(7.3.12)$$

1) There are n individuals at every generation $t = 0, 1, 2, ...$
2) Every individual is of type A or type B, with $A(t)$ denoting the number of type A individuals at time t, so $B(t) = n - A$.
3) On generation $t+1$ each of the n individuals independently attains a new type A with probability $A(t)/n$; and type B with probability $B(t)/n = 1 - A(t)/n$.

These assumptions mean that on each generation we clear away all n individuals and re-populate with n new individuals according to the previous generation's respective A and B counts. Using the rule (3) above we can establish an $(n+1)$-by-$(n+1)$ dimensional transition probability matrix T, having binomial distribution components:

$$(7.3.13)$$

T_{ij} = Prob{j type A individuals appear at time $t+1$,

$\quad\quad\quad\quad$ given that i type A individuals existed at time t}

$$= \frac{n!}{j! \, (n-j)!} (\frac{i}{n})^j (1 - \frac{i}{n})^{n-j}$$

where both i and j range from 0 to n, inclusive. At any time t we denote by $p_k(t)$ the probability that $A(t) = k$. Denote by p the $(n+1)$-dimensional vector:

$$p(t) = \{p_0(t), p_1(t), ..., p_n(t)\} \quad\quad\quad (7.3.14)$$

Then the Markov process is determined by the evolution equation:

$$p(t) = T^t \, p(0) \quad\quad\quad (7.3.15)$$

Note that $p(0)$ will typically be a vector $\{0, 0, ...,1, ...0\}$; i.e. we start with "1" in some single component, meaning that there are initially $A(0) = i$ type A individuals. We have termination, i.e. extinction of either type A or type B, when and only when $A(t) = 0$ or $A(t) = n$. We say that the absorbing states are therefore $p = \{1, 0, 0, ..., 0\}$ and $p = \{0, 0, ..., 0, 1\}$. Through careful analysis it can be shown that the expectation of time-to-termination is derivable from the matrix [Kemeny and Snell 1983]:

$$M = (1 - Q)^{-1} \tag{7.3.16}$$

where Q is the $(n-1)$-by-$(n-1)$ projection of P:

$$Q = \{P_{ij} : 1 \le i,j \le n-1 \} \tag{7.3.17}$$

The interesting property of M is that M_{ij} is, for $A(0) = i$ initial type A individuals, the expectation of the number of generations, prior to termination, at which $A(t) = j$. This phrase "prior to termination" is redundant, since once an absorbing state is reached, i.e. $A(t) = 0$ or n, the state $A(t) = j$ will occur again with vanishing probability. All of this implies that the expected time to termination, given an initial count of $A(0) = i$ individuals, is:

$$< t >_i = \sum_{j=1}^{n-1} M_{ij} \tag{7.3.18}$$

The following session computes the exact expectation $< t >_i$ for i = 1, 2, ..., $n-1$; for $n = 5$ individuals:

$$\tag{7.3.19m}$$

```
n = 5
p[x_,y_] := Binomial[n,j] (x/n)^y * (1-x/n)^(n-y)
q = Table[p[i,j],{i,1,n-1},{j,1,n-1}]
Print[q]
q = IdentityMatrix[n-1] - q
t = Inverse[q]
Print[t]
list = Apply[Plus,Transpose[t]]
```

$$\left\{\left\{\frac{256}{625}, \frac{128}{625}, \frac{32}{625}, \frac{4}{625}\right\}, \left\{\frac{162}{625}, \frac{216}{625}, \frac{144}{625}, \frac{48}{625}\right\},\right.$$

$$\left.\left\{\frac{48}{625}, \frac{144}{625}, \frac{216}{625}, \frac{162}{625}\right\}, \left\{\frac{4}{625}, \frac{32}{625}, \frac{128}{625}, \frac{256}{625}\right\}\right\}$$

$$\left\{\left\{\frac{1733385}{789113}, \frac{746240}{789113}, \frac{503840}{789113}, \frac{337060}{789113}\right\},\right.$$

$$\left\{\frac{964290}{789113}, \frac{1896785}{789113}, \frac{954960}{789113}, \frac{676440}{789113}\right\},$$

$$\left\{\frac{676440}{789113}, \frac{954960}{789113}, \frac{1896785}{789113}, \frac{964290}{789113}\right\},$$

$$\left.\left\{\frac{337060}{789113}, \frac{503840}{789113}, \frac{746240}{789113}, \frac{1733385}{789113}\right\}\right\}$$

$$\left\{\frac{425}{101}, \frac{575}{101}, \frac{575}{101}, \frac{425}{101}\right\}$$

The output signifies, for example, that if we start with $A(0) = 3$ type A individuals, then the expected time to termination (extinction of either A or B) is exactly 575/101 generations. The point of this exercise is to show that empirical results such as the plot of Figure 7.3.4 can be given a rigorous treatment. In fact, if we take $n = 10$ individuals in (7.3.19m) and add a simple ListPlot[] statement, we can plot the precise expectation of the time-to-terminate, the result being Figure 7.3.5.

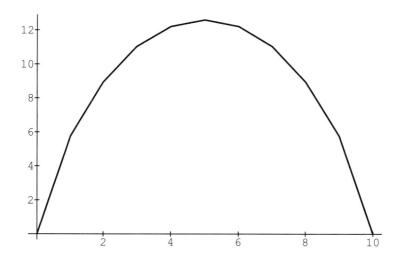

Figure 7.3.5: Exact expectation of time-to-terminate (vertical axis) vs.
             initial number of type *A* individuals (horizontal axis). The
             plot lends credence to the related gamete evolution
             experiment depicted in Figure 7.3.4.

A glimpse into the analytical complexity of this Markov process is afforded by
a typical, exact result. Indeed, for this $n = 10$ the maximum expectation (for
$A(0) = 5$ in Figure 7.3.5) has the approximate value 12.6, but actually has the
exact rational value:

$$<t>_5 \; = \; 2540334305767609095 \; / \; 201765667296121472 \qquad (7.3.20)$$

Some of the complex aspects of the Markov chain calculations disappear for
very large *n*. In particular the assumption that the asymptotic expectation plot
(Figure 7.3.5 but for large *n*) is parabolic gives rise to an interesting line of
analysis. In this connection see [Kimura 1955].

7.4 Neurobiology

A classic problem in neurobiology involves the propagation of action potentials along a nerve axon.

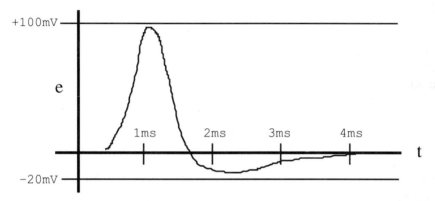

Figure 7.4.1: Schematic appearance of an action potential $e(t)$, adapted from [Jack, et. al. 1975]. The trace is typical for squid nerve at 18.5 degrees Celsius.

As shown in Figure 7.4.1 the voltage $e(t)$ tends to rise to the order of 100 millivolts, then exhibit undershoot of the order of 10 millivolts, finally reaching the resting potential asymptotically. Strong temperature dependence of most pulse configuration parameters is, however, the rule. One of the interesting problems is the derivation, originally due to Hodgkin and Huxley, of the propagation velocity u of such a pulse. The Hodgkin-Huxley system can be derived through proper application of Ohm's Law and cable theory, together with certain assumptions about the behavior of potassium and sodium channels. One assumes that the membrane potential $e(x,t)$, a function of position x and time t, exhibits traveling wave behavior, that is $e(x,t) = e(x - ut)$. The resulting differential equation connecting the membrane potential $e(t)$ (at the spatial origin) and the propagation velocity u is [Junge 1976]:

$$(7.4.1)$$

$$\frac{1}{r_a u^2}\frac{d^2 e}{dt^2} = c_m\frac{de}{dt} + g_K n^4(e - e_K) + g_{Na}m^3 h(e - e_{Na}) + g_l(e - e_l)$$

where the nomenclature is as follows:

$$(7.4.2)$$

r_a = resistance per unit length of the nerve interior
u = propagation velocity
$e(t)$ = membrane potential
c_m = membrane capacitance per unit length
e_K, e_{Na}, e_l = equilibrium potentials for potassium, sodium, leakage
g_K, g_{Na}, g_l = peak conductances of potassium, sodium, leakage
n, m, h = phenomenological functions of e and t

We adopt the various constants and phenomenological n, m, h relations of [Cronin-Scanlon 1981] as:

$$(7.4.3)$$

c_m = 1.0 microfarad per cm^2
g_K = 36 mmho/cm^2
g_{Na} = 120 mmho/cm^2
g_l = 0.3 mmho/cm^2
e_K = −12 mV
e_{Na} = 115 mV
e_l = 10.5988 mV
$dm/dt = a_m(e)(1{-}m) - b_m(e)\,m$
$dh/dt = a_h(e)(1{-}h) - b_h(e)\,h$
$dn/dt = a_n(e)(1{-}n) - b_n(e)\,n$
$a_m(e) = 0.1(25{-}e)/(\exp(0.1(25{-}e)){-}1)$
$b_m(e) = 4\exp(-e/18)$
$a_h(e) = 0.07\,\exp(-e/20)$
$b_h(e) = 1/(\exp(0.1(30{-}e)){+}1)$
$a_n(e) = 0.01(10{-}e)/(\exp(0.1(10{-}e)){-}1)$
$b_n(e) = 0.125\,\exp(-e/80)$

The idea is to find the propagation velocity u for which a potential $e(t)$ is a well-behaved solution to the Hodgkin-Huxley system (7.4.1). We shall integrate the second order differential equation in straightforward Euler fashion. The following session shows how to start with upper and lower bounds on the squared-velocity parameter $vi = r_a u^2$, then to effect a binary search algorithm for the subsequent estimates of vi. The action potential plot will diverge upward or downward indicating in this way the next choice for vi:

$$(7.4.4m)$$

```
cm = 1.0
gk = 36
gna = 120
gl = 0.3
ek = -12.0
ena = 115.0
el = 10.5988
am[V_] := 0.1 (25-V)/(Exp[0.1*(25-V)]-1)
bm[V_] := 4 Exp[-V/18.0]
ah[V_] := 0.07 Exp[-V/20]
bh[V_] := 1/(Exp[0.1*(30-V)]+1)
an[V_] := 0.01*(10.0-V)/(Exp[0.1*(10-V)]-1)
bn[V_] := 0.125 Exp[-V/80.0]
For[ct = 0, ct<=100, ct++, data[ct] = 0.0]
dt = 0.001;
vlow  = 9.169921875
vhigh = 9.17041015625
While[True,
      ct = 0;
      vi = (vlow+vhigh)/2.0;
      n = an[0]/(an[0]+bn[0]);
      m = am[0]/(am[0]+bm[0]);
      h = ah[0]/(ah[0]+bh[0]);
      e = 0.1;
      edot = 0;
      For[t = 0, t < 10, t = t + dt,
            edotdot = vi*(cm edot +
                      gk n^4 (e-ek) +
                      gna m^3 h (e-ena) +
                      gl (e-el));
      dm = am[e] (1-m) - bm[e] m;
      dh = ah[e] (1-h) - bh[e] h;
      dn = an[e] (1-n) - bn[e] n;
            m += 3 dm dt;
            h += 3 dh dt;
            n += 3 dn dt;
```

```
            edot += edotdot dt;
            e += edot dt;
            ++ct;
      If[e>150, vhigh = vi; Break[]];
      If[e<-50, vlow = vi; Break[]];
        If[Mod[ct,100]==0,data[ct/100] = e];
    ];
    Print[t];
  ListPlot[Table[data[j],{j,50}], PlotJoined->True];
]
```

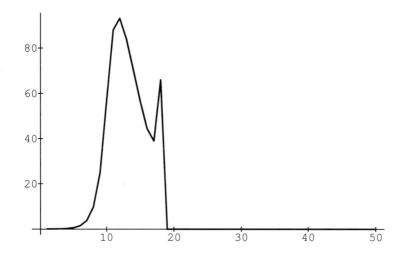

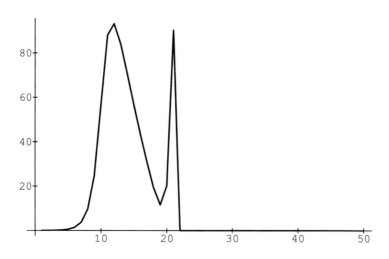

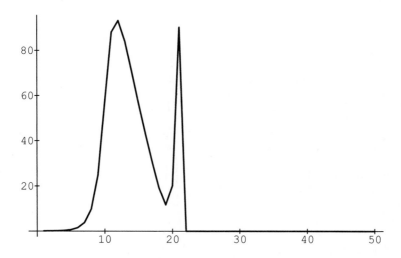

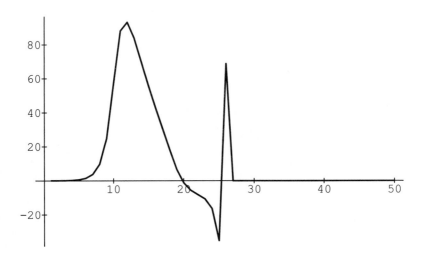

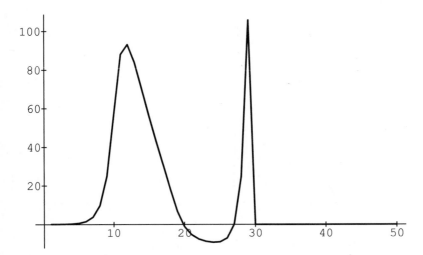

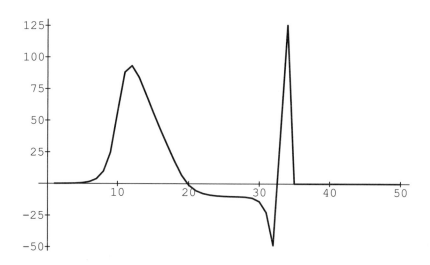

Figure 7.4.2: Snapshots of the Hodgkin-Huxley system, iteratively
solved for the propagation velocity of the action potential.
The last few pictures exhibit the expected undershoot
phenomenon.

It should be noted that as the squared-velocity parameter *vi* is sought in binary
search fashion, many pictures are output, only a few of which are exhibited in
Figure 7.4.2. The squared-velocity parameter upon which this *Mathematica*
session converges (by the time the last plot of Figure 7.4.1 is generated)
happens to be:

$$vi = r_a u^2 = 9.17038979949109 \qquad\qquad (7.4.5)$$

To convert such a computed velocity to physical units is an intricate matter,
partly because axon resistance r_a is not always constant as current varies. In
spite of such difficulties with the electrical model, not to mention the inherently
phenomenological character of the ion-channel assumptions, the original
treatment of Hodgkin and Huxley, which results through such calculations in
experimentally valid propagation velocities on the order of 20 meters/sec at
room temperatures, has dominated the field for several decades [Cronin-
Scanlon 1981].

7.5 Further explorations

E7.1) Implement a general *Mathematica* enzyme kinematics package along the lines of [Atkinson, et. al. 1987] or another appropriate reference.

E7.2) Implement a general pH calculation package.

E7.3) Implement a general titration curve package.

E7.4) For the helium atom, obtain better bounds on the ground state by assuming a non-separated wave function $\Psi = e^{-Zr_1 - Zr_2} (1 + wr_{12})^a$ and minimizing the expectation of the Hamiltonian with respect to Z, w, and a. Note that (7.2.9) must be modified for this more general type of Hamiltonian operator, because derivatives with respect to r_{12} –or some other equivalent extra coordinate–must now appear.

E7.5) Implement a Hartree-Fock self-consistent field (SCF) package.

E7.6) Analyze logistic population equations for *n* species in competition; e.g., $dp_i/dt = p_i(K_i - \Sigma_k C_{ik}p_k)$ where *C* is some "competition matrix". Discrete versions of these models should exhibit chaotic behavior in some regimes; while continuous models will usually exhibit smooth approach to equilibrium.

E7.7) Study time-to-extinction probabilities for a single species occupying at time *t* some number $n = n(t)$ of niches out of a constant total of *N* niches. Any niche is to have either zero or one organism. Assume that the birth rate (applying to currently empty niches) is $b(n)$, while the death rate (applying to currently occupied niches) is $d(n)$. For interesting choices of the *b*, *d* functions determine the mean time to extinction as a function of the initial population $n(0)$.

E7.8) Study trasnsmission line dynamics for axons presented with, say, unit step functions under various clamp conditions.

E7.9) Re-work the Hodgkin-Huxley action potential analysis of this chapter using the more efficient Runge-Kutta methods of Section 5.1.

Chapter 8:
Electronics and signal processing

8.1 Electronic circuits

Mathematica techniques may readily be applied to linear circuits, in which case symbolic solutions are often possible; or to the more difficult non-linear circuits which generally admit only of numerical solution. A good starting example in the linear domain is the LC tank circuit of Figure 8.1.1.

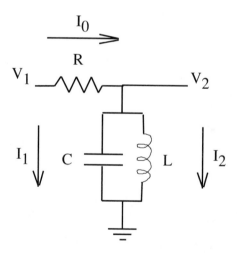

Figure 8.1.1: LC tank circuit which, like any sufficiently simple linear circuit, can be solved symbolically for its steady-state solutions.

The equations for the time-dependent voltages and currents are:

$$(V_1(t) - V_2(t)) = I_0(t)\, R \qquad\qquad (8.1.1)$$

$$I_0 = I_1 + I_2$$

$$C \frac{dV_2}{dt} = I_1$$

$$L \frac{dI_2}{dt} = V_2$$

A key question pertaining to such a circuit is: "For a given input $V_1(t)$, what is the output $V_2(t)$?". The equations (8.1.1) alone are *not* enough to completely determine the output $V_2(t)$, for the simple reason that initial conditions must also be posited. If, for example, we were to require that both V_2 and its time derivative vanish at $t = 0$, then a delta-function impulse $V_1(t) = \delta(t)$ would give rise to a certain transient solution V_2 called the impulse response of the circuit. We can say that the system (8.1.1) completely determines such sufficiently defined transient behavior. It is possible with fairly sophisticated *Mathematica* analysis to analyze transient solutions directly in the time domain, sometimes in closed form, but for this example circuit we choose a steady-state analysis (which is, at least formally, equivalent to impulse analysis).

Happily, the equation system (8.1.1)–even without any supposition of initial time conditions–completely defines the steady-state response, which loosely speaking is the output $V_2(t)$ for a given sinusoidal input $V_1(t) = e^{i\omega t}$, after, of course, all transients have damped out. The LC tank circuit can be seen to be equivalent to the damped, driven oscillator of Section 6.1, with a driving force proportional to the time derivative of V_1. Here, we approach such a system a little differently, by solving the equations (8.1.1) symbolically for the steady state. In a steady state all voltage and current components are assumed oscillatory:

$$\{V_1, V_2, I_0, I_1, I_2\} = \{1, v_2, i_0, i_1, i_2\} e^{i\omega t} \qquad (8.1.2)$$

Any phase lead-lag information will be embodied in the five time-independent complex amplitudes of the right-hand side. Note that our input signal V_1 is assumed to be a unit complex oscillator of angular frequency ω. What we seek is the response amplitude v_2. The following program finds this response:

```
                                                              (8.1.3m)
output = Solve[{ E^(I w t)  - v2 E^(I w t)  ==
               i0 E^(I w t) r,
               i0 == i1 + i2,
               c D[v2 E^(I w t),t]  == i1 E^(I w t),
               l D[i2 E^(I w t),t]  == v2 E^(I w t)},
               {v2,i0,i1,i2}]
Simplify[output]
```

```
                                                       2
                 I l w                          1 - c l w
{{v2 -> --------------------- ,  i0 -> --------------------- ,
                          2                               2
        r + I l w - c l r w            r + I l w - c l r w


                    2
               c l w
     i1 -> -(---------------------),
                              2
             r + I l w - c l r w


                   1
     i2 -> ---------------------}}
                              2
           r + I l w - c l r w
```

The result can be summarized thus: for input voltage $V_1(t) = e^{i\omega t}$ in Figure 8.1.1, the output voltage (after transients have died out) is:

$$V_2(t) = \frac{iL\omega\, e^{i\omega t}}{R + iL\omega - RLC\omega^2} \qquad (8.1.4)$$

As an example of a real-world possibility, let $C = 1$ microFarad and $L = 1$ milliHenry. We learn in early electronics training that the resonance angular frequency should be about $\omega_r = 1/\sqrt{(LC)}$, or about 3.2×10^4 sec^{-1}. What is less elementary is that the quality factor, that is the "sharpness" of the resulting bandpass resonance, is a certain function of the resistance R. We can plot various curves for $R = 100$ ohms to $R = 10$ kilOhms:

```
                                                       (8.1.5m)
Plot[Release[
            Table[Abs[v2 /. output[[1]]]] /.
```

```
                {c->10^(-6), l->10^(-3),
                 r->10^s}, {s,2,4,0.3}
          ]
     ],
     {w,20000,40000}, PlotRange->{0,1}
]
```

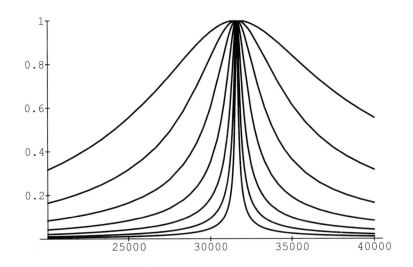

Figure 8.1.2: Response curves for the output amplitude v_2 for the tank circuit of Figure 8.1.1. The family of curves is obtained by varying resistance R and therefore the quality factor of the resonance.

Of course the steady-state solution could have been found by replacing the time-domain formalism embodied in (8.1.1) with a (time-independent) impedance formalism:

$$v_1 - v_2 = i_0 R \qquad\qquad (8.1.6)$$

$$i_0 = i_1 + i_2$$

$$i\omega C v_1 = i_1$$

$$i\omega L = v_2$$

This system is comprised of four linear equations in four complex unknowns. The results will be the same as in (8.1.3m) and (8.1.4). We adopted the initial approach (8.1.1) to show how, with *Mathematica*, to bridge the gap between the impedance formalism and the time-dependent formalism. Another way to analyze a time-dependent system is to use complete steady-state formulae together with Fourier analysis. In general, if $v_2(\omega)$ denotes, as in our LC tank example, the steady-state response for a unit oscillator input of frequency ω, then an arbitrary input voltage

$$V_1(t) \; = \; \int_{-\infty}^{\infty} u(\omega) \, e^{i\omega t} \, d\omega \qquad (8.1.7)$$

will, subject to appropriate causality and growth conditions, give rise to an output voltage

$$V_2(t) \; = \; \int_{-\infty}^{\infty} v_2(\omega) \, u(\omega) \, e^{i\omega t} \, d\omega \qquad (8.1.8)$$

That is to say, each frequency component $u(\omega)$ of the input is filtered according to the response $v_2(\omega)$. In this regard *Mathematica* Fourier transforms, which we discuss in a later section, can prove quite useful.

When linear circuits become sufficiently complicated it is best to stick with the impedance formalism. This approach is quite effective when applied to the popular and ever-so-practical class of linear circuits called active filters. These are circuits that perform sharp filtering via "active" elements such as operational amplifiers. The advent of such circuits in the 1960's changed irrevocably the nature of analog design. One of the important results of introducing gain elements in filter circuits was to obviate, notably in low-frequency cases, the need for unwieldy and costly inductors. What is more, amplifiers with virtually infinite input impedance effectively isolate passive R-C stages from each other when this isolation is desired.

Let us analyze a certain active filter which was constructed using the

CircuitBuilder application on the NeXT Computer. As described in Section 2.2., this application generates, via Kirchhoff's and Ohm's Law, a self-consistent equation system. Figure 8.1.3 shows the circuit in question.

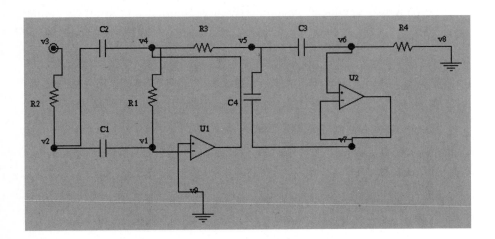

Figure 8.1.3: Active filter designed with the CircuitBuilder application on a NeXT Computer. This piece of the application window shows the result of iconic circuit construction. A self-consistent equation system may be fed to *Mathematica* for symbolic analysis, the idea being to find the output *v7* (lower right) as a function of frequency ω as presented at *v3* (upper left).

The circuit equations generated by the application, for the circuit of Figure 8.1.3, are:

$$(8.1.9m)$$

```
solutions = Solve [{
i1[0] + i1[1] + i1[2] == 0.0,
i2[0] + i2[1] + i2[2] == 0.0,
v3 == 1.000000,
i4[0] + i4[1] + i4[2] + i4[3] == 0.0,
i5[0] + i5[1] + i5[2] == 0.0,
i6[0] + i6[1] + i6[2] == 0.0,
i7[0] + i7[1] + i7[2] == 0.0,
v8 == 0.0,
v9 == 0.0,
i9[0] == 0.0,
```

```
i1[0]  ==  0.0,
v9  ==  v1,
i2[0]  ==  -i1[1],
i2[0]  ==  (v2-v1)*I*w*C1,
i2[1]  ==  -i3[0],
i2[1]  ==  (v2-v3)/R2,
i2[2]  ==  -i4[1],
i2[2]  ==  (v2-v4)*I*w*C2,
i4[2]  ==  -i5[0],
i4[2]  ==  (v4-v5)/R3,
i6[0]  ==  0.0,
i7[0]  ==  0.0,
v6  ==  v7,
i5[1]  ==  -i6[1],
i5[1]  ==  (v5-v6)*I*w*C3,
i7[2]  ==  -i5[2],
i7[2]  ==  (v7-v5)*I*w*C4,
i1[2]  ==  -i4[3],
i1[2]  ==  (v1-v4)/R1,
i6[2]  ==  -i8[0],
i6[2]  ==  (v6-v8)/R4
},{
v1,i1[0],i1[1],i1[2],
v2,i2[0],i2[1],i2[2],
v3,i3[0],
v4,i4[0],i4[1],i4[2],i4[3],
v5,i5[0],i5[1],i5[2],
v6,i6[0],i6[1],i6[2],
v7,i7[0],i7[1],i7[2],
v8,i8[0],
v9,i9[0]
}]
```

Note that the variable $v3 = 1$, corresponding to an input signal $1*e^{i\omega t}$. The desired output is $v7$ (lower right op-amp output of Figure 8.1.3). The various current terms ix[y] represent the outgoing currents numbered y at various circuit junctions numbered x: the relations amongst these currents amount to Kirchhoff's Law applied to respective junctions. When (8.1.9.m) is run in *Mathematica* the results are voluminous, the interesting part being the formula for the output $v7$:

```
                          2
0. - (1. C1 C3 R1 R4 w ) /

   (-1 + -I C1 R2 w + -I C2 R2 w + -I C3 R3 w +

                                                  2
    -I C4 R3 w + -I C3 R4 w + C1 C2 R1 R2 w  +

                  2                 2                 2
    C1 C3 R2 R3 w  + C2 C3 R2 R3 w  + C1 C4 R2 R3 w  +

                  2                 2                 2
    C2 C4 R2 R3 w  + C1 C3 R2 R4 w  + C2 C3 R2 R4 w  +

                          3                         3
    I C1 C2 C3 R1 R2 R3 w  + I C1 C2 C4 R1 R2 R3 w  +

                          3
    I C1 C2 C3 R1 R2 R4 w )
```

In technical terms, this response is that of a second-order bandpass stage, followed by a high-pass stage. A typical response amplitude graph for realistic resistor and capacitor component values is obtained as follows:

$$(8.1.10m)$$

```
v7s = v7 /. solutions[[1]] /. {
          R1 -> 8000, R2 -> 500, R3 -> 50,
          R4 -> 1000, C1-> 10^-7, C2 -> 10^-7,
          C3 -> 10^-9,C4 -> 10^-8}
```

```
                                -10  2
                          8. 10    w
0. - -------------------------------------------------------
                                      2
          -2031 I           8031 w              31 I          3
    -1 + -------- w + ------------ + --------------- w
          20000000    200000000000   500000000000000
```

This is evidently a third-order filter, whose response can be plotted like so:

$$(8.1.11\text{m})$$

```
Plot[Abs[v7s], {w, 0, 20000}]
```

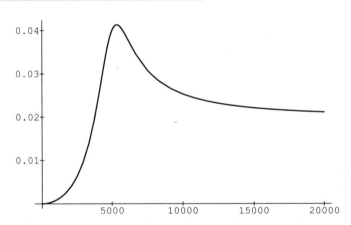

Figure 8.1.4: Response amplitude for the filter of Figure 8.1.3, with component values as in (8.1.10m).

As exemplified in these examples, the complete solution for the steady-state frequency response of a linear circuit can be obtained in principle via linear algebra in *Mathematica*.

What about non-linear circuits? One may almost always assume that numerical methods are the only recourse. Consider the seemingly trivial circuit of Figure 8.1.5, a resistor-diode combination.

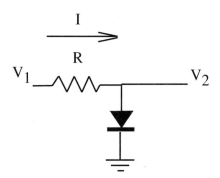

Figure 8.1.5: A simple, nevertheless unsolvable in any exact sense,
non-linear circuit.

The equations for such a circuit read:

$$(8.1.12)$$

$$(V_1 - V_2)/R = I$$
$$I = I_0 (e^{qV_2/kT} - 1)$$

The latter equation is the familar I-V relation for a diode junction, where q is the fundamental electron charge, T is the absolute (Kelvin) temperature, and k is the Boltzmann constant.   The proportionality constant I_0 is the leakage current, usually on the order of 10^{-8} to 10^{-10} amperes. For a given input V_1, the relations (8.1.12) imply a transcendental equation for the output V_2. Let us proceed to solve a particular situation numerically. The problem we pose is this: if a 12 volt supply (with some fluctuation dV_1) is applied as V_1, with $R =$ 100 ohms and room temperature = 298 K., what is the output V_2 and what is its fluctuation dV_2? The answer is obtained numerically as follows:

$$(8.1.13m)$$

```
i0 = 10^(-10)
r = 10^2
k = 1.39 10^(-23)
t = 298
q = 1.6 10^(-19)
a = q/(k t)
sol1 = FindRoot[(12.0-v2)/r == i0 (E^(a v2)-1),{v2,0.5}]
```

```
sol2 = FindRoot[(12.1-v2)/r == i0 (E^(a v2)-1),{v2,0.5}]
Print[sol1," ",sol2," "]
0.1/((v2 /. sol2) - (v2 /. sol1))
```

{v2 -> 0.540027} {v2 -> 0.540252}

445.5864720103533

The results mean that, for 12.0 volts in, the output V_2 is 0.540027, while for input 12.1 volts the output is V_2 = 0.540252. Thus, the diode sustains about 1/2 volt, while the attenuation of ripple fluctuation is about 445. This numerical experiment shows why diodes are usually assumed to have about 0.5 volts bias in forward conduction; and also shows how to begin designing a voltage regulator that rejects much of the fluctuation of the input supply voltage.

These non-linear numerical techniques may be applied to transistor circuits that are near to, or fully in the throes of, saturation. One interesting application is in the theory and practice of matched transistor pairs, which amount to active diode circuits where two or more diodes have "exactly" identical leakage currents, giving rise to convenient symmetries during the numerical analysis.

It goes without saying that the most notable success of non-linear circuitry has been the explosion of computer electronics. It is instructive to work out an example–albeit a trivial one–of digital logic. Consider the gate circuit of Figure 8.1.6, for which we desire to know the output z as a function of two inputs x and y.

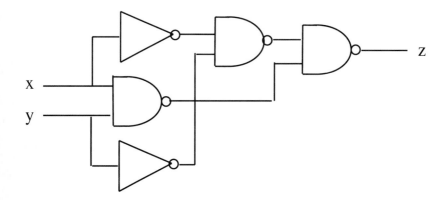

Figure 8.1.6: Gate logic circuit consisting of three nand gates and two
inverters.

All we need to know for this example is that an inverter takes its input *i* into the
Boolean (not *i*), while the nand function of (*i*, *j*) is the Boolean (not(*i* and *j*)).
The logic problem for this circuit is easily solved by generating a truth table via
Mathematica:

(8.1.14m)

```
nand[x_,y_] := !(x && y)
Table[x=(a>0); y=(b>0);
              {a,b,nand[nand[x,y],nand[!x,!y]]},
              {a,0,1},{b,0,1}
] // TableForm
```

0	0	True	1	0	False
0	1	False	1	1	True

This resulting truth table is seen to be that of an "exclusive-nor" operation, with
output *z* given by:

$$z = \text{not} \ (x \text{ or } y \text{ but not both}) \tag{8.1.15}$$

The two examples we have seen, diode and logic circuits, by no means properly
sample the universe of non-linear circuits. For example, there is interesting

modern research into chaotic circuits [Hasler 1987][Wu 1987]. It is a good question, whether after many more decades there will be anything left to say for the linear cases, what with the astounding complexity, applicability, and fascination of the non-linear ones.

8.2 Applications of the FFT

The functional Fourier[ ] is the standard *Mathematica* routine for computing Fourier transforms. One performs such a transform on a signal array of specified length. This array will actually be a *Mathematica* List, and there are special considerations for signal lengths and signal indices, so it is best to begin with a description of the precise calculation that Fourier[ ] is performing. As is customary in engineering scenarios, assume a signal x consists of complex numbers $x[0], x[1], x[2], ..., x[n-1]$, where n is the signal length. The Discrete Fourier Transform (or DFT) yields another signal Fx (which we call the spectrum), also having n components, the k-th such component defined by:

$$Fx[k] \; = \; \sum_{j=0}^{n-1} x[j] \, e^{-2\pi ijk/n} \tag{8.2.1}$$

with k running from 0 through $(n-1)$ inclusive. This is what might be called the "engineer's definition" of the DFT. Given the spectrum Fx, one may recover the original signal elements via the inverse transform:

$$x[j] \; = \; \frac{1}{n} \sum_{k=0}^{n-1} Fx[k] \, e^{+2\pi ijk/n} \tag{8.2.2}$$

By Fast Fourier Transform (FFT) we mean a special algorithm class for calculating the DFT or its inverse rapidly. The Fourier[ ] and InverseFourier[ ] functionals differ somewhat from these transforms, but can be used in any situation to provide an equivalent operation. Here are some rules to observe when using the *Mathematica* transforms:

(8.2.3)

1) A signal $x[0], x[1], ..., x[n-1]$ must first be put in the form of a *Mathematica* list. When we ponder the *Mathematica* transforms we must remember that the first list component $x[[1]]$ means the 0-th signal (or spectrum) component.

2) The InverseFourier[ ] functional is related to the *forward* engineer's transform (8.2.1) in the following way. InverseFourier[x] creates a new list equivalent to the formal description $(Fx)/\sqrt{n}$. Thus InverseFourier[ ] results, when multiplied through by $\sqrt{n}$, will yield the DFT result (8.2.1).

3) The Fourier[ ] functional operating on a known spectrum Fx likewise produces the *inverse* engineer's DFT (8.2.2) up to a scaling factor $\sqrt{n}$.

4) The scaling factors in *Mathematica* cancel overall when forward and inverse transforms are chained. Thus for example, InverseFourier[Fourier[theList]] produces an identical copy of theList (up to possible round-off errors).

5) Fourier[ ] and InverseFourier[ ] are usually fastest when the signal length (i.e. the list length) n is a product of small primes to powers. When possible one should endeavor to use lengths $n = 2^k$. Sometimes one should pad a signal with trailing zeros to force an efficient signal length.

The rules 2,3 appear abstruse so it is perhaps best simply to observe the following algorithms for computing the "engineer's" transforms in *Mathematica*:

To compute the engineer's DFT (8.2.1) given signal components $x[0], x[1], ...x[n-1]$:

(8.2.4)

1) Create a list y having n elements, such that $y[[j+1]] = x[j]$ for $j = 0,1,...,n-1$.
2) Obtain a transformed list, say $z = $ InverseFourier[y]; then multiply each element of the z list by $\sqrt{n}$. This final list has $z[[j+1]] = Fx[j]$.

To compute the engineer's inverse DFT (8.2.2) given spectrum components $Fx[0], Fx[1], ...Fx[n-1]$:

(8.2.5)

1) Create a list y having n elements, such that $y[[j+1]] = Fx[j]$ for $j = 0,1,...,n-1$.

2) Obtain a transformed list, say z = Fourier[y]; then divide each
   element of the z list by $\sqrt{n}$. This final list has $z[[j+1]] = x[j]$.

There is one more observation that is sometimes useful. The *Mathematica* transform directions are related in the following way:

Fourier[theList] gives the same result as the sequence: (8.2.6)

1) Conjugate each element of theList,

2) theList = InverseFourier[theList],

3) Conjugate each element of theList.

The same equivalence of the single and triplet of operations occurs if Fourier[ ] and InverseFourier[ ] are interchanged.

The above algorithms are written out primarily for elucidation: often one does not need to worry about scaling factors or transform directions at all. For example, when computing the convolution of two sequences by Fourier methods, one may simply apply transforms whose directions cancel, without regard for any scaling. Also, if you want to know just the amplitude or power plot of some spectrum when pure-real data is given, a direct call of either Fourier[ ] or InverseFourier[ ] on the signal data will give a correct result up to unimportant scaling.

There are important symmetries connected with the transforms when special conditions are true of the data (or spectrum). One of the most important symmetries arises when the signal data are pure real. In this case:

When all signal components are real: (8.2.7)

1) The spectrum is Hermitian-symmetric, i.e. $Fx[k] = Fx[n-k]^*$.

2) $Fx[0]$ is real.

3) If n is even $Fx[n/2]$ is real.

4) It follows that, for n even, the spectrum components $Fx[n/2+1]$,
   $Fx[n/2+2],...,Fx[n-1]$ are redundant; i.e. they can be recovered
   from knowledge of previous components.

The symmetries hold equally well for the corresponding list components obtained, as in (8.2.4), upon application of InverseFourier[ ] to the signal; provided one keeps in mind that list indexing goes from 1 through n.

Again in the case of pure-real signals, one may effectively double the transform speed by transforming two signals at once. If x and y are pure-real signals, then a transform of the complex signal $x + iy$ actually contains enough information to recover the separate transforms of x and y. We do not go into details here, but the reader may consult references such as [Press, et. al. 1988].

Before going on to actual applications we should clarify a question that is asked often of teachers everywhere, and which, this author believes, has (when not sufficiently answered) prevented many aspiring engineers from getting more interested in these transforms. One way to put this question is: "If the $x[j]$ represent a time-dependent signal and I compute the spectrum values $Fx[k]$, how can k be a frequency?...I thought k was an *integer*." There is one simple formula that answers this question neatly. The idea is that the signal x itself is presumed to be sampled at some rate, call this f_s, which can be thought of as a sampling frequency. Thus $x[j]$, $x[j+1]$ are thought of as separated by a sampling time $1/f_s$. Then the single relation we require is:

$$(8.2.8)$$

real-world frequency associated with component $Fx[k]$
$$= k f_s / n$$

Another way to state this is to observe: the frequency for the k-th spectral component is $k/(nt)$, where t is the sampling time. A simple mnemonic is to just remember that the frequency domain resolution, i.e. the separation between consecutive transform components, is f_s /n. These observations in turn reveal another way to look at the redundancy of the second half of the spectrum, as in (8.2.7): there is no meaningful spectrum data for k indices above about $n/2$. But this is an artifact of the celebrated result that for sampling rate f_s, the maximum meaningful bandwidth for sampled signals is the Nyquist value $f_s/2$ [Ahmed and Natarajan 1983].

A good way to get started with Fourier applications is to create general routines for the plotting of the spectra of pure-real signals. Let x denote a pure-real signal list and create a function that yields a list of meaningful spectral amplitudes, together with a plotting routine:

$$(8.2.9m)$$

```
ampSpectrum[x_List] := Block[{j, len, y, max},
                    len = 1 + Floor[Length[x]/2];
                    y = Take[InverseFourier[x],
                        {1,len}
                        ];
                    y = Abs[y];
                    y /= Max[y];
                    Return[y];
                  ]
SpectrumPlot[x_List] :=
     ListPlot[ampSpectrum[x],PlotJoined->True,
         PlotRange->{0,1}
     ]
```

The ampSpectrum[ ] routine produces a list of spectrum amplitudes | *Fx*[*k*] | (8.2.1), with these absolute values normalilzed so that the maximum amplitude is 1. This normalization is convenient if one wishes to plot, say, simultaneous spectra; in which case multiple plots will fit into the vertical plotting range {0,1}. Note that Fourier[ ] could have been used just as easily as InverseFourier[ ] because of the assumption of pure-real data, a fact easily inferred from (8.2.6). The SpectrumPlot[ ] routine will plot the meaningful part of the amplitude spectrum; all you have to do is pass SpectrumPlot[ ] an appropriate signal list. Clearly, this approach can be worked into a general spectral analysis package along programming guidelines as in [Maeder 1989].

A classic example of spectral plotting occurs when the signal *x* is a square wave. We can plot a square wave and its amplitude spectrum as follows:

$$(8.2.10m)$$

```
sig[j_] := 2 Mod[Floor[j/32.0],2] - 1
x = Table[sig[j],{j,256}]
ListPlot[x,PlotJoined->True]
SpectrumPlot[x]
```

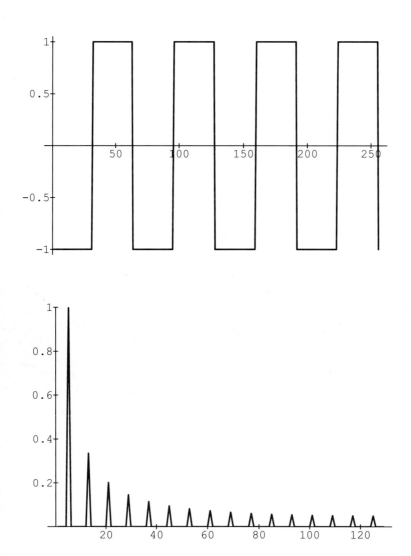

Figure 8.2.1: Square wave signal (upper) and its amplitude spectrum
(lower), revealing the well-known appearance of odd harmonics.

Figure 8.2.1 shows the interesting and often quoted result that odd harmonics appear. There are spikes in at approximate frequencies k_0, $3k_0$, $5k_0$, $7k_0$, ... where k_0 denotes the fundamental square wave frequency. Also interesting is that, at least for a square wave of infinite duration, the amplitudes decay theoretically as the sequence 1, 1/3, 1/5, 1/7, ...; a fact well approximated by the present (finite duration) example. It is instructive to work out a numerical example of the real-world relation (8.2.8) for this case. Say that the square wave signal (upper part of Figure 8.2.1) has been sampled at a rate $f_s = 2560$ samples/sec. Then a square wave period, which is 64 samples in our construction, has therefore a fundamental frequency of $2560/64 = 40$ Hz. But from the lower plot of Figure 8.2.1, the fundamental is at index $k_0 = 4$. The key formula (8.2.8) gives the frequency corresponding to this k_0, and run length 256, as $f_s k_0/256 = 40$ Hz., so everything is consistent.

As a second example, consider a tone burst having duration only a fraction of the total sampling period:

$$(8.2.11m)$$

```
sig[j_] := Sin[2 Pi j/5.0] /; j < 45
sig[j_] := 0 /; j>=45
x = Table[N[sig[j]],{j,256}]
ListPlot[x,PlotJoined->True]
SpectrumPlot[x]
```

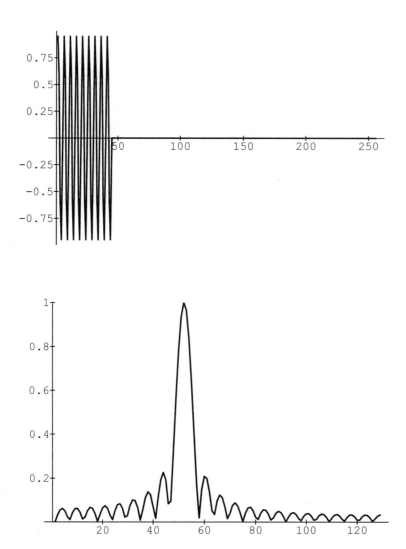

Figure 8.2.2: Tone burst signal (upper) and its amplitude spectrum (lower).

The lower plot of Figure 8.2.2 shows a clear isolated sinusoidal component, but
also shows rippling sidebands. These sidebands turn out to be an artifact of the
finite duration of the tone. One way to smooth out such a plot is to use
windowing technique to remove the effects of the sharp start- and stop-edges of
the burst envelope. To this end one may use a von Hann window (amongst

many possible practical windows), which amounts to multiplying the original signal by a $\sin^2$ "pinch" envelope [Strum and Kirk 1988]. The idea is that a signal element $x[j]$ is replaced by $x[j] \sin^2(\pi j/(n-1))$ where $j = 0, 1, 2, ..., n-1$. This distortion of the signal has the advantage that the abrupt ends of the original burst (upper part of Figure 8.2.2) are smoothed. The windowing technique is exemplified by the following sequence:

(8.2.12m)

```
sig[j_] := Sin[2 Pi j/5.0] /; j < 45
sig[j_] := 0 /; j>=45
HannW[j_,n_] := Sin[Pi (j-1)/(n-1)]^2
x = Table[N[sig[j] HannW[j,45]],{j,256}]
ListPlot[x,PlotJoined->True]
SpectrumPlot[x]
```

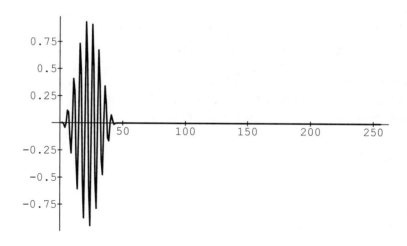

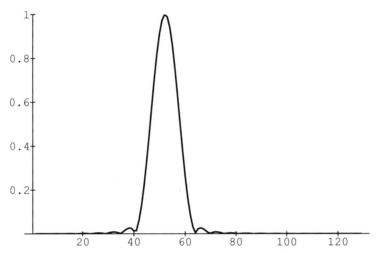

Figure 8.2.3: The tone burst signal of Figure 8.2.2 is premultipled by a von Hann window. The resulting amplitude spectrum reveals markedly reduced sideband ripple.

The utility of spectrum plots is made especially evident in the circumstance that one is looking for components at special frequencies. In the following example, we plot a digitized, modulated sine wave:

$$x(t) = (1 + \frac{1}{10} \cos\frac{2\pi t}{30}) \sin\frac{2\pi t}{15} \qquad (8.2.13)$$

where t will be the list index, 1 through 512 inclusive. As often happens, the signal plot is a hard-to-decipher sequence of dots. But the subsequent spectrum plot, which we now do in a decibel scale, clearly shows the sidebands caused by the modulation:

$$(8.2.14m)$$

```
sig[j_] := Sin[2 Pi j/15.0] (1 + 0.1*Cos[2 Pi j/30.0])
x = Table[N[sig[j]],{j,512}]
ListPlot[x]
x = ampSpectrum[x]
x = 20 Log[10,x]
ListPlot[x, PlotJoined->True,PlotRange->{-60,0}]
```

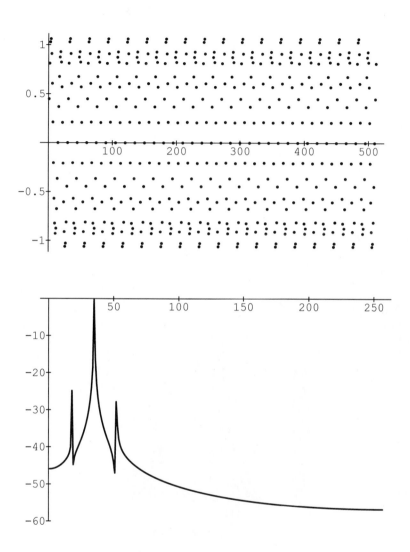

Figure 8.2.4: A digitized amplitude modulated carrier (upper) is seen,
via a decibel plot (lower), to possess double sideband structure.

Because our general functional ampSpectrum[ ] has normalized amplitudes so
that the maximum amplitude is 1, the decibel plot is easily arranged by
replacing any amplitude A with $20 \log_{10} A$, corresponding to a maximum
amplitude of 0 db.

Now we turn to a real-world FFT application for which actual laboratory data was acquired. Using a NeXT Computer's microphone input, a file of digitized sound was created. The word spoken was "mathematica":

(8.2.15m)

```
f = OpenRead["mathematica.sound"]
sound = ReadList[f,Byte]
Close[f]
Length[sound]
```

12000

The file has 12000 bytes of sound data. A plot of the data is effected thus:

(8.2.16m)

```
ListPlot[sound,Axes->None,PlotJoined->True]
```

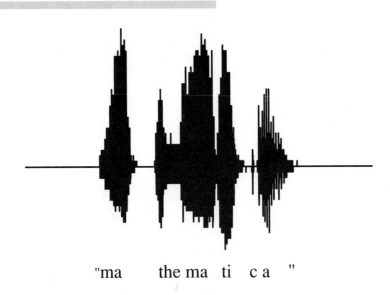

"ma   the ma   ti   c a   "

Figure 8.2.5: The word "mathematica" spoken into a microphone and acquired digitally by a NeXT Computer.

The last syllable of the waveform can be plotted like so:

(8.2.17m)

```
syllable = Take[sound,{7500,9548}]
ListPlot[syllable,Axes->None,PlotJoined->True]
```

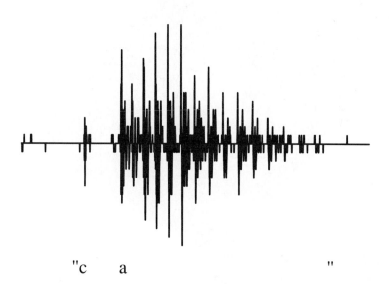

"c   a   "

Figure 8.2.6: The last syllable "...ca" from the sound wave of Figure 8.2.5.

Now that the last syllable data is resident in the list "syllable", we can proceed to create a 3D spectrogram, by taking successive FFTs of length 64 on a partitioned list:

(8.2.18m)

```
list = Partition[syllable, 64]
list = Map[Fourier, list]
list = Abs[list]
amp[b_,k_] := list[[b+1,k+1]] /; k>0
amp[b_,k_] := 0 /; k==0
Plot3D[amp[Round[x],Round[y]],{x,0,31},{y,0,32},
          PlotPoints->32,ViewPoint->{15,-10,25}
]
```

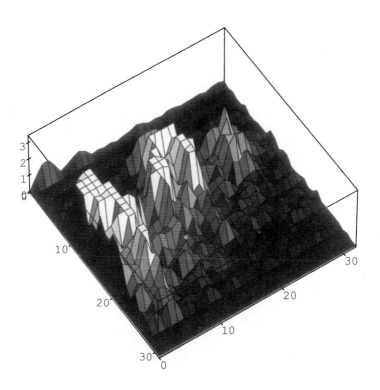

Figure 8.2.7: A 3D spectrogram of the syllable of Figure 8.2.6. The
time axis moves from northwest to southeast. Frequency
is plotted from southwest to northeast. The height of the
surface is the spectrum amplitude for the given length-64
FFT and given time segment.

Note that we have rejected the unimportant DC average of the signal by forcing
the first spectrum amplitude to zero. Figure 8.2.7 shows the fricative "c",
actually a "k" sound, as a wideband (about four grid cells wide) peak centered
at the northwest face of the figure (time $t \sim 5$). Then the "a" sound comes in,
showing at least one fairly steady component: the ridge running from the west
corner to the south corner of the figure. Many of these features are easier to
analyze using a so-called amplitude sonogram:

(8.2.19m)

```
DensityPlot[-amp[Round[x],Round[y]],{x,0,31},{y,0,32},
        PlotPoints->32]
```

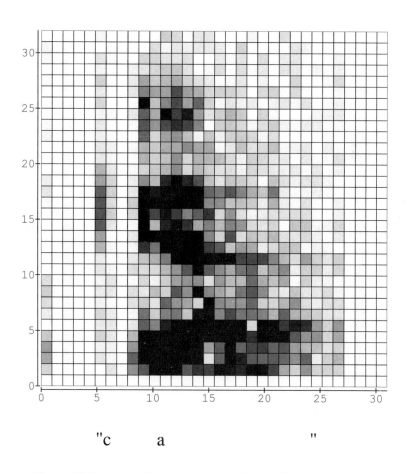

"c   a   "

Figure 8.2.8: An amplitude sonogram of the "ca" syllable, the horizontal
axis being time and the vertical axis being frequency. Darker
regions correspond to greater amplitudes in this plot. One can
see the fricative "c" as a light wideband streak above time = 5.
Strong formant frequencies for the "a" sound are evident.

The sonogram Figure 8.2.8 shows several clear features. The fricative "c" at time = 5 on the horizontal axis is fairly wideband, i.e. stretches vertically a fair distance. As for the final vowel "a", we can see formant frequencies, at rough indices 6, 12 and 18. This kind of graphical analysis is suggestive of further experiments in which such important measures as pitch period, dispersion, envelope and zero-crossing rate may be estimated. These measures are of special interest in the difficult field of speech recognition.

In many branches of engineering, not to mention even fields of abstract science, an important operation is that of convolution of two sequences. There is also the very similar operation of correlation. We have touched upon convolution sums in Section 4.4 and shall mention them again in the next section on digital filters. It is worthwhile to state explicity at this juncture that the method of convolving of Section 4.4 is completely applicable to signals and images. The basic idea, that convolution in signal space is equivalent to a certain multiplication in spectral space, holds across all fields of inquiry.

8.3 Digital filters

The basic idea of digital filtering is that filtering of analog data can be mimicked by numerical operations on a digital facsimile of said data. A typical scenario is this: in a laboratory, data $\{x[j]\}$ are acquired through an analog-to-digital converter, and one wishes to create a filtered version of this signal as a sequence $\{y[j]\}$. Computer programs can perform operations on the x sequence to yield an appropriate y sequence. For example, maybe one wants y to be some sort of running average of x values. An analog low-pass filter built from passive components produces this kind of average. The power of digital filtering is that virtually any linear analog circuit can be approximated via sheer numerical operations. A general scheme, called a Linear Time Invariant (LTI) digital filter, is schematized in Figure 8.3.1.

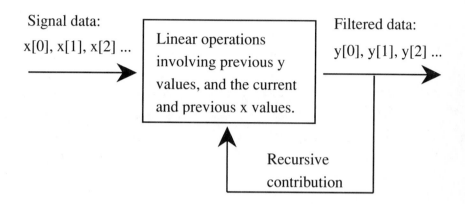

Figure 8.3.1: A general digital filtering scheme. A digitized signal having
            components $x[0]$, $x[1]$, ... is turned into a filtered signal having
            components $y[j]$ that depend linearly on $y[j-1]$, $y[j-2]$, ... and
            $x[j]$, $x[j-1]$, $x[j-2]$, ...

The general linear relation for the digital filter of Figure 8.3.1 is [Strum and
Kirk 1989]

$$y[j] \;=\; \sum_{k=1}^{p} a[k]\, y[j-k] \;+\; \sum_{k=0}^{q} b[k]\, x[j-k] \tag{8.3.1}$$

where the first sum is referred to as the recursive part and the second sum as the
non-recursive part of the filter. It is convenient for computing purposes to
define, for $m = \max(p, q)$, the first m values $\{y[0], ..., y[m-1]\}$ to be zero; after
which all values $\{y[m], y[m+1], ...\}$ are then unambiguously determined by
(8.3.1). From these various assumptions we can obtain the frequency response
of the filter. Let the input data be oscillatory with angular frequency ω, that is
$x[j] = e^{i\omega j}$ and denote the steady-state solution by:

$$y[k] \;\sim\; A(\omega)\, e^{i\omega k} \quad ; \quad \text{large } k \tag{8.3.2}$$

where A is a complex amplitude representing the filter response function vs.
frequency. This amplitude is often written $A = H(e^{i\omega})$ in signal processing
literature. From these assumptions it follows readily from (8.3.1) that the filter

response is:

$$A(\omega) \;=\; \frac{b[0] \;+\; \displaystyle\sum_{k=1}^{q} b[k]\, e^{-i\omega k}}{1 \;-\; \displaystyle\sum_{k=1}^{p} a[k]\, e^{-i\omega k}} \qquad\qquad (8.3.3)$$

The general idea in digital filter design is to find the *a,b* coefficient sequences such that $A(\omega)$ approximates in some suitable sense the desired filter response. We take up the design problem later, turning now instead to a worked example of a tunable bandpass filter. Consider the filter defined by the recursion:

$$y[j] \;=\; 2cg\, y[j\!-\!1] \;-\; c^2\, y[j\!-\!2] \;+\; x[j] \;-\; d\, x[j\!-\!1] \qquad (8.3.4)$$

where $0 < c \le 1$ and $-1 < g < 1$ are constants that completely determine the filter, given $d = 2cg/(1+c^2)$. It turns out that this bandpass filter has a resonant frequency and half-power bandwidth given approximately by:

$$\omega \,\sim\, \text{arc cos}\,(g(1+c^2)/2c) \qquad\qquad (8.3.5)$$
$$\Delta\omega \,\sim\, 2(1-c)$$

The approximation is best for *c* near 1. This filter also has the convenient property that $A(\pi) = A(0)$; i.e., that the amplitude response is the same for the extreme low and high band frequencies. These resonant and bandwidth values can actually be obtained exactly by analyzing the absolute square of (8.3.3) for this case, but the algebra is not too illuminating and for practical purposes (8.3.5) will usually suffice. Incidentally, a useful mnemonic for converting such formulae as (8.3.5) for real-world frequencies is this: for sampling rate f_s of the original data *x*, the value $\omega = \pi$ corresponds to the Nyquist frequency $f_s/2$. Let us plot the filter response amplitude $|A(\omega)| = |H(e^{i\omega})|$ for the values *c* = 0.95, *g* varying from 0 to 0.9:

$$(8.3.6m)$$

```
c = 0.95
Clear[g]
a = {2 c g,-c^2}; p = Length[a]
```

```
b = {-(2 c g)/(1+c^2)}; q = Length[b]; b0 = 1
A[w_] := (b0 + Sum[b[[k]] E^(-I w k),{k,q}]) /
           (1  - Sum[a[[k]] E^(-I w k),{k,p}])
Plot[Release[Table[Abs[N[A[w]]],{g,0.,0.9,0.1}]],{w,0,Pi},
     PlotRange->{0,15}]
```

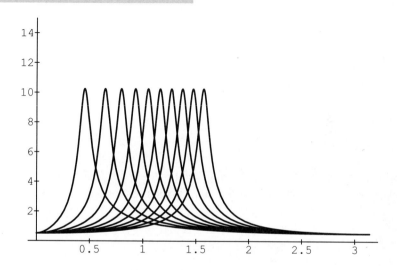

Figure 8.3.2: A family of digital bandpass filter curves for the
recursion (8.3.4). The parameter $c = 0.95$, while parameter
g varies from 0 to 0.9 in steps of 0.1. The resonant frequency
ω approximately satisfies $\cos \omega = g$.

Needless to say, we used prior knowledge [Strum and Kirk 1988] of the
bandpass filter class to establish the particular coefficients of (8.3.4). What
does one do to determine the *a,b* coefficient sequences from scratch when a
given filter response is desired? It turns out to be easier to ponder only non-
recursive filters in which the *a*[ ] sequence is empty.

Let us sketch a design algorithm for non-recursive filters, in which case (8.3.1)
simplifies to:

$$y[j] \;=\; \sum_{k=0}^{q} b[k]\, x[j{-}k] \qquad\qquad (8.3.7)$$

In the design process we shall consider, for some positive integer K, real finite coefficient sequences $b[0] = 0, b[1], \ldots, b[2K+1]$. For suitable time translation of the x signal, the problem comes down to approximating the formal system defined by:

$$y[j] \;=\; \sum_{k=-\infty}^{\infty} h[k]\, x[j{-}k] \qquad\qquad (8.3.8)$$

The h coefficients comprise a so-called unit impulse response. Whereas the h sequence will turn out generally to be non-vanishing for infinitely many indices, in our approximation $b[k] = h[k{-}K{+}1]$ for $0 \le k \le 2K$ and $b[k] = 0$ otherwise. The theoretical filter (8.3.8) has a response:

$$A(\omega) \;=\; \sum_{k=-\infty}^{\infty} h[k]\, e^{-i\omega k} \qquad\qquad (8.3.9)$$

from which it follows formally that

$$h[m] \;=\; \frac{1}{2\pi} \int_{-\pi}^{\pi} A(\omega)\, e^{-i\omega m}\, d\omega \qquad\qquad (8.3.10)$$

To ensure real valuedness of the h sequence, we assume further that A satisfies $A(\omega) = -A(\omega)$. A filter design algorithm may now be established:

(8.3.11)

1) Choose a real-valued, even function filter response $A(\omega)$ defined for $-\pi < \omega < \pi$, noting that for any ω, real-world frequency $f = \omega f_s / 2\pi$.
2) Determine for some integer K (the larger this K the better the eventual approximations) the coefficients $h[-K]$, ..., $h[0]$,... $h[K]$ from (8.3.10).
3) Set $b_0 = 0$ and $b[k] = h[k-K+1]$ for $1 \leq k \leq 2K+1$.
4) Now the digital iteration (8.3.7) will give rise to a y sequence that is an approximate filtering, with amplitude response $\sim A(\omega)$, of the x sequence.

A typical design procedure starts with the bandpass response shown in Figure 8.3.3.

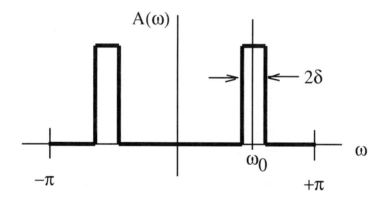

Figure 8.3.3: Digital filter design procedure for non-recursive cases
starts with an assumption of a symmetrical filter response
$A(\omega)$. In this case a bandpass filter with resonance frequency
ω_0 and width 2δ is desired.

From (8.3.10) the unit impulse response for the Figure 8.3.3 design is not hard to establish as:

$$h[m] \quad = \quad \frac{2}{m\pi} \cos m\omega_0 \, \sin m\delta \qquad (8.3.12)$$

Once again it is worth noting that the real-world resonant frequency of this filter will be $\omega_0 f_s / 2\pi$. Let us plot the frequency response amplitude for this resonance, with width $\delta = 0.2$, noting item (3) of (8.3.11):

$$(8.3.13m)$$

```
sinc[y_] := Sin[y]/y /; y!=0
sinc[y_] := 1 /; y==0
b = Table[N[Cos[m Pi/6.0] sinc[0.1 m]],{m,-40,40}]
q = Length[b]; b0 = 0
A[w_] := b0 + Sum[b[[k]] E^(-I w k),{k,q}]
Plot[Abs[N[A[w]]],{w,0,Pi},PlotRange->{0,20}]
```

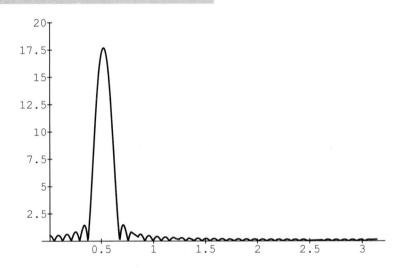

Figure 8.3.4: A designed bandpass filter response $|A(\omega)|$, starting from
Figure 8.3.3 with $\omega_0 = \pi/6$, $\delta = 0.1$; and $K = 40$ from (8.3.11).

To try out this filter on a particular signal, we note that (8.3.7) requires $2K+1 =$ 81 coefficients $b[j]$. An instructive test signal is a sine wave of frequency ω_0 buried in a random noise:

$$x[j] = \sin \frac{2\pi j \omega_0}{12} + n[j]$$

$$(8.3.14)$$

The idea is that the digital bandpass filter should pick the sinusoidal signal out of the noise signal $n[j]$:

(8.3.15m)

```
sinc[y_] := Sin[y]/y /; y!=0
sinc[y_] := 1 /; y==0
b = Table[N[Cos[m Pi/6.0] sinc[0.1 m]],{m,-40,40}]
q = Length[b]
x = Table[N[Sin[2 Pi j/12.0] + 5*Random[]],{j,256}]
n = Length[x]
y = Table[0.0,{j,n}]
Do[
  Do[y[[j]] += b[[k]] x[[j-k]],
    {k,q}
  ],
  {j,q+1,n}
]
ListPlot[x,PlotJoined->True]
ListPlot[y,PlotJoined->True]
```

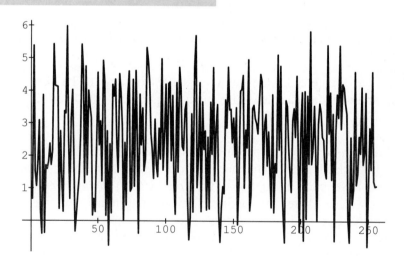

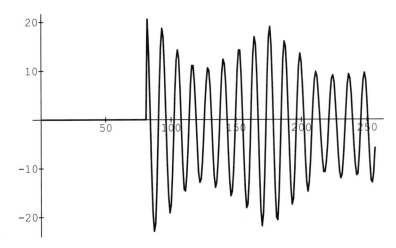

Figure 8.3.5: Digital bandpass filter in action. A sinusoidal
signal plus noise (upper) is filtered via the 81-tap filter
of Figure 8.3.4, yielding sharp noise reduction (equivalently,
reinforcment of the sinusoidal signal) in the output (lower).

Note that in Figure 8.3.5 the output signal is defined to be zero until the
horizontal time index has moved far enough, in this case to $j = 2K+2 = 82$, that
the sum (8.3.7) is well-defined.

Digital filter options are voluminous and sometimes, especially in the recursive
cases, complicated. Many references describe design algorithms; some of these
do not involve explicit integration of the type (8.3.10) [Quinn 1990][Parks and
Burrus 1987].   There also exist efficient algorithms for the practical
computation of aperiodic convolutions such as the standard filter convolution
formally described by (8.3.8). One approach is to pre-compute the FFT of a
finite, appropriately zero-padded impulse response h, and use this with
repetitive computation of the FFT of subsequences of the input x, each
subsequence also being zero-padded. This Fourier approach turns out to be
superior to the direct summation we used in (8.3.15m) when the aperiodic
convolution size (such as $2K+1$) as sufficiently large. Other approaches include
overlap-add and overlap-save finite convolutions, and the optimized Winograd
convolution [Burrus and Parks 1985].

8.4 Image processing

A primary task in image processing is to represent an image by a suitable data array.   One way to proceed is to read in an array of image pixels as a *Mathematica* list, after which one may use appropriate arithmetic to find, for example, the pixel value at coordinates (x, y).   In the following example an image file had been created in "neutral format". This particular file begins with the integer values of width and height, in ASCII, followed by a total of width*height 8-bit pixel intensities, arranged lexicographically such that the first row of pixels crosses the top scan line starting from the upper left. This arrangement, whereby the origin is at the upper left, is a common one for computer images. Such a file may be read into a list as follows:

$$(8.4.1m)$$

```
f = OpenRead["transamerica.neut"]
w = Read[f,Number]
h = Read[f,Number]
Read[f,Byte]   (* Some systems will require this newline
                   read. *)
image = ReadList[f,Byte]
Close[f]
Print[w," ",h," ",Length[image]]
```

```
198 197 39006
```

At this point, the image file "transamerica.neut" has been read in, with width = 198 pixels, height = 197 pixels. The list length is, as expected, 39006 = 198*197. By defining an appropriate intensity function pixel[ ] of Cartesian coordinates we may display the image via direct density plotting:

$$(8.4.2m)$$

```
pixel[x_,y_] := N[image[[Round[x]+1+w*(h-Round[y]-1)]]]
DensityPlot[pixel[x,y],{x,0,w-1},{y,0,h-1},Mesh->False,
     PlotPoints->{w,h}]
```

Figure 8.4.1: An image has been read into a *Mathematica* list
and displayed via DensityPlot[ ]. The list contains pixel
intensity values (black = 0), arranged lexicographically,
starting at the upper left corner of the image.

The pixel arithmetic used in this example depends on the following definitions.
Let $p(a, b)$ be the pixel intensity (0 = black, 1 = white) at *integer* coordinates
(a, b), where $(0,0)$ is the lower left origin of the image. Then the intensity p is
related to elements of the image list by:

$$p(a, b) = \text{image}[[a+1 + w*(h-b-1)]] \qquad (8.4.3)$$

Thus we have defined our function pixel$[x, y]$ as $p(\text{Round}[x], \text{Round}[y])$, so
that graphical references to pixel[ ] will produce density, contour, or relief plots
as desired.

A straightforward image processing problem is that of edge detection, whereby sharp intensity transitions are enhanced relative to slow transitions. A classic way of enhancing edges is to replace an image function pixel[x, y] by its discrete Laplacian:

$$4 \text{ pixel}[x, y] - \text{pixel}[x+1, y] - \text{pixel}[x-1, y] \qquad (8.4.4)$$
$$- \text{pixel}[x, y-1] - \text{pixel}[x, y+1]$$

The result of this filtering is exhibited in the following sequence:

$$(8.4.5m)$$

```
image2 = image
Do[image2[[j]] = 4 image[[j]] - image[[j+1]] -
          image[[j-1]] - image[[j-w]] - image[[j+w]],
   {j,w+1,h*w-w}
]
pixel2[x_,y_] := N[image2[[Round[x]+1+w*(h-Round[y]-1)]]]
DensityPlot[pixel2[x,y],{x,0,w-1},{y,0,h-1},Mesh->False,
      PlotPoints->200]
```

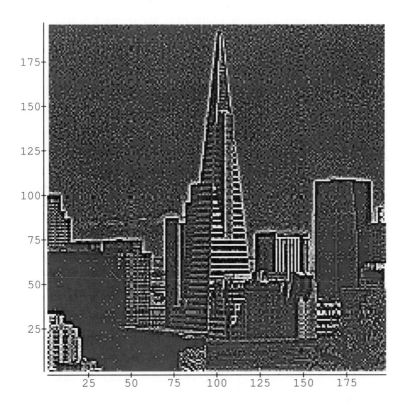

Figure 8.4.2: Laplacian edge detection filtering applied to the original
image of Figure 8.4.1. Sharp white-black scores appear
at the relatively strong intensity gradients.

It is entirely possible–and often preferable–to define instead a two-dimensional
image list for such image calculus. For example one may define a list called
image2[], partitioned into scan lines such that image2[[a,b]] is the pixel value at
horizontal scan line a, column b, using the enumeration implicit in (8.4.3) to
handle the fact of pixel origin (0,0). This approach is definitely superior when
one performs transforms, such as 2D FFTs, on the image. With the two-
dimensional list representation, automatic mapping of Fourier[] can be effected
as in (8.2.18m) on horizontal or (after a Transpose[] operation) vertical scan
lines. For this book we have adopted the one-dimensional representation, since
it is slightly easier for the elementary Laplacian example.

The possibilities for image filtering and general processing abound. Regardless of one's image list representation, one may perform 2D transforms via *Mathematica* by following a very simple rule: given a rectangular array of intensity values (such as the image just analyzed), the 2D FFT may be obtained by transforming each horizontal scan *in place*, then, on this complex-valued image, transforming each vertical scan *in place*. The 2D transforms are especially useful for Optical Character Recognition (OCR) technology, in which one may convolve known symbol images, via 2D FFTs, with regions of text in order to isolate particular characters. Another image processing challenge is to "de-blur" images by adroit application of high-pass filtering, of which the Laplacian edge detection is a rudimentary example. This de-blurring can be very effectively implemented for both motion blur (the camera was exposed to a moving image) and lens blur (the camera is defocused) [Beauchamp and Yuen 1979].

8.5 Further explorations

E8.1) Analyze the transient response of a linear circuit of choice. For example, take the circuit of Figure 8.1.1, assuming quiescence; i.e. $V_2(0) = dV_2/dt(0) = 0$. Let $V_1(t) = \delta(t)$, a delta-function impulse. Then the desired output $V_2(t)$ for positive t will be the desired "impulse response". In this regard (8.1.7) and (8.1.8) are useful.

E8.2) Work out general design packages for the important filter classes: low-pass, high-pass, band-pass, phase-shift, and notch filters. The most useful package would allow for user determination of various pass-band ripple constraints, roll-offs, and characteristic frequencies.

E8.3) Create a general *Mathematica* package for the analysis of logic circuits made up of gates from the following selection: nand, and, or, nor, and inverter. Ideally, the user would somehow input the wiring scheme and the gates so wired, obtaining a complete truth table (if such exists). The most difficult cases involve past-dependent circuits such as latches made up of input-crossed nor's, etc. It is a good idea therefore to separate all (legal) circuits into two classes: those that admit of deterministic solutions and those that exhibit hysteresis.

E8.4) Investigate de-blurring algorithms as follows. Load in a picture and motion-blur it intentionally in the x direction, by replacing every pixel with the average of some fixed number of its neighbors along the same scan line. Then work out possible algorithms to de-blur such a blurred image. One approach is to find a digital filter for scan line data that essentially "undoes" the blurring operation. Another is to de-convolve the blurred image with respect to the blurring convolution. A different line of research is to assume focus blur instead, in which case an out-of-focus lens is assumed to be the culprit.

E8.5) Attempt Optical Character Recognition (OCR) experiments using 2D FFTs, as follows. Take the 2D FFT of some text image (a short paragraph say) of given 2^k-by-2^k frame size. Choose a solitary letter, and take the 2D FFT of this character sitting alone at the upper left origin of the same frame size image. Then multiply componentwise the two FFTs, finally taking the inverse 2D FFT of the componentwise product spectrum. The result should be sharp diffraction points lying exclusively on those letters that match the solitary character.

Chapter 9:
Great problems of history

9.1 Problems solved and unsolved

Many investigators harbor, either privately or outwardly, their own preferred list of favorite problems of history. Some such problems were solved with tremendous finesse. Some have not been seriously dented after hundreds of years of intensive research. What are perhaps the most populous stars in the galaxy of difficult problems are those for which partial solutions exist, often as a result of great effort by many thinkers.

Mathematica techniques can be used effectively to explore this special domain, the great problems of history. In parallel with the above categorization of such problems, we have the options: replay the machinations of our ancestors and see how the problem was solved, or get some feeling for why the problem is so very hard, or obtain partial solutions in the historical style.

The author requests the liberty to claim that practitioners of modern culture should continually and resolutely appreciate the mathematical achievements of ancestors. One who appreciates the problems of history is often enough pained to be asked, even if indirectly, what good are the theories of numbers, complex functions, or gravitation? Let us put the answer in an intentionally blunt but canonical form: without Fermat, Gauss, Riemann, and Einstein you might neither have a car to drive nor a place to shop. There is no telling where a mathematical idea, however deeply entrenched in the symbolism of a given era, may eventually lead.

The following selection covers some of the author's favorite great problems of history. If the problem is a solved one, we can glimpse the beauty of the past analysis. When the problem is unsolved or partially solved, we can see how barriers were made to recede. In any case it becomes evident that the modern processing power of *Mathematica* can teach lessons of history.

9.2 Fermat's "Last Theorem"

The eminent Pierre Fermat did, in 1637, claim the theorem that for $n>2$ the Diophantine equation

$$x^n + y^n = z^n \tag{9.2.1}$$

has no solutions in positive integers (x, y, z). The allure of this problem is due in part to its extreme difficulty, and in part to the famous anecdote that Fermat wrote out this claim as a marginal note in his copy of Bachet's works of Diophantus [Hardy and Wright 1979]. The legend is augmented further by Fermat's reason for not giving us his proof: he claimed there was not sufficient space in the margin to write out the logic. To this day we face two stifling blockades: we do not know if Fermat had a proof, and we do not know whether his claim–the impossibility of (9.2.1) for $n>2$–is true. It is more often than not believed that Fermat could not have had a proof, what with the great numerical thinkers of 200 years since all coming up short.

Note that it would suffice to show the impossibility of (9.2.1) for all prime exponents, because if (9.2.1) happened for exponent $n = ap$ where p is prime, then the triple (x^a, y^a, z^a) would be a solution for exponent p. The pioneering mathematician Kummer, over the period 1847-1850, used his profound theory of cyclotomic fields to establish a certain class of primes called *regular* primes [Koblitz, ed. 1982]. For such primes Kummer's result is that

$$x^p + y^p = z^p \tag{9.2.2}$$

has no solutions in positive integers (x, y, z). Now one definition of regular is that

$$p \text{ does not divide any numerator of } B_2, B_4, ..., B_{p-3} \tag{9.2.3}$$

where the B_{2k} are the even-indexed Bernoulli numbers. This must certainly have been exciting to discover, for now an inspection of a finite list of Bernoulli numerators will often settle completely the Fermat question for exponent p. For one thing, the first few primes are regular, i.e. they do not divide (the numerator of) any member of their respective sets of Bernoulli numbers. However, as Kummer found, at least the primes

$$p = 37, 59, 67, 101, 103, 131, 149, 157 \qquad (9.2.4)$$

are irregular. It is known that there exist an infinity of irregular primes; in fact it is a plausible conjecture that only an asymptotic fraction $1/\sqrt{e} \sim 0.6$ of all primes are regular [Ribenboim 1988].

Let us do a *Mathematica* investigation of these wonderful partial results on Fermat's "Last Theorem". First, we check the "Theorem" for the exponent $p = 7$:

$$(9.2.5m)$$

```
Print[BernoulliB[2], "     ", BernoulliB[4]]
```

```
1        1
-      - (--)
6       30
```

Because 7 divides neither of the numerators, this trivial *Mathematica* segment proves the special case $p = 7$ of Fermat's "Last Theorem". It should be pointed out that to determine

$$x^7 + y^7 = z^7 \qquad (9.2.6)$$

has no positive triplet solutions (x, y, z), as we have just done, is highly non-trivial if done with some rudimentary method such as investigating the appropriate number field directly. For such reasons one appreciates the power of Kummer's regularity criterion.

Next we verify that the prime $p = 37$ is irregular. In fact, we go:

$$(9.2.7m)$$

```
Print[BernoulliB[32]]
```

```
  7709321041217
-(-------------)
       510
```

and then:

$$(9.2.8m)$$

```
Mod[Numerator[%],37]
```

0

showing that 37 divides the numerator of B_{32}. Of course, preknowledge of the correct index 32 was used in this case, so we turn to a more unified treatment of the Bernoulli numbers that will give rise to results for general p.

How do we go through the proper list of Bernoulli numerators, checking each one (mod p)? There are many ways to do this, but we shall investigate a method that, when optimized in a certain fashion described later, is asymptotically (large p) quite efficient. Note that the Bernoulli numbers can be defined in terms of a generating function:

$$\frac{t}{e^t - 1} = \sum_{n=0}^{\infty} \frac{B_n}{n!} t^n \qquad (9.2.9)$$

The left-hand side will be used to precision $O(t^{p-3})$, so that in the series expansion of the denominator $e^t - 1$ the coefficients are of the form $1/k!$ for $k = 1$ through $k = p - 1$. It follows that the expansion of $(p - 1)! \, t / (e^t - 1)$, through order $O(t^{p-3})$, will yield integer coefficients on the right-hand side. Indeed, we go:

$$(9.2.10m)$$

```
p = 37
s = Normal[Series[Factorial[p-1]*t/(Exp[t]-1),{t,0,p-3}]]
```

```
3719933267899012174679994481508352000000000 -
  18599666339495060873399972407541760000000000*t +
```

```
30999443899158434788999954012569600000000*t^2 -
51665739831930724648333256687616000000000*t^4 +
12301366626650172535317442068480000000000*t^6 -
30753416566625431338293605171200000000*t^8 +
77660142845013715500741427200000000*t^10 -
196568346908075008831546982400000*t^12 +
4978214284936776634662912000000*t^14 -
126093845018321576243527680000*t^16 +
3193957788339335451033600000*t^18 -
80903664250783627309056000*t^20 +
2049312289416696944640000*t^22 -
51909677420475942144000*t^24 +
1314887430899448806400*t^26 -
33306487341550536960*t^28 +
843663177746409600*t^30 -
21370237926253524*t^32 + 541314450257070*t^34
```

It is evident that $p = 37$ divides an even-indexed Bernoulli number up through B_{p-3} if and only if it divides a non-zero coefficient in the above series data. There is a compact way that *Mathematica* can tell us about the nature (mod p) of a coefficient, which is to simply use the Mod[ ] function which in the present situation reduces each polynomial coefficient (mod p):

$$(9.2.11m)$$

```
s = Mod[s,p]
```

```
36 + 19*t + 3*t^2 + 24*t^4 + 10*t^6 + 9*t^8 + 25*t^10 +
24*t^12 + 35*t^14 + 12*t^16 + 36*t^18 + 28*t^20 + 18*t^22
+ 8*t^24 + 4*t^26 + 6*t^28 + 34*t^30 + 4*t^34
```

That the coefficient of t^{32} is missing indicates that, indeed, $p = 37$ is irregular because it divides (the numerator of) B_{32}. Proceeding in this way we can use *Mathematica* to prove Fermat's "Last Theorem" for all exponents p less than some limit, *except* for the irregular primes.

What does one do then, when p is irregular, as in the cases (9.2.4)? The irregular primes such as $p = 37$, require more work. A criterion of Vandiver gives, happily, a side calculation that actually uses the discovered irregularity indices $2k$, where B_{2k} are the Bernoulli numbers whose numerators were divisible by p. This side calculation has never been known to fail for irregular cases, but there is as yet no rigorous guarantee of this (or we would have a proof of the general "Theorem"!). The criterion is as follows [Wagstaff 1978]. Let p be an irregular prime that divides the numerators of $\{B_{2k}\}$ for some set of irregularity indices $\{2k\}$. Suppose that $P = rp + 1$ is a prime less than $p(p - 1)$. Let u be a positive integer such that $u^r \pmod{P} \neq 1$. For each irregularity index $2k$, define

$$Q_{2k} = u^{-rd/2} \prod_{b=1}^{m} (u^{rb} - 1)^{b^{p-1-2k}} \tag{9.2.12}$$

where $m = (p-1)/2$ and

$$d = \sum_{j=1}^{m} j^{p-2k} \tag{9.2.13}$$

If, for each irregularity index $2k$, $Q_{2k}{}^r \pmod{P} \neq 1$, then Fermat's "Last Theorem" holds for p. We are finally in a position to establish proof for the irregular cases such as $p = 37$:

$$\tag{9.2.14m}$$

```
p = 37   (* Prime exponent under test *)
twokList = {32}   (* List of irregularity indices 2k *)
r = 0
Do[bigp = r*p+1;
   If[PrimeQ[bigp], Break[]],
   {r,2,p-2,2}
]
r = r-2
If[PrimeQ[bigp], Print["Prime P = ",bigp,",  r = ",r]]
u = 2
If[PowerMod[u,r,bigp] != 1, Print["u = 2 works"]]
m = (p-1)/2
Do[twok = twokList[[w]];
   d = Sum[j^(p-twok),{j,m}];
   bigq = Mod[
               PowerMod[u,-r*d/2,bigp] *
                 Product[
                     PowerMod[PowerMod[u,r*b,bigp]-1,
                              b^(p-1-twok),bigp],
                 {b,m}
```

```
                ],bigp
        ];
   If[PowerMod[bigq,r,bigp] != 1,
          Print["Criterion holds for ",p,", ",twok]],
   {w,Length[twokList]}
]
```

```
Prime P = 149, r = 4
u = 2 works
Criterion holds for 37, 32
```

So Fermat's "Last Theorem" holds for exponent $p = 37$. As a second example of the Vandiver criterion, one might invetsigate tthe irregular $p = 157$ which is a new kind of case in that 157 divides two relevant Bernoulli numbers; viz. B_{62} and B_{110}. In such a case we define the list of indices by

$$(9.2.15m)$$

```
twokList = {62,110}   (* List of irregularity indices 2k *)
```

and by running (9.2.14m) with this modification obtain the output:

$$(9.2.16m)$$

```
Prime P = 1571, r = 10
u = 2 works
Criterion holds for 157, 62
Criterion holds for 157, 110
```

Proceeding in this way, Fermat's "Last Theorem" can be settled for $p < 200$ in *Mathematica* without much trouble. However, by using fast algorithms on dedicated machines running optimized code one can settle prime exponents through $p < 10^6$ as the author and collaborators have recently done. We used more exotic Bernoulli expansions that can be derived from (9.2.9). One such is obtained by differentiation in the t variable, followed by application of some hyperbolic function identities to yield:

$$\frac{t^2}{\cosh t - 1} = -2 \sum_{n=0,\, n \text{ even}}^{\infty} \frac{(n-1)\, B_n}{n!}\, t^n \qquad (9.2.17)$$

Then we write the cosh function as a power series to order t^{p-1} in order to check sufficiently many B_n (mod p). The denominator of (9.2.17) is a finite polynomial, whose reciprocal can be established rapidly using Newton's method modulo p as exemplified in Section 4.4. In this way we obtain the right-hand side of (9.2.17) as a polynomial of degree $(p-3)$, in even powers of t, where each coefficient is, apart from unimportant factors, B_{2k} (mod p). There are even better expansions, ones that split the right-hand side of (9.2.17) into various congruence class sums; e.g. $n = 0,2,4,6$ (mod 8). When used in practice to generate the Bernoulli numbers (mod p) these "multi-sectioned" expansions turn out to provide even faster performance.

With these accelerations for computing B_{2k} (mod p) it is possible to establish Fermat's "Last Theorem" for p into the thousands with *Mathematica*. We took these methods (which, incidentally, were developed via *Mathematica*) and wrote fast C routines on the NeXT Computer in order to push the known limit p < 150000 [Tanner and Wagstaff 1987] further. The current situation is that a network of NeXT Computers claims, via regularity checks followed in the irregular cases by applications of the Vandiver criterion, that Fermat's "Last Theorem" is true for all exponents p < 1000000 [Buhler and Crandall 1989]. During this work we found isolated truths; for example, that the equation:

$$x^{2000291} + y^{2000291} = z^{2000291} \qquad (9.2.18)$$

is impossible in positive (x, y, z). This may be the largest known settled case, although the Newton's method polynomial expansion is so efficient that to better this case takes only a few hours on any decent workstation of today. We also found that the prime $p = 527377$ divides the numerators of *six* Bernoulli numbers, this six amounting to the highest known irregularity index. But, as was also the case in our experiments for each prime < 10^6, the Vandiver criterion was sufficient to settle this irregular prime exponent.

If there is a moral to these experiments on Fermat's great conjecture, it is that

Mathematica can be used not only to establish rigorous proofs for simple cases, but also to lay the groundwork for fast machine attacks on such deep problems.

9.3 The Riemann Zeta function and prime numbers

Riemann's Zeta Function $\zeta(s)$ is a rich, profound entity that in many ways embodies the essence of the set of integers. In fact the Zeta function for complex s, $Re(s) > 1$ is defined as a certain sum over all positive integers:

$$\zeta(s) = \sum_{n=1}^{\infty} \frac{1}{n^s} \tag{9.3.1}$$

which sum converges absolutely for $Re(s) > 1$.   For $Re(s) \leq 1$, $s \neq 1 + 0i$, the complete Zeta function is the analytic continuation of (9.3.1).   The elegant Euler identity for Zeta, valid for $Re(s) > 1$, reads

$$\zeta(s) = \prod_{p \text{ prime}} \frac{1}{1 - p^{-s}} \tag{9.3.2}$$

where p runs through the primes 2,3,5,7,... .   When one expands the series $1/(1-x)$ for $x = p^{-s}$, and performs the product of (9.3.2), one neatly obtains the formal series (9.3.1) for Zeta, due to the unique factorization of each integer n of (9.3.1) into unique products of prime powers.   It is instuctive to use *Mathematica* to exemplify this manipulation, where for ease in symbolic manipulation we use $-s$ as the relevant universal power. We start with a partial expansion of the product formula (9.3.2):

$$\tag{9.3.3m}$$

```
proofLimit = 15
f[x_, deg_] := Normal[Series[1/(1-x),{x,0,deg}]]
z[s] := Product[
                f[Prime[m]^s,
                  Floor[N[Log[Prime[m],proofLimit]]]
```

```
                ],
        {m,1,6}
    ]
z[s]
```

```
(1 + 2^s + 2^(2*s) + 2^(3*s))*(1 + 3^s + 3^(2*s))*
   (1 + 5^s)*(1 + 7^s)*(1 + 11^s)*(1 + 13^s)
```

This last result is a portion of $\zeta(-s)$, where the primes p = 2,3,5, ...13 are involved. We next expand the product for z:

$$(9.3.4m)$$

```
t = Expand[z[s]]
```

```
1 + 2^s + 2^(2*s) + 2^(3*s) + 3^s + 2^s*3^s +
   2^(2*s)*3^s + 2^(3*s)*3^s + 3^(2*s) + 2^s*3^(2*s) +
   2^(2*s)*3^(2*s) + 2^(3*s)*3^(2*s) + 5^s + 2^s*5^s +
   2^(2*s)*5^s + 2^(3*s)*5^s + 3^s*5^s + 2^s*3^s*5^s +
   2^(2*s)*3^s*5^s + 2^(3*s)*3^s*5^s + 3^(2*s)*5^s +
   2^s*3^(2*s)*5^s + 2^(2*s)*3^(2*s)*5^s +
   2^(3*s)*3^(2*s)*5^s + 7^s + 2^s*7^s + 2^(2*s)*7^s +
   2^(3*s)*7^s + 3^s*7^s + 2^s*3^s*7^s + 2^(2*s)*3^s*7^s +
   2^(3*s)*3^s*7^s + 3^(2*s)*7^s + 2^s*3^(2*s)*7^s +
   2^(2*s)*3^(2*s)*7^s + 2^(3*s)*3^(2*s)*7^s + 5^s*7^s +
   2^s*5^s*7^s + 2^(2*s)*5^s*7^s + 2^(3*s)*5^s*7^s +
   3^s*5^s*7^s + 2^s*3^s*5^s*7^s + 2^(2*s)*3^s*5^s*7^s +
   2^(3*s)*3^s*5^s*7^s + 3^(2*s)*5^s*7^s +
etc...
```

Where the output display is truncated for the sake of brevity. Let us try to express this partial product of prime powers as an expression in integer powers as seen in (9.3.1). We wish to display terms such as n^s that comprise the last output t. So we invoke rules for reduction of terms:

$$(9.3.5m)$$

```
t = t /. {
          x_^a_ y_^a_ -> Re[x*y]^a,
          x_^a_ y_^(2a_) -> Re[x*y^2]^a,
```

```
x_^a_ y_^(3a_) -> Re[x*y^3]^a,
x_^(2a_) ->Re[x^2]^a,
x_^(3a_) ->Re[x^3]^a
}
```

The Re[] function is used to assure that in this experiment *Mathematica* will not split apart certain forms such as 6^s into $2^s\ 3^s$. The output arising from *several* consecutive applications (several are required to reduce terms such as $a^s\ b^s\ c^s$ completely) of this rule reduction is:

$$(9.3.6m)$$

$$1 + 2^s + 3^s + 4^s + 5^s + 6^s + 7^s + 8^s + 9^s + 10^s + 11^s +$$

$$12^s + 13^s + 14^s + 15^s + 18^s + 20^s + 21^s + 22^s + 24^s +$$

$$26^s + 28^s + 30^s + 33^s + 35^s + 36^s + 39^s + 40^s + 42^s +$$

$$44^s + 45^s + 52^s + 55^s + 56^s + 60^s + 63^s + 65^s + 66^s +$$

$$70^s + \ldots$$

This output is displayed in attenuated form for brevity, the actual last term being 360360^s for this run. The identity of (9.3.1) and (9.3.2) is certainly justifed in this last output. In fact, the first missing terms are 16^s, due to the lack of 2^{4s} in the output of (9.3.3m), and 17^s, due to the lack of the prime 17.

We have seen with the previous manipulations how the Zeta function and the integers, especially the primes, are related. It was Riemann's inspiration to allow the variable *s* to attain complex values. The resulting analytic continuation that formally defines Zeta has been an object of intense scrutiny for about a century. One reason for the interest is that theorems about the Zeta function turn into theorems about integers, about primes in particular. As a simple example, the fact that $\zeta(s)$ diverges (i.e. has a pole) at $s = 1 + 0i$ implies that there exist infinitely many primes. Indeed, if there were only finitely many primes, the product (9.3.2) could not be infinite at $s = 1$. The celebrated Prime Number Theorem, that the number of primes $\pi(x)$ not exceeding x admits of asymptotic behavior:

$$\pi(x) \;\sim\; \frac{x}{\log x} \qquad\qquad\qquad (9.3.7)$$

can be shown to be equivalent to the statement that $\zeta(s)$ has no zeros on the line $Re(s) = 1$ [Wiener 1958]. Though (9.3.7) was proven at the turn of the century, deeper problems remain open. Not the least of these is the Riemann Hypothesis, that the only zeros of $\zeta(s)$ in the "critical strip" $0 < Re(s) < 1$ lie precisely on the "critical line" $Re(s) = 1/2$. This Hypothesis, which remains open to this day, implies many strong number-theoretic relations. We next turn to *Mathematical* investigations of the Zeta function in complex regions.

A surface plot of $1/|\zeta(x+iy)|^2$ over part of the critical strip is instructive, in that zeros should appear as divergences. Consider a finite section of the critical strip restricted by $10 < y < 24$:

$$(9.3.8m)$$

```
Plot3D[1/Abs[Zeta[x+I y]]^2, {x,0,1}, {y,10,24},
          PlotPoints->40, PlotRange->{0,40},
          Shading->False
]
```

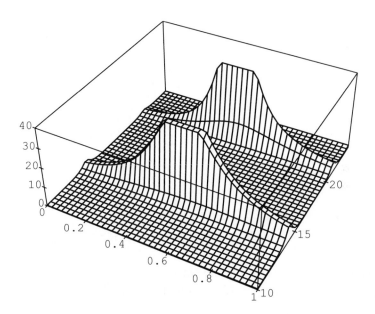

Figure 9.3.1: The inverse absolute square $1/|\zeta(x+iy)|^2$ is plotted for part of the "critical strip": $0 < x < 1$, and $10 < y < 24$. The existence of zeros of ζ at $y \sim 14$ and $y \sim 21$ is suggested.

Figure 9.3.1 shows graphical evidence of zeros on the critical line $Re(s) = 1/2$. The graph cannot show infinite values of $1/|\zeta(s)|^2$, so we adopted a cutoff. The zeros at $y \sim 14$ and $y \sim 21$ are really there. It was proved by G. H. Hardy in 1915 that infinitely many zeros of ζ do lie precisely on the line $1/2 + iy$ [Titchmarsh 1967]. The first two zeros correspond to the peaks of Figure 9.3.1 for $x = 1/2$. We can envision the first zeros more clearly by fixing $Re(s) = x = 1/2$ and plotting Zeta directly along part of the critical line:

$$(9.3.9m)$$

```
Plot[Abs[Zeta[1/2+I y]],{y,0,30}]
```

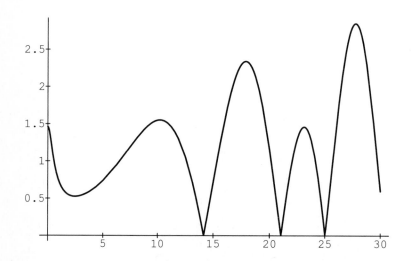

Figure 9.3.2: The magnitude | $\zeta(1/2 + iy)$ | for $0 < y < 30$. The
first few zeros (of infinitely many) are evident.

One way to zoom in on a zero is to use Newton's method in the following way,
where the example zero near $y = 15$ is approached rapidly:

$$(9.3.10m)$$

```
eps = 10^(-8)
y = 15
Do[y = y - eps *Zeta[0.5+I y]/
          (Zeta[0.5+I (y+eps)] - Zeta[0.5 + I y]);
   Print[N[y,20]],
   {j,5}
]
```

```
14.25523018100763 - 0.2739226122586387 I
14.10008832341813 + 0.019087540596111506 I
14.1342556540614 - 0.0004412172215592369 I
                                             -8
14.13472531188594 + 2.370839376149335 10    I
                                             -14
14.13472514173474 - 3.722288413555814 10     I
```

It can be checked that $\zeta(1/2+iy)$ for this last y estimate is of the order of 10^{-14}.
Mathematica has a built-in option for this kind of procedure. One may perform

FindRoot[Zeta[1/2 + I t]==0, {t,{t0,t1}}] to obtain similar results.   The Newton's iteration of (9.3.10m) is "rolled out" for reasons of pedagogy.

Over the years several powerful methods have been developed for numerical analysis of the zeros [Edwards 1974]. It has been claimed that the first *billion* zeros in the upward critical strip indeed lie *exactly* on the line 1/2 + *iy* [Riesel 1985]. But this is not a proof that all critical zeros are on the line. Nor is the proven fact that infinitely many zeros lie on the line too compelling–all we need to demolish the Hypothesis is but a single zero with real part between 0 and 1 but ≠ 1/2.

One way to perform numerical analysis on the Zeta function is to use partial sums. This can be done with rigor if one is careful to deal with floating-point errors. Note first that if $s = \sigma + it$ but the real part $s \leq 1$ in (9.3.1), the sum does not converge absolutely so it will not do, for example, to sum the powers n^{-s} directly for s on the critical line $\sigma = 1/2$. However, the Zeta function in such regions is defined as an analytic continuation, and something *can* be proved about how Zeta behaves with respect to finite sums.   One result [Titchmarsh 1967] is the following. Let $s = \sigma + it$, $t > 0$ and let x be half an odd integer, with $x > t/2\pi$. Then Zeta can be written:

$$\zeta(s) = \sum_{n=1}^{n<x} \frac{1}{n^s} - \frac{x^{1-s}}{1-s} + E(s, x, t) \qquad (9.3.11)$$

where the error term E is bounded by:

$$|E| < 2x^{-\sigma}/(2\pi - t/x) \qquad (9.3.12)$$

This rigorous result allows us to approximate any given $\zeta(s)$ arbitrarily well, provided we take x large enough (i.e., allow the partial sum in (9.3.11) to have enough terms). The error term (9.3.12), if used with proper care, can be used to ensure accuracy. Let us compute $\zeta(1 + 10\,i)$ using these observations:

```
s = 1 + 10.0 I                          (9.3.13m)
k = Ceiling[2 Pi Im[s]]
x = k + 1/2
```

```
approxZeta[s_] := N[Sum[n^(-s),{n,1,k}] - x^(1-s)/(1-s)]
error[s_] := N[2 x^(-Re[s])/(2 Pi - Im[s]/x)]
Print[approxZeta[s],",  errorBound = ",error[s]]
```

1.39021 - 0.10986 I, errorBound = 0.00514162

Sure enough, the value of $\zeta(s)$ at $s = 1 + 10\ i$ is, to six significant figures, 1.39029 - 0.109785 *i*. So the error bound 0.00514... arising from (9.3.12) is consistent. Formula (9.3.11) can be used now to establish zero-free regions in the following way. Assume that $\zeta(s) = 0 + 0\ i$, in which case

$$\left|\sum_{n=1}^{n<x} \frac{1}{n^s} - \frac{x^{1-s}}{1-s}\right| < E(s, x, t) \qquad (9.3.14)$$

For $s = 1/2 + it$, we can do a simple *Mathematica* analysis of some zero-free parts of the critical line. We express the left- and right-hand sides of (9.3.14), and then plot their difference:

$$(9.3.15m)$$

```
lhs[k_, t_] := Abs[N[Sum[n^(-1/2-I t),{n,1,k}] -
                  (k+1/2)^(1/2 - I t)/(1/2 - I t)]]
rhs[k_, t_] := N[2 (k+1/2)^(1/2)/(2 Pi (k+1/2) - t)]
tmax = 25
c[t_] := 1 + Ceiling[t/(2 Pi)]
Plot[lhs[c[t],t] - rhs[c[t],t],{t,0,tmax}]
```

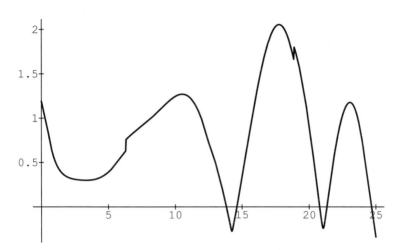

Figure 9.3.3: A "proof" plot for zero-free parts of the critical line $\sigma = 1/2$.
Assuming that floating-point error can be rigorously quantified,
the parts of the horizontal t-axis for which the plot is *positive*
cannot possess any zeros due to the rigorous inequality (9.3.14).

The output Figure 9.3.3 should be compared with the direct plot 9.3.2. We have shown, subject to a requisite analysis of calculation errors, that, for example, there are no zeros of $\zeta(1/2 + it)$ for $0 < t < 13$. Of course, the first two zeros, at $t \sim 14.1347251417$ and $t \sim 21.022039638$, lie at points in Figure 9.3.3 at which the plot is *negative*.

This analysis of zero-free regions is much simpler than the modern analyses that have established aforementioned results concerning the first billion zeros. But the fundamental notions are the same; all such analyses to date require some sort of rigorous error bound.

Let us turn to one more method for analyzing zeros. We are not merely beating the subject of critical zeros to death; rather, we reveal yet more *Mathematica* techniques that loom useful for this most difficult of problems. The approach we shall take would possibly be futile if one wanted state-of-the-art results. But again, it is the *Mathematica* technique at issue. In fact, the following approach is one the author arranged as part of a *Mathematica* test suite. Perhaps only a physicist (the author admits to being one of these) would dream of such a baroque approach, which is to relate the problem of the zeros with the theory of quantum oscillators. Various quantum Hamiltonian formalisms have already been brought to bear on the Riemann Hypothesis [Berry 1988] so there is some precedent for the interdisciplinary approach. The method concerns integrals with oscillatory integrands. Riemann himself had shown that the Hypothesis can be stated thus: that for a certain function f, the integral

$$X(t) = \int_0^\infty f(u) \cos ut \ du \qquad (9.3.16)$$

have only *real* zeros in the t variable [Titchmarsh 1967]. The particular function f is defined by:

$$f(u) = \sum_{n=1}^\infty (2n^4\pi \, e^{9u/2} - 3n^2 e^{5u/2}) \, e^{-n^2\pi \, e^{2u}} \qquad (9.3.17)$$

The first few critical zeros can be found numerically in *Mathematica* by performing a numerical integration (9.3.16) on the sum for f (9.3.17). But we adopt a more instructive path: by expanding the f function in a certain manner, the critical zeros can apparently be approximated *as the roots of polynomials of sufficiently large degree*.

In the quantum theory of the harmonic oscillator, one becomes familiar with the notion of expanding square-integrable functions such as $f(u)$ in an Hermite eigenfunction basis:

$$f(u) = \sum_{n=0}^\infty a_n H_{2n}(ku) \, e^{-k^2 u^2/2} \qquad (9.3.18)$$

where k is a constant, and the even-indexed Hermite polynomials H_{2n} are sufficient because $f(0) \neq 0$. Now a remarkable fact about cosine integral transforms of the type (9.3.16) on Hermite expansions is that the coefficients $\{a_n\}$ are essentially preserved, but with alternating sign factors. It turns out to be enough to find the zeros of the function

$$Y(t) = \sum_{n=0}^{\infty} (-1)^n \, a_n \, H_{2n}(t/k) \, e^{-t^2/2k^2} \qquad\qquad (9.3.19)$$

The author was especially intrigued by this analysis when he observed that if $f(|x|)$ is thought of as an initial wave function for a certain harmonic oscillator potential (this wave function having no zero crossings), then at a certain finite time later, the Schroedinger equation will have propagated this original wave function into a chaotic one, essentially $Y(x)$, whose zeros are precisely the critical zeros (meaning infinitely many zero-crossings as we already know). In this regard there is some hope for new results on the Riemann Hypothesis, if one considers that all the apparatus of quantum theory could conceivably be brought to bear on the problem of critical zeros.

Armed with (9.3.19) we observe that if the expansion is truncated after finitely many summands, and we set $Y(t) = 0$ and cancel the exponential factor, then the resulting polynomial equation will have roots that we expect are approximations to the Riemann zeros. This analysis proves somewhat difficult numerically, in part because the coefficients $\{a_n\}$ are not easy to compute. But *Mathematica* can certainly be used to approximate the first few zeros in this way. We define the f function and choose a fortuitous constant k for the expansion (9.3.18):

$$(9.3.20\text{m})$$

```
f[u_] := Sum[N[(2 n^4 Pi E^(4.5 u) - 3 n^2 E^(2.5 u)) *
                E^(-Pi n^2 E^(2 u))],{n,1,4}]
k = 48.0
sk = Sqrt[k]
max = 8
Do[a[j+1] = NIntegrate[f[x] HermiteH[2 j,x sk]
                Exp[-k x^2/2],
                {x,0,2.5}]/N[2^(2 j) Factorial[2 j]];
    Print[a[j+1]],
    {j,0,max-1}
]
```

0.021732
0.00226624

```
0.000105241
0.00000285975
            -8
4.96481 10
            -10
5.52403 10
            -12
3.46622 10
            -15
2.59451 10
```

Next, we form the Y function from (9.3.19), $n = 0,1,...,\text{max}-1$ and plot this function:

$$(9.3.21m)$$

```
g[t_] := Sum[N[a[i+1] (-1)^i  HermiteH[2 i,t]],
             {i,0,max-1}
            ]
Plot[g[t/sk],{t,0,34},PlotRange->{-0.002,0.005}]
```

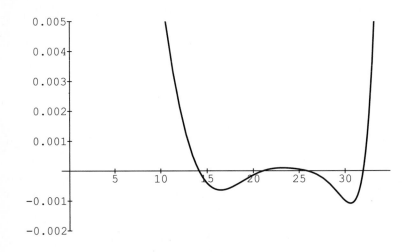

Figure 9.3.4: A quantum oscillator formalism is applied to the problem of critical zeros. For a truncated Hermite expansion of the relevant wave function, the polynomial zeros approximate the true critical zeros of the Riemann Zeta function.

We verify that the first polynomial zero of Figure 9.3.4 is a good guess:

$$(9.3.22m)$$

```
FindRoot[g[t/sk],{t,14}]
```

```
{t -> 14.13543524008105}
```

The precise zero being 14.134725..., the method at least gives this first value to one part in 10^5.

The above exercise in Hermite expansions would acquire more power if we could ascertain conditions on the coefficients $\{a_n\}$ in (9.3.19) that would imply relations for the zeros. This is an open problem as far as the author knows.

Next we use *Mathematica* to investigate the historical connections between the Riemann Zeta function and prime numbers. Riemann had established a connection involving $\pi(x)$, the number of primes not exceeding x. Let $R(x)$ be defined by:

$$R(x) \;=\; \sum_{m=1}^{\infty} \frac{\mu(m)}{m}\, Li(x^{1/m}) \qquad\qquad (9.3.23)$$

where μ is the Moebius function and *Li* denotes the logarithmic integral [Ribenboim 1988]. One of many seminal results due to Riemann is that the prime-counting function $\pi(x)$ is given exactly by:

$$\pi(x) \;=\; R(x) \;-\; \sum_{\rho} R(x^{\rho}) \qquad\qquad (9.3.24)$$

where ρ runs through the zeros of $\zeta(s)$ in the critical strip $0 < Re(s) < 1$. If, on the Hypothesis, all such zeros have real part 1/2, it can be shown that

$$\pi(x) \;=\; \frac{x}{\log x} \;+\; O(x^{1/2} \log x) \qquad\qquad (9.3.25)$$

which is presumably the strongest possible form of the Prime Number Theorem, which theorem is customarily expressed in the less specific asymptotic form (9.3.7). One convenient series expansion for the function R is the following:

$$R(x) \;=\; 1 \;+\; \sum_{m=1}^{\infty} \frac{1}{m\zeta(m+1)} \frac{(\log x)^m}{m!} \qquad\qquad (9.3.26)$$

This function is in the sense of (9.3.24) a first approximation to $\pi(x)$. Let us do an experiment, endeavoring to approximate the number of primes less than $x = 4 \times 10^{16}$.

$$\qquad\qquad\qquad\qquad\qquad\qquad\qquad\qquad\qquad (9.3.27m)$$

```
r[x_] :=1 + Sum[N[Log[x]^n/(n Factorial[n] Zeta[n+1]),30],
               {n,1,150}]
x = 4 10^16
Print[Round[r[x]]]
```

1075292778742170

The actual number of primes less than 4×10^{16} has been reported [Riesel 1985] as

$$\pi(4 \times 10^{16}) = 1075292778753150 \qquad\qquad (9.3.28)$$

The discrepancy between the first order Riemann estimate (output of 9.3.27m) and the exact result is $R - \pi = -10980$. This is an error of the impressive minitude of one part in 10^{11}. The Zeta zeros in the sum (9.3.24) can render even more accuracy, especially if one develops some measure of "overall accuracy" for a given range of x.

As for the Prime Number Theorem itself, (9.3.7), we have mentioned before that it is enough to prove that $\zeta(s)$ has no zeros on the line $Re(s) = 1$. Some credibility is lent to the Prime Number Theorem when we plot $\zeta(s)$ along part of the line $Re(s) = 1$:

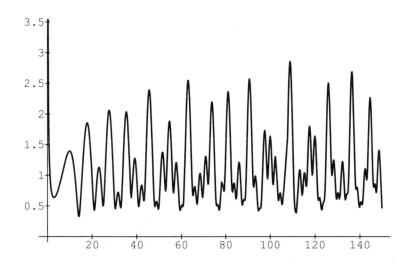

Figure 9.3.5: The absolute value of the Zeta Function $\zeta(s)$ on the line
$Re(s) = 1$, for $\varepsilon < Im(s) < 150$. That $\zeta(1+it)$ has no zeros
is an equivalent statement of the Prime Number Theorem.

Treatments of the fact of non-vanishing ζ on $Re(s) = 1$ are exemplified in the statement that, for $\sigma > 1$ [Apostol 1986],

$$\zeta^3(\sigma) \mid \zeta(\sigma+it) \mid^4 \mid \zeta(\sigma+2it) \mid \geq 1 \qquad\qquad (9.3.29)$$

from which it is not too hard to conclude that $\zeta(1+it)$ cannot vanish. To date, the best analyses have only pushed the region for which ζ has (provably) no zeros slightly to the left of the line $Re(s) = 1$. The Riemann Hypothesis thus stands as a substantially deeper result even than the Prime Number Theorem.

9.4 Theories of gravitation

Newton's classical development of gravity contained as a particularly aesthetic passage the proof that a uniform solid spherical mass, viewed from a remote vantage point, gravitates precisely as if all mass were concentrated at the sphere's center. It suffices to show that any infinitesimally thin spherical shell gravitates in this way, since a sphere may be built up from concentric shells. Consider the setting of Figure 9.4.1, in which a shell of radius a and unit surface mass density gives rise to a gravitational potential at a distance r from the origin:

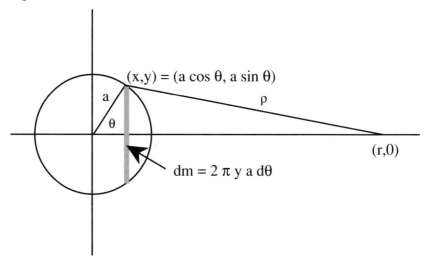

Figure 9.4.1: The setting for a proof of Newton's result that a sphere viewed remotely gravitates as if from its center. A shell of radius a causes a potential at point $(r,0)$ due to the summed potentials from "bands" of mass dm.

Assume that the gravitational potential due to a *point* mass m at distance R is, in some system of units, $-Gm/R$, where G is a universal constant. Then for the shell of Figure 9.4.1 the gravitational potential $\phi(r)$ at $(r,0)$ will be a sum over infinitesimal masses dm:

$$\phi(r) \ = \ -G \int \frac{dm}{\rho} \tag{9.4.1}$$

Now the absolute distance ρ is given by the Law of Cosines as

$$\rho = \sqrt{(a^2 + r^2 - 2ar \cos \theta)} \tag{9.4.3}$$

and the mass of the thin "band" of fixed x-coordinate is

$$dm = (2\pi \, a \sin \theta) \, a \, d\theta \tag{9.4.4}$$

We are ready to perform the relevant integral (9.4.1) via *Mathematica*:

$$\tag{9.4.5m}$$

```
integral = Integrate[a (2 Pi a Sin[u])/
              (r^2+a^2-2*a*r*Cos[u])^(1/2),{u,0,Pi}]
```

```
            2               2
-2 Pi a Sqrt[a  - 2 a r + r ]
-------------------------------- +
             r


          2             2
 2 Pi a Sqrt[a  + 2 a r + r ]
 ----------------------------
             r
```

This resulting expression for the potential is the correct formal integral for the problem, but we need rules to simplify the Sqrt[] expressions. The usual definition of the square root of a square is that $\sqrt{(z^2)} \ = \ |z|$ for real z. Our symbolic processor does not necessarily assign such a root in this way, because in some problems one wants $\sqrt{(z^2)}$ to simplify down to just the symbol z. Furthermore, that our radicands are real is an artifact of the particular problem. One way to force *Mathematica* to adopt the proper definition in our case is:

                                                                    (9.4.6m)

```
integral = Simplify[integral /.
            {Sqrt[b_^2 + 2 b_ c_ + c_^2] -> Abs[b+c],
            Sqrt[b_^2 - 2 b_ c_ + c_^2] -> Abs[b-c]
            }
          ]
```

```
-2 Pi a (Abs[a - r] - Abs[a + r])
---------------------------------
                r
```

This peculiar result actually yields the exact potential for *all* distances r. The procedure has given us a surprise bonus. By inspection of the Abs[] functions the potential can be written as follows. Recalling that the shell has unit mass density so that shell mass is $m = 4\pi a^2$, we have:

$$\phi(r) = \;-Gm/r \;\; ; \;\; \text{if } r \geq a \qquad\qquad (9.4.7)$$
$$-Gm/a \;\; ; \;\; \text{if } r < a$$

In the first case the vantage point $(r, 0)$ is outside the shell and the potential behaves as r^{-1}. In the second case the potential is constant. This is the bonus result, which can be interpreted as meaning the gravitational force (on an infinitesimal test mass), which is the gradient of the potential, *vanishes inside the shell.* When we contemplate a solid sphere as a collection of concentric shells, we infer that the exterior force behavior is r^{-2}, while the interior force is linear, as r itself.

Another Newtonian triumph was the deduction that planetary orbits are conic sections. In particular, all bounded orbits are elliptical. Let us derive the general orbit trajectory for a moving mass m attracted to a (very much larger hence unmoving) mass M. Assume a gravitational potential energy $V(r) = -GMm/r$. For a planar orbit in polar coordinate (r, θ) representation, we can write conservation relations involving the conserved angular momentum L and the conserved total energy E:

$$mr^2 \frac{d\theta}{dt} = L \qquad (9.4.8)$$

$$\frac{m}{2}\left(\left(\frac{dr}{dt}\right)^2 + r^2\left(\frac{d\theta}{dt}\right)^2\right) - \frac{GMm}{r} = E$$

One approach from this point is to find explicit time-independent formulae for the time derivatives, then to obtain the spatial derivative:

$$\frac{dr}{d\theta} = \frac{\dfrac{dr}{dt}}{\dfrac{d\theta}{dt}} \qquad (9.4.9)$$

In this way we shall be left with a differential equation for the geometrical orbit. We proceed first by solving (9.4.8) for the time derivatives:

$$(9.4.10\text{m})$$

```
derivs = Solve[{ (m/2)(rDot^2 + r^2 thetaDot^2) -
                 G M m/r == E,
                 m r^2 thetaDot == L}, {rDot, thetaDot}
           ]
```

```
                              2
                             L
            Sqrt[2 G M m -  --- + 2 E r]
                            m r                             L
{{rDot ->  -------------------------------, thetaDot -> ----},
                 Sqrt[m] Sqrt[r]                            2
                                                          m r
                              2
                             L
            Sqrt[2 G M m -  --- + 2 E r]
                            m r
   {rDot -> -(-----------------------------),
                 Sqrt[m] Sqrt[r]
```

```
                 L
   thetaDot  ->  ----}}
                  2
               m r
```

Taking the first solution for {*dr/dt*, *d*θ/*dt*}, the other in the long run offering nothing really new, we use (9.4.9) to get the angular derivative:

$$(9.4.11\text{m})$$

```
drdtheta = (rDot /. derivs[[1]][[1]]) /
                     (thetaDot /. derivs[[1]][[2]])
```

```
                                     2
          3/2                        L
Sqrt[m]  r      Sqrt[2 G M m - --- + 2 E r]
                                m r
-----------------------------------------------
                     L
```

This last output being *dr/d*θ, one is tempted to integrate (1/(*dr/d*θ)) immediately to find the angle θ as a function of *r*. The resulting expression, although correct, is unwieldy. Instead, we adopt a fortuitous change of variables *r* = 1/*u*. On the subject of variable substitution within integrals, assume we have some *Mathematica* integral defined as Integrate[f[r], r]. Then under the substitution *r* = *g*(*u*), the integral can be written in the equivalent form Integrate[f[g[u]] D[g,u], u]. We use this method to establish a trajectory {*u*, θ} as follows:

$$(9.4.12\text{m})$$

```
r = 1/u
thet = Integrate[ D[r,u]/drdtheta, u]
```

```
              2
           G M m
        - (------)  + L u
            L
  -ArcSin[-------------------]
                    2   2   4
                   G   M   m
          Sqrt[2 E m + --------]
                          2
                         L
```

This integral is an exact trajectory expression for the angle $\theta - \theta_0$, where θ_0 is an appropriate constant of integration. The only steps left are to solve for u, then use $r = 1/u$ to get the polar coordinate representation of the orbit:

$$(9.4.13m)$$

```
soln = Solve[Sin[theta] == -Sin[-thet], u]
r = 1/u /. soln
```

```
                       L
{---------------------------------------------}
      2                    2   2   4
  G M m                   G   M   m
  ------  -  Sqrt[2 E m + --------] Sin[theta]
    L                        2
                            L
```

This is the correct orbit equation [Goldstein 1965], and can be put in the conic form:

$$r = \frac{1}{a - A \sin \theta} \tag{9.4.14}$$

for appropriate initial conditions (that force $\theta_0 = 0$). Here, $a = GM/h^2$ where h is the angular momentum per unit mass L/m; and A/a is the eccentricity of the orbit, which can be found explicitly from the output of (9.4.13m). The orbit (9.4.14) can be an hyperbola, a parabola, an ellipse, or a circle; depending on the eccentricity. It should be noted that we could have invoked the substitution $r = 1/u$ earlier in the game; in fact the equation of the trajectory can be derived from the fundamental Euler-Lagrange equations of motion as:

$$\frac{d^2u}{d\theta^2} + u = a \qquad (9.4.15)$$

This is an interesting formulation of general Newtonian orbits: the reciprocal radius is a simple periodic function (an offset sinusoidal function) of the polar angle θ. When we study the corresponding orbits in Einstein's gravity, the formulation (9.4.15) is in some ways more natural, as we next investigate.

Schwarzschild derived, following Einstein's theory of gravity, the orbit equation analogous to (9.4.15) [Keener 1988]. This is the theory that presumably predicts correctly the precession of the perihelion of planet Mercury. One starts with a special planar-motion ($\phi = 0$) case of the Schwarschild metric:

$$ds^2 = (c^2 - 2GM/r)\, dt^2 - dr^2/(c^2 - 2GM/r) - r^2\, d\theta^2 \qquad (9.4.16)$$

One looks for geodesic arcs, i.e. space-time trajectories that extremize total s under this metric. This formalism can be thought of as a correct generalization of our "launched clock" problem of Section 5.3. After some interesting textbook analysis, the result for the polar coordinatized trajectory turns out to be:

$$\frac{d^2u}{d\theta^2} + u = a + \frac{3GMu^2}{c^2} \qquad (9.4.17)$$

where a is now defined slightly differently as GM/h_1^2, with $h_1 = r^2 d\theta/ds$ [Keener 1988]. On the idea that orbits will generally precess in all but certain central potential problems, we dilate the angular coordinate θ to first order in a certain perturbation parameter b. Setting $b = 3GM/ac^2$ and $x = (1 + bg)\,\theta$ for a constant g we obtain:

$$(1 + bg)^2 \frac{d^2u}{dx^2} + u = a(1 + bu^2) \qquad (9.4.18)$$

Now assume that the first terms in the perturbation series for $u(x)$ are:

$$u(x) = a - A \sin x + b\, u_1(x) + ... \tag{9.4.19}$$

in which the first two Newtonian terms are evident. We proceed to solve (9.4.18) to first order in b:

$$\tag{9.4.20m}$$

```
u = a - A Sin[x] + b u1[x]
rel = LogicalExpand[
      Normal[Series[(1 + b g)^2 D[D[u,x],x] +
            u,{b,0,1}]] ==
            Expand[Normal[Series[a (1 + b u^2),{b,0,1}]]]
]
```

```
a + b (2 A g Sin[x] + u1[x] + u1''[x]) ==

        3       2               2            2
   a + a  b - 2 A a  b Sin[x] + A  a b Sin[x]
```

The output relation will now be inspected for the implicit coefficients of powers of b:

$$\tag{9.4.21m}$$

```
rel /. b->0
```

```
True
```

So we are on the right track: the zeroth-order terms agree, as expected from the Newtonian approximation $u \sim a - A \sin x$. The first-order relation involving b^1 is obtained by:

$$\tag{9.4.22m}$$

```
rel2 = D[rel,b] /. b->0
```

```
2 A g Sin[x] + u1[x] + u1''[x] ==

    3         2              2              2
   a   - 2 A a  Sin[x] + A  a Sin[x]
```

This relation turns out to be possible for a certain value of the constant g, and appropriate function u_1. One of many ways to proceed is to force the coefficients of $\sin x$ to cancel:

(9.4.23m)

```
rel3 = D[rel2 /. Sin[x] ->snx, snx] /. snx->0
```

```
2*A*g == -2*A*a^2
```

implying that $g = -a^2$. To obtain the final relation for the function u_1, we proceed:

(9.4.24m)

```
Eliminate[{rel2, rel3}, g]
```

```
                           3    2           2
A != 0 && u1[x] == a  + A  a Sin[x]   - u1''[x] ||

                       3
    A == 0 && u1[x] == a   - u1''[x]
```

The differential equation for u_1 is embodied in this output. One could solve for u_1 with further analysis, but the main effect of the relativistic precession is embodied in the constant g. For the record, the solution for u_1 is:

$$u_1(x) = a^3 + A^2a/2 + (aA^2\cos 2x)/6 \qquad (9.4.25)$$

as one may readily verify using the output of (9.4.24m). The relativistic analogue of the orbit trajectory (9.4.14) we have found to be:

$$r = \frac{1}{a - A\,\sin((1-ba^2)\,\theta) + bu_1}$$ (9.4.26)

to first order in the parameter $b = 3GM/(c^2a)$. The dilation of the angular coordinate thus gives rise to a precession of the major axis of the ellipse at a rate of about $6\pi aGM/c^2$ radians per revolution.

For planet Mercury, the eccentricity is $A/a = 0.205$, the orbital dimension is fixed by $a = 1.80 \times 10^{-11}$ meters^{-1}, and the precession works out to 5.0×10^{-7} radians per revolution. This accumulates to about 43 seconds of arc per century, one of the currently supported, spectacular achievements of Einstein's gravitational theory. We can graph a mythical example in which Mercury has the same orbital scale and dimension, but the central mass is, say, 10^6 Solar Masses. Using (9.4.26) we plot this mythical Mercury's orbit for about five revolutions:

(9.4.27m)

```
G = 6.67 10^(-11)       (* Universal Gravitation. *)
M = 1.99 10^30 10^6     (* One million Solar Masses. *)
c = 3 10^8              (* Speed of light. *)
a = 1.80 10^(-11)       (* Orbital parameter of Mercury. *)
e = 0.205               (* Eccentricity of orbit. *)
b = 3 G M/(c^2 a)
u1[x_] := a^3 (1 + e^2/2 + e^2/6 Cos[2 x])
rad[the_] := Block[{x},
                x = (1 - a^2 b) the;
                Return[1/(1 - e Sin[x] + b/a u1[x])]];
             ]
ParametricPlot[{rad[th] Cos[th], rad[th] Sin[th]},
                {th,0,10 Pi}, AspectRatio->Automatic
]
```

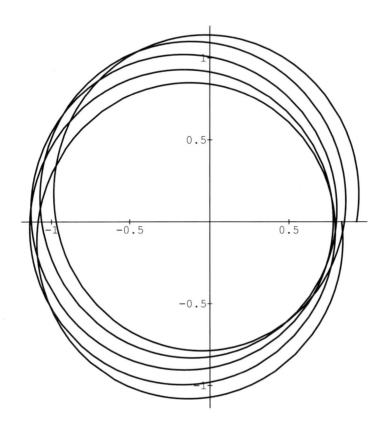

Figure 9.4.2: If Mercury had its usual orbital dimensions, but around a
        star of one million solar masses, the relativistic precession would be
        evident: the perihelion would advance one-half radian per revolution.

9.5 Further explorations

E9.1) As a practical matter, just how large an isolated prime exponent p can you resolve via *Mathematica* in Fermat's "Last Theorem"?

E9.2) As a practical matter, how high can you take N rigorously, in the statement "The first N zeros of $\zeta(\sigma+it)$ in the critical strip $0<\sigma<1$, ordered by positive t values, all have real part $\sigma = 1/2$."? See [Edwards 1974][Riesel 1985] and references therein.

E9.3) Work out a scheme by which Zeta zeros are computed and then used numerically in (9.3.24) to obtain sharper approximations to $\pi(x)$ than, say, (9.3.27m) affords. Study *ranges* of x, because for some x (9.3.24) is specifically disappointing and therefore better interpreted in an average sense.

E9.4) Investigate numerically Landau's 1903 equivalent statement of the prime number theorem: that for real $c > 1$, the vertical line integral along $(c-i\infty, c+i\infty)$ of $[\log \zeta(s)\, x^s\, ds/(2\pi i s)]$ is asymptotic (large x) to $x/\log x$. This classic result shows that deep enough properties of Zeta to the *right* of $Re(s) = 1$ are enough to establish the Prime Number Theorem [Apostol 1986].

E9.4) For a flat uniform-density circular disc of matter, the gravitational potential at some remote test point does not generally act as if arising from the disc's center. Describe how the "effective" gravitational center moves about in space as a function of the remote test point.

E9.5) Investigate other problems of historical import, for example Hilbert's Tenth Problem, which asks for an algorithm (if one exists) that would successfully seek all solutions to an arbitrary Diophantine equation. Use *Mathematica* to provide as much as possible of the modern proof that *no such algorithm exists* [Davis 1982].

E9.6) Attempt to use *Mathematica* in partial (or complete!) re-enactments of the great irrationality and transcendency proofs of history; e.g. to prove that e, π, $\log 2$, $2^{\sqrt 2}$ or other interesting numbers are irrational or even transcendental. You might, for example, prove that e has an infinite simple continued fraction representation and so is irrational.

References

Abbott P 1990, private communication

Abramowitz M and Stegun I, eds. 1970, *Handbook of Mathematical Functions*, Dover Publications, Inc. New York

Ahmed M and Natajaran T 1983, *Discrete-time Signals and Systems* Reston Publishing, Inc.

Aho A, Hopcroft J, and Ullman J 1974, *The Design and Analysis of Computer Algorithms*, Addison Wesley Publishing, Inc.

Anderson J and Yamamoto B 1988, private communications from NeXT Software Group

Andrews G 1986, *Trans. Amer. Math. Soc.* **293** 1 113-134

Apostol T 1986, *Introduction to Analytic Number Theory*, Springer-Verlag

Aref H and Flinchem E 1984, *J. Fluid Mech.* **148** 477-497

Atkinson D, et. al. 1987, *Dynamic Models in Biochemsitry*, Benjamin/Cummings Publishing, Inc.

Beauchamp K and Yuen C 1979, *Digital Methods for Signal Analysis*, George Allen & Unwin Ltd., London

Bense B 1990, private communication from San Diego SuperComputer Center Consultant's Group

Berry M 1988, *Nonlinearity*, **1**(3) 399-407

Borwein J and Borwein P 1987, *Pi and the AGM*, John Wiley & Sons, Inc.

Brent R and Pollard J 1981, *Math. Comp.* **36** 627-630

Buchler J, Perdang J, and Spiegel E, eds. 1985, *Chaos in Astrophysics*, D. Reidel Publishing Company, Amsterdam, Holland

Buhler J and Crandall R 1989, in preparation

Burrus C and Parks T 1985, *DFT/FFT and Convolution Algorithms*,
        John Wiley & Sons, Inc.

Cejtin H, et. al. 1990, *MathTalk* software authors

Cohen H and Lenstra H 1984, *Math. Comp.*, **42**, 297-330

Crandall R 1990, *Computers in Physics*, Mar/Apr

Crandall R and Buhler J 1987, *J. Phys. A: Math. Gen.* **20** 5497-5510

Crandall R and Colgrove M 1990, *Scientific Applications for NeXT Computers*,
        Addison-Wesley Publishing, Inc. , in prep.

Crandall R and Reno M 1982, *J. Math. Phys.* **23**(1) 64-70

Cronin-Scanlon J 1981, *Mathematics of Cell Electrophysiology*,
        Marcel Dekker, Inc.

Davis M 1982, *Computability and Unsolvability*, Dover Publications,
        Inc., New York

Devaney R 1986, *An Introduction to Chaotic Dynamical Systems*,
        Benjamin/Cummings Publishing, Inc.

Devaney R 1990, *Chaos, Fractals, and Dynamics*, Addison-Wesley
        Publishing, Inc.

Doenias J and Crandall R 1989, ExpressionBuilder application authors

Drazin P and Johnson R 1989, *Solitons: an introduction*,
        Cambridge University Press

Dudman J 1990, private communication

Edwards H 1974, *Riemann's Zeta Function*, Academic Press, New York

Feynman R, Leighton R and Sands M 1979, *The Feynman Lectures in Physics,
        Volume II, 6th ed.,* Addison-Wesley Publishing, Inc.

Glasser M and Zucker I 1980, *Theoretical Chemistry:
        Advances and Perspectives*, **5** 67-139, Academic press, Inc.

Goldberg, Schey and Schwartz 1967, *Am. J. Phys.* **35**(3)

Goldstein H 1965, *Classical Mechanics,* Addison-Wesley Publishing, Inc.

Gottfried K 1989, *Quantum Mechanics Volume I: Fundamentals*,
    Addison-Wesley Publishing, Inc.

Gradshteyn I and Ryzhik I 1965, *Table of Integrals Series and Products*,
    Academic Press, Inc.

Gray T 1989, RealTimeAlgebra application author

Gray T 1990, private communication

Hardy G and Wright E 1979, *An Introduction to the Theory of Numbers*
    Oxford University Press, New York

Hasler M 1987, *Proceedings of the I.E.E.E.* **75**(8) 1009-1021

Holden A, ed. 1986, *Chaos*, Princeton University Press, Princeton, New Jersey

Jack J, Noble D, and Tsien R 1975, *Electric Current Flow in Excitable
    Cells,* Oxford University Press

Junge D 1976, *Nerve and Muscle Excitation*, Sinauer Associates, Inc.

Kaplan R 1988, private communication

Keener J 1988, *Principles of Applied Mathematics*, Addison-Wesley
    Publishing, Inc.

Kemeny J and Snell J 1983, *Finite Markov Chains*, Springer-Verlag, New York

Kimura 1955, *Proc. Nat. Acad. Sci*, **41**:144-150

Knuth D 1969, *The Art of Computer Programming, Vol. 2: Seminumerical
    Algorithms*, Addison-Wesley Publishing, Inc.

Koblitz N 1987, *A Course in Number Theory and Cryptography,*
    Springer-Verlag, New York

Koblitz N, ed. 1987, *Number Theory Related to Fermat's Last Theorem,*
    Birkhauser

Koonin S and Meredith D 1990, *Computational Physics: FORTRAN Version*,
    Addison-Wesley Publishing, Inc.

Lenstra A, Lenstra H, Manasse M and Pollard J 1990, *STOC Proceedings*, to
    appear

Lenstra H 1986, Report 86-18, Mathematisch Instituut, Universiteit
        van Amsterdam

Lightman A et. el. 1975, *Problem Book in Relativity and Gravitation*,
        Princeton University Press, Princeton, New Jersey

Lydgate C and Crandall R 1989, CircuitBuilder application authors

Maeder R 1990, *Programming in Mathematica*, Addison-Wesley
        Publishing, Inc.

Manasse M and Lenstra A 1990, general network announcement of
        15 June 1990

Misner T, Thorne K, and Wheeler J 1973, *Gravitation*,
        W. H. Freeman and Company, new York

Montgomery P 1987, *Math. Comp.* **48** 243-264

Morrison M and Brillhart J 1975, *Math. Comp.* **29** 183-205

Parker L and Christenson S 1989, private communication from S.C.

Parks T and Burrus C 1987, *Digital Filter Design*, John Wiley & Sons, Inc.,
        New York

Pomerance C, Smith J, and Tuler R 1988, *SIAM J. Comput.*, **17** 387-403

Press W, et. al. 1988, *Numerical Recipes in C: The Art of Scientific
        Programming*, Cambridge University Press

Quinn R 1990, *Personal Engineering and Instrument News*, March, 39-44

Ram-Mohan L, et. al. 1990, *Computers in Physics* Jan/Feb

Ribenboim P 1988, *The Book of Prime Number Records*, Springer-Verlag

Riesel H 1985, *Prime Numbers and Computer Methods for Factorization*,
        Birkhauser Boston, Inc.

Russell P 1986, *Genetics*, Little, Brown & Company (Canada) Limited

SawHill B 1990, private communication

Schiff L 1968, *Quantum Mechanics 3rd. ed.*, McGraw-Hill, Inc.

Schroeder M 1986, *Number Theory in Science and Communication*,
   2nd ed., Springer-Verlag

Skiena S 1990, *Implementing Discrete Mathematics: Combinatorics and
   Graph Theory with Mathematica*, Addison-Wesley Publishing, Inc.

Strum R and Kirk D 1988, *Discrete Systems and Digital Signal Processing*,
   Addison-Wesley Publishing, Inc.

Stump D 1986, *Am. J. Phys.* **54**(12) 1096-1100

Tanner J and Wagstaff S Jr. 1987, *Math. Comp.* **48** 341-350

Titschmarsh E. 1967, *The Theory of the Riemann Zeta Function*,
   Oxford University Press

Truhlar D, ed. 1988, *Mathematical Frontiers in Computational Chemical
   Physics*, Springer-Verlag

Wagstaff S Jr. 1978, *Math. Comp.* **32**(142) 583-591

Wiener N 1958, *The Fourier Integral and Certain of its Applications*,
   Dover Publications, Inc., New York

Wolfram S 1988 *Mathematica: A System for Doing Mathematics by Computer*,
   Addison-Wesley Publishing, Inc.

Wu S 1987, *Proceedings of the I.E.E.E.* **75**(8) 1022-1057

Zucker I 1984, *SIAM J Math Ann* **15** 2 406-413

Index

Addison-Wesley Publishing Company

Books About *Mathematica*®

Stephen Wolfram, ***Mathematica: A System for Doing Mathematics by Computer Second Edition*** (HB: 0-201-51502; PB: 0-201-51507, 1991)

Roman Maeder, ***Programming in Mathematica, Second Edition*** (HB: 0-201-54877, PB: 0-201-54578, 1991)

Richard Crandall, ***Mathematica for the Sciences*** (HB: 0-201-51001, 1991)

Steven Skiena, ***Implementing Discrete Mathematics: Combinatorics and Graph Theory with Mathematica*** (HB:0-201-50943, 1990)

Theodore Gray and Jerry Glynn, ***Exploring Mathematics with Mathematica*** (HB: 0-201-52809, PB: 0-201-52818, 1991)

Ilan Vardi, ***Computational Recreations with Mathematica*** (PB: 0-201-52989, 1991)

 If you'd like additional information about any Addison-Wesley scientific computing title, simply fill out and mail the postage-paid card below. You'll receive the latest information on new titles and special offers from Addison-Wesley's Advanced Book Program.

Name: _____ (100)
Title: _____
School/Company: _____
Department: _____
Street Address: _____
City: _____ **State:** _____ **Zip:** _____
Daytime Telephone: _____

Title and author of this book: _____
Date purchased: _____

Where did you buy/obtain this book?
☐ Bookstore   ☐ Mail Order   ☐ School (for class use)
☐ Campus Bookstore ☐ Toll-Free Number   ☐ Professional Meeting
☐ Other _____   ☐ Addison-Wesley Representative

☐ If you're currently writing a book, please check this box if you'd like to discuss your project with us and indicate your subject area: _____

...or call toll-free 1-800-447-2226 to order

Available Versions of *Mathematica*®

Apple Macintosh:
- Standard (does not require numeric coprocessor)
- Enhanced (requires 68020/30 and numeric coprocessor; 4 MB memory recommended)

386-based MS-DOS systems:
- 386 (does not require numeric coprocessor)
- 386/7 (requires 287 or 387 numeric coprocessor)
- 386/Weitek (requires Weitek coprocessor)
  (640KB and 1MB memory required; supports CGA, EFA, VGA, MCGA, AT&T, 8514a, and Hercules graphics standards, PostScript, LaserJet, Epson FX/LQ, IBM Proprinter, and Toshiba P3 printer standards.)

386-based Unix systems:
- 386/ix and V/386

Convex:
- C1 and C2 series

Data General:
- AViiON

Digital Equipment Corporation:
- ULTRIX (VAX and RISC)
- VAX/VMS

Hewlett-Packard/Apollo:
- HP 9000/300 series
- HP/9000/800 series
- DN 2500 through 4500
- DN 10000

IBM:
- RS/6000
  (see above for PC compatibles)

MIPS:
- RISComputer and RISCstation

NeXT:
- The NeXT Computer

Silicon Graphics:
- Personal IRIS
- 4D Series (supports real-time 3D graphics)

Sony:
- NEWS

Sun Microsystems:
- Sun-3
- Sun-386i
- SPARCstation and Sun-4

All versions of Mathematica are fully compatible. Mathematica front ends (also available separately) can be connected to remote Mathematica kernels. Educational and student discounts are available. All specifications are subject to change without notice. Mathematica is a registered trademark of Wolfram Research, Inc. Mathematica is not associated with Mathematica, Inc., Mathematica Policy Research, Inc. or MathTech, Inc. All other trademarks are owned by their respective companies.